BETWEEN FRIENDS

James Branch Cabell in 1916

BETWEEN FRIENDS

LETTERS OF
JAMES BRANCH CABELL
AND OTHERS

EDITED BY

PADRAIC COLUM

AND

MARGARET FREEMAN CABELL

WITH AN

INTRODUCTION

BY

CARL VAN VECHTEN

HARCOURT, BRACE & WORLD, INC.   NEW YORK

ACKNOWLEDGMENTS

For permission to reprint letters herein, grateful acknowledgment is made to Wilson Follett, Robert M. McBride, Vincent Starrett, Donald Ogden Stewart, Deems Taylor, Louis Untermeyer, Carl Van Vechten; also to the following for letters from: William Rose Benét—James Benét; Thomas Beer—Miss Alice Baldwin Beer; Ernest Boyd—Mrs. Madeleine Boyd; Theodore Dreiser—the Trustees of the Dreiser Trust; Mr. and Mrs. F. Scott Fitzgerald—Mrs. Samuel Lanahan and Harold Ober Associates; Garrard Glenn—Garrard W. Glenn; Joseph Hergesheimer—Mrs. Dorothy Hergesheimer; Guy Holt—Mrs. Rackham Holt and Robert M. McBride Company; Sinclair Lewis—Ernst, Cane, Berner and Gitlin, Executors of the Lewis Estate, and Doubleday and Company; Arthur Machen—Mrs. Janet Davis and Yale University Library; H. L. Mencken—August Mencken and Mercantile-Safe Deposit and Trust Company, Executors of the Mencken Estate; George Jean Nathan—Mrs. Julie Haydon Nathan and Cornell University Library; Frances Newman—Mrs. Margaret Newman Patterson and Louis D. Rucher; Burton Rascoe—Mrs. Hazel Rascoe; Eugene Saxton—Mrs. Martha P. Saxton and Doubleday and Company; Carl Van Doren—the Estate of Carl Van Doren; Hugh Walpole—Rupert Hart-Davis. The Chicago *Tribune* has also kindly granted permission to reprint the material on the Cabell-Rupert Hughes contretemps.

The editors also wish to express their thanks to the following: John Cook Wyllie, Book Editor, Richmond *News Leader* and Librarian of the Alderman Library, University of Virginia; Miss Louise Savage, Associate Librarian, Alderman Library; Francis L. Berkeley, Jr., and Miss Anne Freudenberg, Alderman Library; George H. Healey, Curator, The Wordsworth Collection, Cornell University Library; George Freedley, Curator, The Theatre Collection, New York Public Library; Robert W. Hill, Keeper of Manuscripts, New York Public Library; Edward G. Freehafer, Librarian, New York Public Library; R. L. De Wilton, The Macmillan Company; Philip Kaplan; Edmund Wilson; Mrs. Neda M. Westlake, Curator, Rare Book Collection, University of Pennsylvania Library; Thomas Yoseloff, Director of the University of Pennsylvania Press; Donald Gallup, Curator, Collection of American Literature, Yale University Library, and Richard Colles Johnson, Assistant to the Curator, Yale University Library; Alexander P. Clark, Curator of Manuscripts, Princeton University Library;

Julian P. Boyd, Princeton Library; Mrs. Dorothy C. Rieger; Rudolph Hirsch, Curator, Rare Book Collection, University of Pennsylvania Library; Lewis F. Ball, Book Editor, Richmond *Times-Dispatch;* Virginius Dabney and Karl V. Hoffman, Editors, Richmond *Times-Dispatch;* Mrs. William R. Trigg, Jr.; Miss Ellen W. Tompkins; Mrs. Mary M. Harrison, Reference Department, Richmond Public Library; Edgar E. MacDonald, Professor of English, Randolph-Macon College; The Reverend G. M. Brydon; Littleton Wickham; Catherine McCarthy; Richmond Public Library; Virginia State Library; Library of the University of Texas.

CONTENTS

AN INTRODUCTION WITH CANDOR
AND SOME LITTLE TRUTH

When Margaret Cabell invited me to write the introduction to the pages that follow, she offered a curious but indubitably sincere explanation: "You are, perhaps, the only well-known author still living who was intimately acquainted with the writers of these letters." If Margaret's dubious position can be regarded as in any degree worthy of attention, my compliance, outside of actual rudeness, seemed to be a matter of necessity. I had known all these writers with some measure of intimacy. The men were my companions in the Twenties: they were friends I frequently broke bread with at Pogliani's or the Hotel Knickerbocker, and with whom I occasionally overdrank, illegally. We often discussed current literary affairs together and it was the custom of several of them to inform me of the details of their peculiar tastes and of their varied manners of composition.

I had visited Joseph Hergesheimer many times in his Dower House on the road opposite the Golf Club and in the Victorian mansion in West Chester he had occupied during the reconstruction of Dower House. I had sat in his office on the Main Street of that town where he was wont to write his overupholstered novels, famous novels of the period: *The Three Black Pennys, Java Head,* and *Linda Condon,* the latter dedicated to me. I had drunk a forgettable number of Daiquiris in his classically correct formal dining room and I had heard him repeat often his most familiar phrase, "There are only a few of us left," sometimes in the presence of others when Joe was giving more attention to his manners than to his sense of actuality. In any case, the phrase might be spoken about that period much more reasonably now. Joe was fantastic in dress, extravagant in conversation; more, he was brilliant. His flamboyant personality and literary style are conveyed to the observer with extraordinary exactitude in Florine Stettheimer's painting, now the property of the Yale Library. He writes Cabell, "I am not rich but extravagant. Turning so flatly from magazines, from the easy magnificence of their returns, I must have three things at least: the support of a small handful of friends, something not entirely foreign to a degree of satisfaction in myself, and then a number of books sold." From the point of view of literary value, his letters are easily the best. They are not dashed off. They are created with an eye on posterity.

In the *Smart Set* office, and later in the office of the *American Mercury*, I had discussed papers I had written with the generously abundant Henry Mencken; I had drunk countless seidels of dark German beer with him in his favorite bar in Hackensack, or was it Weehawken? I had photographed him and his wife, Sara Haardt, who was a devoted friend of my wife, Fania Marinoff. He had dined with us at various New York apartments and we had dined with him at his favorite Baltimore restaurant, Schellhase's, where, of course, terrapin was served. We met even more frequently at our publisher's, Alfred A. Knopf. I was as familiar with his style as with his hair, combed in the middle of his head, so that I could detect his addition of one word in the contribution of any of his various authors. We frequently discussed music, as he urged me to write saucy essays about the scandalous lives of singers and conductors. Or he was ecstatic about Beethoven and Johann Strauss, while I was more enthusiastic about Ravel or Stravinsky. As a letter writer he was *sui generis,* unique, and frequently bawdy or sacrilegious. In his letters to Cabell, he is not in his best unbuttoned form.

Sinclair Lewis, known to chronologically different groups as "Red" or "Hal," I had met when I first came to New York in 1906, when we each had a room in a rooming house at 39 West Thirty-ninth Street. I believe he was still to publish his first book. Certainly, he had yet to achieve any kind of fame. Later, I met him again with his first wife, Grace Hegger, now the Countess Casanova. I also knew his second wife, Dorothy Thompson, and I had encountered his two sons at least once. I was familiar with his writing and gave my unstinted admiration to *Dodsworth.* He paid me the compliment of using my novel *The Tattooed Countess* as part of the plot in his novel, *Gideon Planish.* He was egocentric and loved practical jokes, disguises, and imitations. He frequently parodied political speakers endlessly at dinner parties and once, at the Langners', he answered the bell, took the coats from the guests and hung them in the closet, as if he were a glorified footman. On another occasion, in the pulpit of a well-known Kansas City church, he had the effrontery (and the vanity) to challenge God to strike him dead, while he held a stopwatch. He was much admired by young ladies, in spite of a disastrous complexion, and it was not uncommon to discover him surrounded by bevies of them. His letters in this volume are unaffected and unmannered. They deal with practical projects.

Theodore Dreiser, with his handkerchief-folding mannerism, I had also met soon after my arrival in New York. As the editor of the *Broadway Magazine,* now long defunct, he had invited me to compose a paper about Richard Strauss's *Salome,* to be presented for the first time in New York that January (1907) at the Metropolitan Opera House. This was probably my first periodical appearance. Thereafter, we met only occasionally, but he was a sometime guest at our apartment in the "block beautiful" on East Nineteenth Street. I attended parties at his apartments, first on St. Luke's Place and later at 200 West Fifty-seventh Street. One of the parties on St. Luke's Place, when an uninvited Scott Fitzgerald appeared with a bottle of champagne, furnished the town with gossip for a month, and was eventually described with a good deal of imagination by three writers, each with his own version. I photographed Dreiser most successfully, and one of the photographs exhibits him laughing, a unique item. On one occasion, at Dr. Brill's, we had discussed endlessly, it would seem, the relation of the consumption of various drugs to the composition of literature, an experiment both of us had made unsuccessfully.

There are letters from Hugh Walpole in the pages that follow. All of us knew him, some better than well. He came to see us often at our apartment on East Nineteenth Street, and later at 101 Central Park West. He introduced me to some hitherto obscure authors whom later I enjoyed writing about, Baron Corvo and M. P. Shiel among others. Once I visited him at Brackenburn on Derwent Water, one of the English Lakes near the Scottish border, and I still possess the silver shell dish he had presented me as a souvenir of the occasion. His behavior was suitably Scottish when I desired to telephone my wife in London. The telephone, it seemed, had never before been used for long distance.

Scott Fitzgerald, too, became an intimate friend, together with Zelda. In an early visit to Hollywood, circa 1929, we lived in adjoining bungalows on the Hotel Ambassador lawn and shared each other's pleasures and many meals. He was making an early and even then unsuccessful attempt to write scenarios for motion pictures and I was taking a Hollywood vacation. We spent many amusing evenings in one another's company and met at many parties. At this period, his principal dread was of reaching the age of thirty, which he confused with old age, "when everything would be over." I visited him once or twice in the great house (the drawing room was one hundred feet long) he occupied for a short time on the Delaware, near Wilmington, and I recall a Christmas there when the kitchen was overflowing with colored people, servitors and their relatives, including many children—a real Southern custom. In a letter to Cabell, he characteristically misspells "Menken" and "Drieser." Quite late in Scott's life, I photographed him in front of the Algonquin Hotel, photographs which have since been published more than once in various accounts of his torture-filled life.

I had met James Cabell first, I believe, at Hergesheimer's Dower House, where we were both guests with Priscilla ("Percie") and Fania, but later we met in Richmond at a period when Joe and I were delighted to spend a week now and then in that delectable town. By that time I was more or less familiar with his reticences, his rare enthusiasms, his exclusions, his shyness (he detested New York), and his methods of work. When I first knew James, he lived in Dumbarton Grange, a more or less ramshackle farmhouse on the outskirts of the town that Ellen Glasgow in her novels referred to as Queenborough. However, Dumbarton Grange was such a grandiose appellation for a house of this low character that, when friends in New York asked me to describe it, I recalled instead Ellen Glasgow's magnificent early Victorian mansion with its correct English furniture and its beautiful crystal chandeliers. It helped Cabell's reputation as a rich landowner and a gentleman of taste and it did Ellen no harm.

It is a pity that the time scheme of this book does not permit the inclusion of Cabell's correspondence with Ellen Glasgow, which began at a later date.* He was completely relaxed when he wrote to her and consequently these informal and warm letters were among his best. Since Ellen did become one of the Friends, perhaps it is not remiss for me to quote from some of these later letters which I have had the pleasure of reading. In writing to Ellen re Norman Baskin's recent marriage to their friend Marjorie Rawlings, Cabell quotes her as complaining because Norman had entered the American Field Service. "Why," demanded Marjorie, "did I have to get stuck with a God damn hero?" In another letter he writes: "Still one does get over being desperate and defiant and settle down into some irresponsibility for the universe." Again re the Rawlings-Baskin nuptials James writes Ellen: "I cannot but regard through

* *Editor's note:* Ellen Glasgow and Cabell were both born in Richmond, but, perhaps because of the difference in their ages, there was not much personal meeting until after the beginning of his literary success. And even then, the few notes exchanged between them were very short and formal until some time after the *Jurgen* episode. The great warmth of their friendship, as shown in their later letters, developed only during the last ten years before her death in 1945. It has been suggested that the Glasgow-Cabell correspondence alone would make an interesting volume.

tear-stained eyes anyone who is pledged to share life intimately with an author." He writes: "I type with frozen fingers against a freezing North wind," and again, "I bang on my typewriter day after day, trying to get everybody in my book murdered off by the first of March."

Ellen Glasgow, when she came to New York, usually invited her sister, Mrs. Tutwiler, to accompany her, or at times the chatty Carrie Duke, who sold antique English or American furniture in her shop in Richmond. This was because of Ellen's very considerable deafness. In social intercourse she managed quite well with a hearing aid, but she found it difficult to cope with hotel waiters and bellboys, and especially she found it difficult to cope with the telephone. When the ladies dined with us, which was at least once during every visit they made to New York, we brought out our best silver and our best china, and we invited our best guests. Ellen returned the compliment when I visited Richmond, usually in the company of Joseph Hergesheimer. Curiously enough, on such occasions, shad roe and Virginia ham, served cold with salad and beaten biscuit, always seemed to be in season. Once, at my special request, she had entertained Gertrude Stein, when Gertrude was lecturing in Richmond, at a dinner which Mr. Cabell had attended—a dinner that became very celebrated in its aftermath of gossip and small talk. It was Ellen who invited my first interest in Negro spirituals, when she introduced me to a Negro singing group, The Sabbath Glee Club, who sometimes softly intoned these sweet songs of sorrow under the magnolia in the garden of Ellen's beautiful early Victorian house at 1 West Main Street.

I refrain from drawing a sketch of Louis Untermeyer. He is alive and he can picture himself. Burton Rascoe, probably the most frequent contributor to these epistles, was unreliable in his columns and frequently distorted the facts, twisting them this way or that to suit his own views. He was often indiscreet, repeating the nasty remarks that another had made about the person he was writing to. As a critic he may be summed up by his description of *Manon Lescaut* as a "drooling piece." How the manuscript of *Jurgen* came into his possession, recounted fully herein, sheds light on another phase of his character. However, his excessive admiration of Cabell is obviously sincere. He writes: "the magic of your touch transcends anything in literature." His letters to Cabell expressing his opinions on this subject were so undeniably honest that they were appreciated as such by Cabell himself.

Frances Newman did not enjoy my company and I did not enjoy hers. In a letter to Cabell, I exclaim: "I cannot but think that you much over-praise Frances Newman, both as to acumen and performance; I think perhaps you underpraise Elinor Wylie in the same departments." Louis Untermeyer angrily inquires of James Cabell, "Who *is* Frances Newman anyway?" Later Frances Newman was to write to Cabell: "T. R. Smith [whose letters, strangely enough, are missing from this file] wants me to edit a collection of love stories, very realistic, and of course we'll want one of yours, if you have any sufficiently shocking." Miss Newman herself considered it "murderous" for Middleton Murry to have compared Hugh Walpole to Ouida.

Ernest Boyd was a near neighbor in the Twenties when we both lived on East Nineteenth Street. We saw each other frequently and I listened with delight to his fascinating and endless Irish arguments. Vincent Starrett I had known through his connection with one of the small magazines and for his very great interest in one of my idols, Arthur Machen, a Welsh author who comes off unscathed in the following pages. He is generally praised, while most other writers are generally excoriated or even excommunicated. Lewis Galantière I admired for his great knowledge of French literature. I exposed myself to his charm and erudition as frequently as possible. There are a few letters from Tom Beer, Donald Ogden Stewart, Wilson Follett.

It is interesting to note that in the letters gathered herein almost everyone (and this includes me) seems to be writing a Cabellian prose. Formerly this was Mencken's particular magic, but now Cabell seems to have the same power. In rereading my own letters, I was especially struck by this resemblance. Further, James wrote in a curiously hermetic style, being a past master of equivocation, so that his opinions might be interpreted in several distinctly different manners: one is never entirely certain of his exact meaning or of his precise opinion.

The case over *Jurgen* is now historic. Since that celebrated discussion there has been another controversy over *Lady Chatterley's Lover*, but hardly any other two books have created so much of a stir. There is, of course, throughout, and especially in the middle section, much ado about *Jurgen*, speaking of which Cabell writes Rascoe: "My agreement with Holt was to write the thing as it came to me, and that done, for us to cut out the really impossible portions." Further Cabell in his letter to Rascoe (August 10, 1919) practically outlines how *Jurgen* came into being. A large part of the present volume is devoted to a very lively discussion of this very lively book.

Nancy Mitford has written: "Friendship is something to be built up carefully by people with leisure. It is an art; nature does not enter into it." We were all busy, playing our own games, and we had no time for this kind of ideal friendship, but in spite of that fact we did enjoy a vast deal of social intercourse, some of it on the pragmatic side. A fair amount of this shows up in the following letters, so assiduously devoted to log-rolling. They are replete with literary interest, but most of them are rather rigidly inhuman. Wives and children, or puppies and pussies, or stocks and bonds, seldom come into the picture, which, indeed, for a good deal of the time, exists in a vacuum.

There are human touches, however. Hal Lewis wants James Cabell to live in London and rather insists upon it. Joe Hergesheimer complains to Cabell that the line in *Steel* (Charlotte is speaking to Howard) as published in the *Saturday Evening Post* was: "You've no idea how I've dressed at you." The line in the manuscript reads: "You've no idea how I've dressed and undressed at you." In a letter to Walpole, Cabell begins by explaining: "This handmade letter, Hugh, is in deference to my wife's queer notion that a typewriter is on Sunday immoral, and apt by its clicking to attract the attention of a deity who, I deduce, can hear but not see through a roof." Tom Beer comments to Cabell: "In Sicily there is a demon named Celerri, whose feet are luminous on the soles. This makes his nightly forays doubly interesting as he is obscure when standing flat footed. . . . These facts have been made known to me by Clefante Visella, my gardener." Lewis to Cabell: "There are cliques of Wylieites to whom every word she wrote was perfect, while, of course, you are so right about her terrible *Orphan Angel:* it wasn't merely an orphan; it was a bastard. . . . "

Cabell writes to Lewis regarding *Main Street:* "I mildly regret that you did not permit Carol to be seduced by Eric." Lewis to Cabell: "I, too, wanted Eric to seduce Carol, but she would none of it—for all her aspirations to rebellion she was timorous; she was bound; she would never have endured it." Apropos, Mencken to Cabell: "I agree with you that the girl should have yielded up her person, but I incline to think that the lawyer should have flounced her, rather than the Swede."

I recall an old definition of a literary clique: ten or a dozen authors who live in the same town and who hate each other cordially. This was not true of our group in the Twenties. Many of us did not live in New York, but we at least attempted to love one another. We frequently dined together, wrote each other sporadically or often, according to the interest involved, and sometimes reviewed each other's books. Occasionally we visited together in our respective towns. Actually, it was the nearest approximation to a group that had existed since Hawthorne's day, and certainly there is nothing like it today when occasionally you see a single author struggling with his peers at a cocktail party.

This volume of letters, then, reopens a literary period and throws light on some of its notable authors for a new generation of readers who are permitted to observe various opinions on numerous subjects from center, left, and right center. There is some truth and frankness included herein, but a vast deal of dissimulation. The reader must make his own choices. On the whole, however, the picture is a peaceful one and even the lies light up the truth more balefully.

CARL VAN VECHTEN

New York
November 18, 1961

❧ 1 ❧

THE MAKING OF THE JEST

George H. Doran Company
New York, February 1, 1915

Dear Mr. Cabell:

I have a very difficult letter to write to you, rejecting *In the Flesh*. I am not particularly fond of the role of sage editor, who speaks *ex cathedra* to the humble race of authors out of the abundance of his wisdom, and advises them to go straightway and take out the "love interest," if "love interest" there be; or to put it in if it is lacking.

As a matter of fact, I discovered by reference to *Who's Who* that I am slightly younger than yourself—and naturally I do not need to refer to that charming little volume to discover how very much more important you are than I am.

Nevertheless I have a desire to mount into a pulpit and preach at you with the most savage texts. Let me preface my remarks by saying that some years ago, when I was a reader for Frederick A. Stokes Company, I was the first to read your book, which was afterwards published under the changed title of *The Soul of Melicent*—I am depending on my memory for the title. I said in my opinion on the book that it was the most beautiful love-story I had ever read, and that the firm absolutely must publish it. Furthermore, when I had left Stokes, when I had no "commercial interest" in the book, I insisted that they see to it that, if the book was illustrated, it be nobly illustrated.

Recently there came to me here—where I am no longer merely a reader, but that omnipotent and omniscient divinity, the editor—your book *The Rivet in Grandfather's Neck*. Although I felt that the end of the story straggled badly, I was so much taken with it as a whole, that I insisted upon it having several readings. Then it was rejected by the Chief and now comes *In the Flesh*.

I do not think that *In the Flesh* is a good story. I think it would have made an admirable ten-thousand word short story, but it strikes me as a short story which has sprouted in the cellar of discontent.

3

And I shall probably delight your soul—proving the kinship of all publishers—by saying that the letters on pages 46 and 7, and the burlesque upon the following pages, first amused me, then pleased my sense of ingenuity, but ended by leaving a very bad taste in my mouth. Do you really suppose that any publisher in the country is going to offer such an insult to Dodd, Mead & Company as to publish a book in which they are referred to as "Dead, Mudd & Company?" To say nothing of the insult to my very good friends of the Century Company implied in referring to that company as "The Cemetery Company"? Doubtless if I preferred those firms to my own, I should make an endeavor to be with them instead of with Doran. But the fact that I prefer my own firm does not at all indicate that I have any desire to insult them publicly and unpleasantly: and I should most certainly regard it as a direct affront to them to countenance the publication of a book in which they were referred to as they are in these pages of yours. Nor does the fact that I have loved the sheer beauty of some of your stories, keep me from resenting your reference to Mrs. Wharton's *The Customs of the Country*, as *The Cuspidors of the Countrymen*. This despite the fact that your variation of her name as "Mrs. Seeketh Haut-Ton" is most charmingly ingenious.

Finally I seriously doubt whether any one who is not closely connected with the world of book-making would be in the least amused by these pages. The fact that I reviewed most of these books is a reason why I am able to find most of their prototypes.

I make so much of these few pages—which could, of course, be cut out without trouble, if you consented—because it seems to me that they are more or less typical of the spirit of the book. A book of dreams it is and of very wonderful dreams. But they who dream are in every daylight life rather detestable. Your genealogist in *The Rivet in Grandfather's Neck,* though he too lived in Lichfield, would have been decidedly uncomfortable in this book. So far as I can see the only excuse for disagreeable characters is in realism of the Dutch *genre* school, or as villains in naive literature, which is still unashamed of melodrama.

Nor is that all. I do not believe that this book *lives*. I do not believe that it is indeed in the flesh. The phrase "midnight oil" keeps coming back to me as I read it. And there is another phrase which keeps coming back to me. It is this: "Sore on the world." Are you?

You who can do beautiful things in a country which is not overrun with beauty, we cannot afford to have you "sore on the world."

And there ends my sermon, which is at once *ex cathedra* and decidedly *obiter dictum*—for who am I that I should present the above as any more than a frank personal opinion.

I hope that this letter will not make you angry, I hope that it will not disgust you, I hope that by some happy miracle it may even be of some actual service to you. I think you will realize that it is not customary for bright young men at publishers to dictate letters of such frankness and length. And I think that I in turn realize that there is no particular reason for thus compelling you to be an audience, willing or unwilling, to my ill-tempered, though sincere sermon.

And I think that you will realize that the fact that I have thus lectured indicates that I should be glad at any time to see anything that you write, and that you have more than merely "my good wishes."

Sincerely yours,
SINCLAIR LEWIS

Cabell's answer to this letter appears to be lost, but we know something of its content from Lewis's reply.

From Sinclair Lewis

New York, February 15, 1915

Dear Mr. Cabell:

I am glad indeed to learn from your letter that life is brighter than, from your novel, I had judged it to be. . . .

Your reference to your lacking the rose-colored spectacles of "Mrs. Barclay or—pardon me—Miss Corelli," I take to be a gentle and well-deserved indication that we are not without sin in publishing Miss [Marie] Corelli's books. Far be it from me to condemn one of our own authors, but I fancy that from the fact that I have so much cared for your own work indicates the degree of esteem in which I hold the earnest and lucrative Miss Corelli.

Good luck man—and sometimes dreams of the *sigil!*

Yours sincerely,
SINCLAIR LEWIS

Later on, when Cabell and Lewis met, they got on together excellently. And many years later, Cabell said: "I found that, for my part, it was not possible to help liking and admiring this Sinclair Lewis, even after the droll and deferential boy whom I first knew had turned out to be a world-famous genius."

Also Cabell wrote later, "In April 1915 I paid my first visit to the offices of Robert M. McBride & Company . . . where yet another hitherto unheard-of young person, who signed himself 'Guy Holt,' had been interested by the typescript of *In the Flesh* to the highly non-commital extent of wishing to see something else by its writer. I, who had four unpublished books, was willing to oblige him." As the upshot of this visit, McBride's accepted three of the four— *The Rivet in Grandfather's Neck*, published in 1915, *The Certain Hour*, and a book of poems, *From the Hidden Way*, both published in 1916. But *In the Flesh*, now rechristened *The Cream of the Jest*, still hung fire.

While the three books were being readied for publication, a warm author-editor relationship developed between Cabell and Holt. Cabell spent the summer of 1916 revising *The Cream of the Jest*, and in December Holt called on him in Richmond.

Dumbarton Grange
Dumbarton, December 20, 1916

My dear Holt:

. . . Write me candidly as to "Cabell on the Cosmos" now in your hands. I think it far and away my best work, but that is because I really "let myself loose" in many parts of it: for which sufficient reason you have no earthly call to agree with me. At worst, you will see that your remonstrance against too-clever dialogue, as being unnatural, had been considered by me before our talk . . . And, as I have told you, you make intelligent suggestions, so that I would appreciate and heed any and all admonition short of advice to burn the manuscript. . . .

Yours faithfully,
JAMES BRANCH CABELL

Dumbarton, December 30, 1916

My dear Holt:

This is terrible! You evidently do not think well of *The Cream of the Jest*, and—as I told you—it is either very, very good or very, very bad, with no possible middle-ground. No less, I shall continue to assure myself that it is beautifully written, from the technical side, and so truthful that when it is published, if it ever is, I shall have for the rest of my life the feeling of going about unclothed. All this apart, I have indisputably, again, made the mistake of considering a problem, without appending the precise answer—namely, what is everything up to? Between ourselves, I do not know. . . . However, I shall look for your report. . . .

At all events, you . . . were entirely right as to James Stephens' being an unfailing joy. . . . The book is delightful, and I shall look out for his other work forthwith. I trust that you, in passing, will do as much for Arthur Machen, though I believe that in America his books are practically unprocurable. . . .

Yours faithfully,
JAMES BRANCH CABELL

From Guy Holt

Robert M. McBride Co.,
New York, January 3, 1917

My dear Cabell:

You pay me a poor compliment when you assume that I do not like *The Cream of the Jest,* nor do you encourage me in the occasional fits of reticence to which I like to believe I am prone. I know, indeed, that it is impossible for you to conceive me as hesitating to give an opinion about a subject for the mere reason that I am ill informed on it, but such happens to be the case in this instance at least. . . .

Now I can say I have read it all. And I like it, Greatly! You are right, I believe, in saying that it is the best thing you have done—at least in part—and you will pardon me if I venture to accuse you of being "vital," despite yourself. For this book, however tricked out with fantasticality, is of the very blood and bones of life. It states your problem—and mine, and everyone's—and that it proposes no answer can never be cause for criticism by sensible people. Anyway, Euclid is the only literary man who solved the problems he propounded—and he exhausted his subject.

Kennaston's nocturnal adventures I think are very beautiful. They have the teasing incompleteness of dreams themselves. I think I like them better because they do not satisfy.

But it is in the depiction of Kennaston himself that you have out-stripped (and stripped, perhaps) yourself. He is finely done and he has blood in him!

So much in rebuttal. Now, pray, permit me to carp in my turn. First then, a minor criticism or two: I am a bit afraid of the composite author-ship. . . . Those references to Froser's biography, and the occasional foot-notes—I wonder if they are worth the loss of interest they might occasion. To me the book is too big to need them, and although I fancy that I see why you might wish to make him seem an actual character, I do not see how you can do it. He is—to paraphrase an idea of your own—too true to be real. . . .

My principal quarrel with you, however, is occasioned by Chapter V. Your parodies of publishers' names, and worse still, of the best-sellers of yesterday, as well as of their authors! I cannot believe that you intended them for other than the amusement of publishers' readers. . . . And per-haps one letter of rejection would be enough to quote.

I think, too, that the conversation of Messrs. [Theodore] Roosevelt *et al.* might well be reduced to a mere suggestion, somewhat after the manner of the banquet scene in *La Peau de Chagrin* (I believe that is the book, but it is one of Balzac's), where by fragmentary bursts of talk the reader may deduce babel. . . .

This, I believe, is all I have to make in the way of criticism. I should be tempted to apologize for the heat of my comments were it not that I really detest those two chapters heartily, and that I fear they might prove excellent obstacles to other folks' admiration. And besides—you gave me this box of matches and might reasonably expect a blaze of some sort. Apropos of your comments on symmetry, page 145 or thereabouts: somewhere in Goethe is a bit of theorizing upon the symmetric growth of plants; and a very fine artist I know detects two kinds of symmetry—static, or balanced, and dynamic—the latter based on the spiral.   He has written a book about this and sundry other speculations which will be published when the war ends I hope. Meantime it is not accessible and I mention it only because your speculations are not unlike his theory—with the difference that his work relates only to aesthetics. . . .

Faithfully yours,

GUY HOLT

Dumbarton, January 7, 1917

My dear Holt:

It is rarely I get a more interesting letter than your last, nor, upon the whole, one that gives me greater pleasure. I am—and, indeed, have long known myself to be—very deeply your debtor.

My main end in the complete revision I gave the book last summer was to make Kennaston an individual and real person. Previously the tale was all dreamland. So I tried, leaving his head in the clouds, to get his feet firmly set on earth. If I have done that, I am content. He is, of course, rather loathsome. Some reviewer will probably be discovering some day that he lacks the tonic uplift of Pollyanna and Mrs. Wiggs *et als*.

Meanwhile—do you think there is any real chance of getting the book serialized? Nothing would more delight me. Other matters apart, it would mean getting some actual money for writing a book, and I have always had a liking for novel experiences——

I approve of almost all your fault finding—— The composite authorship is bungling, though far from purposeless—— And we will remove all the footnotes at one sweep, some to oblivion and others to the text proper. Mr. Froser's Biography, I think, may remain without arousing undue worriment—or, at a pinch, the reader can be referred to a little-known masterpiece entitled *The Eagle's Shadow*—— And Harrowby's assertion that fiddling with pen and ink is no fit employment for a grown man, can—and should—be softened to just that dreary suspicion common to all writers once in a while that such may be the case. In fine, it should not be advanced as a belief, but as a doubt which occasionally arises.

I understand your objection to the White House luncheon—though it comes ill from you, who warned me against making my dialogue unnaturally clever. Secure in the knowledge of that chapter's existence I smiled, sir, as you talked—— Now, the table-talk is, almost, a transcript from what they actually said, but, just as my friend Kennaston suspected, it displays no startling originality of thought. My notion, then, would be to remove most of it, and break the remainder into very short paragraphs, to cover not over two book pages at most, and to allure the eye onward by the light look of it—— Is that not what you mean? You see, this platitudinous talk has a quite definite place in the book's scheme, echoed in the dream at Vaux-le-Vicomte and in the call the Kennastons pay the Harrowbys, and duly summed up in the book's peroration. It must be indicated, and indicated as the dull twaddle it is.

Now, as to the publishing chapter, I do not understand. The publishers' letters, if they make too tedious reading, can be summed up in a paragraph—— And the puns on the best sellers and their authors likewise can be altered—— These puns, I must modestly point out, are themselves a species of literary criticism—— Or do you mean that they sound vicious? or that this material would not interest persons outside of the bookmaking business? . . . Suppose you alter that chapter yourself, and let me see specifically what you do mean. I am agreeable to any arrangement which preserves the essential points of the chapter. . . .

Yours faithfully,
JAMES BRANCH CABELL

The United States entered the war against Germany on April 6, but literary matters continued to be of paramount importance. As the spring of 1917 advanced, Cabell, having disposed of *The Cream of the Jest*, except for the correction of proofs, started on another book, as was his custom. Writing to Holt, he said, "I have quit fiction and am writing a book to elucidate my 'aesthetic creed'—being persuaded by you and Mr. Follett *et al.* that I have one—and have found that, subconsciously, it was just what I wanted to write. Some day you will see it, and some day, too, I hope to have your rebuttal. Meanwhile I have invented a new essay-form, and am having a delightful time playing with it."

It was June before he wrote Holt again about his new venture, the book finally published as *Beyond Life*. "The essays go on nicely. . . . You see, I was in Fairhaven recently, and of course called on John Charteris. I spoke to him of your rebuttal, in fact, read it to him, and he replied at considerable length. He is better qualified than I to speak on literary topics, because he has access to all the books of Bookland,—such as all the novels of Arthur Pendennis, a library set of David Copperfield's works, a copy of Beltraffio, and any number of other such masterpieces. And of course he has all the books that were never written—the complete Weir of Hermiston, and Denis Duval, and so on,—as well as the dream-version of every published book, including all the books I meant to write—— So he replied from the dream-versions of my books—these being my real masterpieces—and spoke for, precisely, ten hours—— I enjoyed it not a little, for he proved my theories were entirely correct. So far we have reached two A. M., but he is to talk until dawn—— So in this too we are to collaborate, at your convenience, I hope."

Dumbarton, September 20, 1917

My dear Holt:

To-day I am expressing you what really seems to me a remarkable production. I read the thing in its entirety yesterday for the first time, and was much pleased therewith, as indeed I always am by this author's books, at the first perusal. It is afterward I perceive his botcheries with steadily increasing clearness.

Read it at your leisure. I found, as I think you too will find, that the entire discourse is written at you, in a quite personal way, so that I in particular want your opinion thereupon. I am tempted to explain the tandem of notions I drive therein. But if you don't yourself detect them unaided, no amount of explaining will help now. Of course, I desire all imaginable suggestions.

Meanwhile it is beautifully written. I have pleased myself by doing what I have always wanted to do, in holding the meaning of each sentence in solution for the last word to precipitate. Of course you cannot do that in narrative, certainly not in dialogue. And apropos of my Greek sentences, I am herewith offering you a many lovely samples at which you will swear. But I protest their architecture is noble. . . .

Yours faithfully,

JAMES BRANCH CABELL

From Guy Holt

New York, September 25, 1917

My dear Cabell:

Your letter did indeed achieve that timeliness which you execrate so bitterly, as it reached me a half hour after I reached the office the other day. I shall be glad to see your manuscript and to discover whether you have anticipated my rebuttal. I expect also to admire your Greek sentences in appropriate humility.

Meanwhile you will be interested to learn that following my acquisition of *The Soul of Melicent* (which I like least of your books, despite the *joie de vivre*) I have picked up for the sum of 79¢ *The Line of Love* and *Chivalry*. These bring my collection of "Cabelliana" almost to completion. *The Majors and their Marriages* is still lacking: and I search the 25¢ tables in vain for *The Eagle's Shadow. . . .*

The Cream of the Jest is published tomorrow. . . .

Faithfully yours,
GUY HOLT

Thus, more than two and a half years after it had been submitted, McBride published *The Cream of the Jest.* Commented Cabell in retrospect: "The ways of all publishers, however, I discovered some while ago to be incalculable: and I do not think that any deduction can ever be drawn, through the channels of mere rationality, from any of their actions. It is perhaps the one trait which they share congenially with their authors."

Dumbarton, September 28, 1917

My dear Holt:

This is the hastiest of notes, to express my real pleasure with the get-up of the new book—— I also admire your impudence in not liking *Melicent*. The trouble with you is that you belong to an effete and sophisticated generation. You are not primal and red-blooded, and so your reaction was not what it should be. I, in consequence, do not expect you even to read the other sweet little love-stories on which you squandered $1.58. Instead, you can look at the pictures. . . .

Yours faithfully,
JAMES BRANCH CABELL

Some time before this, Holt had announced in a letter: "Incidentally, you will be interested to know that we have arranged with Arthur Machen for the American publication of his book *The Terror,* which will appear some time this fall." So that when Cabell saw the October *Century* Magazine he wrote to Holt: ". . . First of all, what is the meaning of the Machen story in the *Century?* The book I have not yet seen, but from what you told me this must be the same tale. . . . Apropos, I was right as to the notion of the Limehouse story being closely paralleled in Balzac. You will find that in *La Cousine Bette* Valerie Marneffe persuades four men, apart from her husband, that they are paternally interested in her child. . . .

"By this time, I hope, *Beyond Life* has reached and probably irritated you. A deal of it you cannot possibly like, but I can assure you, from the disadvantage point of age, that it is all perfectly true."

Reactions to *The Cream of the Jest* began to come to Cabell in the form of letters, some from hitherto unknown readers.

H. L. Mencken, who had praised one of Cabell's books as early as 1909, came forth in *The Smart Set* with a pleasingly polite article in which *The Cream of the Jest* was appraised in combination with a novel quaintly entitled *The Three Black Pennys*, by a young Pennsylvanian, Joseph Hergesheimer. Writing from *The Smart Set*, Mencken asked Cabell, "Have you anything on paper that would fit into the above great moral periodical?"

So the group began gradually to come together, if only by means of the United States letter carriers.

Dumbarton, November 26, 1917

My dear Sinclair Lewis:

Your letter pleased me more than anything has done for a long time—— Indeed, your first letter, of near three years ago, likewise delighted me because it raised so much intelligent objection to the original version of *The Cream of the Jest* . . . and pointed out a host of real and removable faults therein. I don't assert, you conceive, that the book as it stands is a masterpiece, but humbly acknowledge that but for your letter it would have been infinitely worse. So it seemed merely civil to take notice of your collaboration.

So much for my laborious paper-spoiling—— But of course, my dear man, *The Job* is excellent. I have read it very slowly and considerately, and with no little envy. It must be great to "do" women in that honest and convincing fashion. Yet I don't know but that fundamentally Mr. Schwirtz and I are almost at one in our literary tastes. Still, I spare you the depressing spectacle of an author "being intellectual about romanticism"—particularly as I have succumbed to the temptation at some length in an unpublished volume, which some day I shall certainly send you. . . .

I shall follow your advice and procure the Hergesheimer book. I don't know him at all, save nominally. In fact, I don't know any of my contemporaries, as reading-matter, and have abandoned all effort to keep up with them. They irritate me by the high (and monotonous) level of their work, no less than by the good things I find therein and resent not having thought of first. Then too in Richmond—I live just on the outskirts of Richmond—we have no real bookstores. It is always possible to see the latest offence by Mrs. Barclay or Mr. Harrison or Mrs. Porter or Mr. Wright,[1] but if you want a real book you have to order it "sight unseen." And I cannot tell whether or no I want a book until I have seen it! So I have withdrawn perforce from the ranks of the book-buying public, and doubtless miss much that is worth while. But what is one to do?

1 Four of the more popular light novelists of the day: Florence Louisa Barclay, Henry Sydnor Harrison, Gene Stratton Porter, Harold Bell Wright.

I was hearing of you only a day or two before your letter came—from Mrs. Bosher (of *Mary Cary* fame), who tells delightful things of you and your wife. Is St. Paul a permanence? It sounds insufferably remote, and I was hoping some day to know you. Somehow I do not think you could be as disappointing to meet as I resentfully feel myself to be—— And the name of the sulky beast is Cabell, in ironic consonance with rabble. I don't wonder you did not know, since I was forced to spend two years in New York under the alias of Cáy-bel and Cay-béll, through the utter impossibility of persuading any Northerner to pronounce my actual name.

"Sixthly and lastly," that appears to be about all. Some day when you have a vacant quarter of an hour, you must read the Sigil frontispiece, which is quite simple and, I fear, truthful.

Yours faithfully,
JAMES BRANCH CABELL

From Sinclair Lewis

516 Summit Avenue,
St. Paul [date?]

Dear Mr. Cabell:

No! St. Paul is *not* a permanence. It is an experiment in living—— I was born in Minnesota, hence have always taken St. Paul seriously—just as you probably could not take it seriously, and as I cannot take Fort Smith, Ark., or Lima, Ohio, or many other places doubtless quite filled with bankers and shoemakers and authors and other worthy persons, at all seriously. My wife and I being for a time less footfree because of the coming of a son some six months ago, decided to try the experiment of living as much like Respectable Persons as possible, for one winter, and chose St. Paul as the place in which to perpetrate that experiment. (In New York, of course, where I know princes and bums, I should never be permitted to be so much or so little as respectable.)

Well—we have succeeded! I am a member of the Minnesota—you know: oak lounging room, with copies of the *Outlook* and the *Illustrated London News* and the papers from Chicago and Omaha on the long tables. We have been decorous with bankers, lawyers, the rector of St. John's, and the secretary of the Welfare League. We are spoken of with respect in the Social Column. I (now and then) wear dinner clothes—neither evening clothes nor a flannel shirt—to Sunday evening suppers. But—— The end approaches. This damned palace which we have rented returns to its owner on April 25th, and then I think we shall go to

Dumbarton Grange or Montana or Cape Cod or Alaska or one of those places, and begin to write perfectly indecent sarcasm about the dear people who have given us their hearts and salt, such being the approved custom of authors after convalescence from respectability.

Anyway we'll go to Dumbarton—some day. In the last three years we have been in Florida, British Columbia, Juarez, Hartford, and other places, so I know we shall sometime be somewhere near Virginia—where we spent our honeymoon, some four years ago.

I am glad, very very glad, to have discovered you.

Servt!

SINCLAIR LEWIS

Hearst's—think of it, *Hearst's!*—has taken a real story by me called "Mother Love," the title being by contraries.

Dumbarton, December 3, 1917

My dear Holt:

. . . Who, to begin with, is Galantière? He writes a charming letter, exactly the sort one hungers to receive, but, in view of his unusual literary discernment, I cannot but suspect his sanity, you conceive. . . . I was much pleased by the Mencken notice—eminently quotable, that—and regard the book I sent him as well invested. Still, our pecuniary parsnips remain unbuttered, and the whole thing is infernally disheartening. . . . Meanwhile I look forward to having Mr. Roscoe [*sic*] call me a Titan, right out in print,—which, when you consider how unpopular the Titans were with the gods, seems plausible.

Sinclair Lewis has written me a long and delightful letter about the book, to which he is more than complimentary. To the other side, this week I had no clippings at all. Hence depression—— However, when you gain time write me as to *Beyond Life*. Make suggestions, particularly as to anything I might add. There were, as I recall, one or two things in the universe to which the manuscript made no reference, and that may seem invidious. Then perhaps this damned war ought to be kept out of it? And above all, if you could refute the whole thing, that would work in nicely as an antepenultimate chapter—what I with sturdy commonsense replied to Charteris, you understand,—then leaving the last word with him. Come now, if you will sketch out such a chapter I will dedicate the book to you, and send you thundering down the ages. That ought to tempt you.

Yours faithfully,

JAMES BRANCH CABELL

From Vincent Starrett

300 N. Lotus Avenue
Chicago, Illinois
December 5, 1917

Dear Mr. Cabell:

I've just finished with reading *The Cream of the Jest,* and I don't know what to write you about it. I am convinced of one thing—that it is a very great book. It leaves me bewildered with the bigness of its vision; in places I had to go back two and three pages and reread before I was sure I understood it—and then I wasn't sure! This, of course, is my fault, not yours. I shall read it again in its entirety; soon, I hope. I would like to write something about it, and if the opportunity is given me, I will. But what shall I say?

It is too bad that a critic cannot cry enthusiastically, "a great book," and be done with it. But he must tell why it is a great book: . . . readers want a synopsis and an analysis—and that's just what I'm sure I can't write about *The Cream of the Jest.* It is Life, of course, the great Puppet-play, with that sardonic kick of Futility in its tail—after all the talisman is the top of a cold cream jar! You see, immediately one becomes incoherent.

It is one of the biggest things I have ever read; I wish I had written it. I wish Machen could read it. Please send him a copy, telling him I asked you to. . . .

Now tell me, are you Kennaston? Have you dreamed those dreams? I have—some of them; I think we all have, although we have never attempted to interpret them. I wish you would tell me what the book means to you, and what led you to write it. I am still bewildered. It seems to be not one book but a hundred. Like a parable, I am sure it has a hundred interpretations; that of one hundred persons no two would say the same thing about it.

I felt this way about Machen, when I read *The Hill of Dreams,* that appallingly desolate record of a life. I felt that I couldn't do him justice; but how I wanted to! I felt that only a man big enough to write that book was big enough to say what it meant. I feel much the same about *The Cream of the Jest.*

Did you see my paper on Machen, by the way? If you have not, I'll send you a copy. But it doesn't begin to do him justice. It has only one merit; it *is* the first authoritative piece of writing about him. . . .

Yours,

VINCENT STARRETT

Dumbarton, December 14, 1917

My dear Mr. Starrett:

Your letter very positively embarrasses me. I had hoped *The Cream of the Jest* might interest you because of the Machen influence, which I at any rate detect therein, from *The Hill of Dreams* and *A Fragment of Life*,—but when it comes to telling me that you think it is a really great book, in such superlatives, I can but be dubious and embarrassed and, above all, delighted. Presently, no doubt, I shall be believing you—— For of course I am Kennaston. Anyone of us, I take it, is Kennaston who does not contract from his associates all his opinions and beliefs, as though they were measles. But when it comes to proclaiming that the book means this or that precisely—that $x + y + z =$ a definite whole number, and no more or less—I am afraid the unknown quantities do not sum up quite so exactly. At least one interpretation you may without much difficulty detect in the Sigil, if you hold it upside down. Even so, "beauty" is a very comprehensive word. Perhaps I had best refer you to Horvendile's declaration at Storisende, that we dreamers hunger for we know not what, and for the exercise of powers we know that we possess, without knowing what they are—— Indeed, I suspect the parable is constructed on the Hans Christian Andersen formula, whereby the moral is sensed but cannot be set down in any explicit black and white. Another great and unappreciated genius, that!

But I too run toward incoherency. There is nothing I would like better than to see your Machen article, so please send it to me, at your earliest convenience. I have never, you can see, read anything about him, and feel in advance that you underrate your efforts in saying you have not done him justice—— Meanwhile, decipher the sigil! and believe me, in anticipation of delight in your article,

Yours faithfully,

JAMES BRANCH CABELL

P.S.—I am following your suggestion as to sending Machen the book, as well as in blaming it entirely on you.

❧ 2 ❧

THE CIRCLE WIDENS

Cabell, in writing to Holt for a business accounting, asked: "And then do you tell me who, if you know, is Vincent Starrett? He has written me such superlatives as to my stupendous genius, &c (I invested a *Cream* in him) that I would like to think him intelligent. Hertzberg, of the Fashion-Art,[1] has also written a ream of private encomiums, and tells me Galantière is head-clerk in 'the best, not the biggest, bookstore in Chicago.' And that is?"

Dumbarton, January 5, 1918

My dear Holt:

It was a comfort to get those accounts at last, however depressing it was to read them, and I am tendering my thanks for your efforts toward making possible this melancholy pleasure. The accounts, however, do not after all tell the main thing I wanted to know, which is how many copies of the *Jest*, approximately, have been sold thus far. So don't forget to tell me this when you next write.

But when—ah, when indeed—do you expect to write me as to *Beyond Life?* We stand just where we did four months ago, as touches that, so that really your verdict ought to be mature. For my part, I have not read a line of the thing since I expressed you the fair copy in September, so that my notions about it are hazy. In consequence, I may be more or less fair-minded.

To the other side, I am, I warn you, quite insufferably conceited since reading the Chicago *Tribune* article, in which, again, I recognize your friendly hand. Rascoe sent me a copy, with a tremendous letter, and the combination has entirely turned my head. The one drawback is that he is only too correct in his contention that newspaper criticism amounts to precisely nothing, even when it is eulogistic. Still, it furnishes me with delightful reading-matter.

---

[1] Hans Hertzberg, editorial writer and one-time editor of the Chicago *Inter-Ocean*. *Fashion Art Magazine* was published in Chicago by the Fashion Art League of America.

I have been shocked to find that Maurice Hewlett has written another good book, in *Thorgils*. My enjoyment was tempered by the circumstance that I purchased it along with *The Little Iliad,* but *Thorgils* is fully worth $2.70. . . .

Yours faithfully,

JAMES BRANCH CABELL

Dumbarton, January 9, 1918

My dear Holt:

We telepathed, so that our letters crossed. Mails now arrive at Dumbarton only as often as Mr. McAdoo thinks may be good for us, so that your rebuttal came last night. One or two questions in my last thus stay unanswered. Meanwhile I am tranquilly annexing your rebuttal as the penultimate chapter of *Beyond Life*—to precede the present Epilogistic—and in return will immortalize you with the volume's dedication when the thing is published. *What, therefore, are your views upon the possibility of getting this book published?* Of course it is quite infernally clever and, though you seem to doubt this, an infernally candid Apologia for my books and incidentally for myself. For consider the splendid elusiveness of the book's scheme, whereby I am enabled to air my naked opinions without incurring any responsibility therefor; since nominally I stay always on the other side! No, here at least I had no reason to pose as what seemed expected.

Your rebuttal, my dear fellow, is so precisely what I wanted, if only to lend an air of fairmindedness! You see, here I shall break in indignantly and say what you say, with brief retorts by Charteris. Your scurrilous onslaught upon my books I shall put in the mouth of Charteris, as a *tu quoque* after my advocacy of gusto: the question of my books' permanency being of course with him a vital matter since his existence hinges on it. And then I shall go on to the end.

I don't find that, after all, we disagree as to much. My theory has its root in cowardice? — Of course, it has: for my part, I am terribly afraid of what it is all up to, and feel that you and I and all of us are in a fearful position. I am at one with Maeterlinck and his perpetual *J'ai peur*— Then too you underhandedly suggest that the method does not matter so long as it tenders nourishment, which is equivalent to saying you had as lief eat from a tin plate as any other. Romance, sir, furnishes the proper service: its silver was mined in the moon (by lunatics, of course) and its napery is woven of dreamstuff— As for gusto! Charteris shall consider its importance immediately after he has done with urbanity—a very fitting moment—in the last chapter. Meanwhile to recommend that I acquire an eager and multifarious and sympathetic disposition is precisely as though you suggested I could improve my appearance by having brown eyes. I purposely spoke of acquirable virtues. Thus wit and humor were not mentioned, nor did I include even the power to depict alien temperaments with sympathy—— No, I see plainly what you mean by gusto; but I do not find it in my favorite pages (just as a tonedeaf person might not notice music, of course), and I do not find it in life, except when I have had a good deal to drink, and I emphatically deny that it is essential. You may recall the fable of the Fox without a Tail?

I shall repeat my former advice: read *Thorgils*, and read reverently. I suspect that this is Hewlett's truest book. That, sir, is life. Then too there is a plotless little story of how the greatest genius the world has known sat in a Stratford garden, among much wasted fruit, and drew conclusions as to the ultimate value of gusto. Finally, if you can sufficiently conquer your aversion to Pater, read his essay upon Mérimée. It suggests, to me, an author in whom I am interested: and it explains with uncomfortable discernment why that author, in whom I am interested, writes the romantic books which irritate you.

Ah, well! please answer all my questions,—and believe me, as always,

Yours faithfully,

JAMES BRANCH CABELL

P.S.—I am wondering if Cicely received the little cup I sent her?—it was the wrong color, in honor of New York's adoption of equal suffrage.

From Guy Holt

New York [date?]

Dear Cabell:

[After replying that Vincent Starrett was a well known critic in Chicago, Holt continued]:

I revert to *Beyond Life*. You misconceive me somewhat when you assume that I ask you to adopt a different attitude. Really, I am not altogether naive. I merely wished to comment (reverently, but not too patently so) that in your work (I always except the *Rivet* and the *Jest*) you have attempted to combine a spirit and a form which do not well agree with one another. For by your own words I learn that the purpose of romance (in its sense of "costume piece") is cheerfully to misrepresent life. You do not do this; and speaking from a base, commercial attitude, I believe that is an excellent reason why you should stick to the type of fiction which is loosely but somewhat accurately styled the "study." Surely this is what all your modern books are—studies. You have been pessimistic enough in these, God knows, with some show of reason. I need not point out to the author of *Beyond Life* why readers are ready enough to accept an undercurrent of despair in stories of their own day and demand a hearty joy in tales of other times. John Charteris will not quarrel with me here.

Therefore, since you, for one, cannot keep up the romantic pretense with any convincing show of sincerity, why not openly join us of the other side, particularly as you have already put in four pretty strokes on our behalf? Wear your own uniform, if you like: you are the best judge of whether or no lace and knee-breeches will encumber you; but fight to make today timeless, regardless of whether the rest of us wear tweeds or nothing at all.

Apropos: do you know "The Shropshire Lad"?

> *Therefore [though] the best is bad*
> *Stand and do the best, my lad—*

Your own attitude, more or less, that of the first line; the second you might paraphrase by suggesting that it is pleasanter to talk of olden times. Only, you do not make it pleasanter. I grow tedious, I suppose, and yet I can't risk pointing out that the moral value of the Cinderella legend is not so great as you think it. Consider the well-known plight of those too well read in romantic literature, who pass through all of the tiny crises which make up life, confident that despite whatever blunders and missteps they make, the happy ending awaits them on the three-hundredth page. I fancy that it is as beautiful, as human (and certainly as interesting) to remember that all men are not brave nor all women beautiful and virtuous (or vice versa, for that matter) as to insist mendaciously that the reverse is true. But it is far better to realize that all of us are living exemplifications of a compromise between the romantic dream and the realistic facts. I think this compromise is truth and humanity, and the artist who recognizes it is the only one who puts both these commodities between covers.

It is precisely here that I take my stand, insisting that the method is unimportant. I do not, for example, believe that Dreiser writes badly because he is a meticulous chronicler of facts; he has merely an untidy mind and no sense of beauty in any degree, save of that most primitive form which recognizes the awful virtue of bigness. The truth is that the modern realist (by the way, he need not be completely detached as Flaubert essayed to be) has undertaken a big task at which he has, with one or two exceptions, invariably failed. But his success, witness *Jean-*

Christophe, is very great indeed, and not a whit lessened by the fact that his hero who begins as a very average man ends as one cast in a larger mold.

It is there that realism and romance imperceptibly merge—for realism seeks cause for wonder in common things (precisely as did Raimbaut, you remember) by throwing upon it the glamour of understanding. While romance—well, what else does Romance do?

Frankly I am tempted to believe that the popular attitude toward these two antagonists is the correct one: John Jones, in doublet and hose, is romance; and Gaston de Puysanges (is that his name?) becomes realism if only you dress him in proper business fashion—— So again, I urge you to pay thus much lip-service to commerce and write of ageless men who live nowadays.

As for your remark about service: may I remind you that treacle served in a silver goblet is treacle for a'that. Give us wine, sir. God knows we need it, and you have some heady stuff in your bottle.

But now I do become tedious. Let me, therefore, vulgarly suggest, *en passant,* that perhaps man first conceived the witch-woman as one who by her magic arts alone could keep him faithful —— and pass on to such unimportant matters as the possible publication of your book.

Your plan of incorporating my comments somewhat dismays me, for as you outline it, it destroys a pet scheme of my own for making *Beyond Life* more publishable and possibly more saleable. You see, as it stands now, it presupposes a familiarity with your other books, which could only be expected of its original audience, and one or two hardened reviewers. But how simple to eliminate James Branch Cabell from the text entirely. Happily Nicolas de Caen is still an historical character, (Rascoe, Hertzberg *et al.* to the contrary, notwithstanding); and Sheridan and Wycherly are accessible in other biographical sources than *The Certain Hour.* Your expositions of Gallantry and Chivalry can be based upon the man not the book—— And, on the whole, you lose only the pleasure of writing more openly about yourself than otherwise you could, a chapter-heading, and acquire a somewhat altered introduction. Charteris may remain himself, if you like—although my original idea was complete anonymity for you—even upon the cover; certainly between them.

What do you think? You would lose, in addition, perhaps, the approximation of your Intended Edition, but you would gain a publisher, the more quickly, a public (you would not be appealing to the Average Novel Reader, remember!) and a more unified book.

Then, too, it might be a good plan to make each chapter more of a separate essay, so that, in a pinch the *Atlantic* or some other magazine, could publish selected portions. The whole would be, perhaps, sub-titled

"An Apology for Romance" or "Conversations with a Romanticist" and could be brought out after the usual delay by—

Well, do you offer it to us, Sir?

I am still (or rather, more than ever) the *fons et origo* of this house, despite many attempts by other publishers, made desperate by the draft, to lure me away. And McBride will, I am sure, bear with me in my unaccountably obstinate attempt to foist your wares upon an unawakened public.

There would be other matters to discuss—a few minor changes, which can wait until I arrive in Richmond early in March—perhaps some contractual stipulations. But these can be postponed.

Do you let me know how my suggestions seem to you; and bear with me while I communicate with you upon your monstrous pessimism. I had thought this was the province of youth, to view God and man with a doleful eye. But here am I upon the verge of twenty-six and with the wisdom of my generation quick within me, looking sadly down upon you from the rosy heights. You are all of a dozen years older than I and should of right be putting Pollyanna to the blush, by this. Instead, behold!

Heigh ho, it is midnight, and I have been writing these two hours. Tomorrow I shall copy this, for it needs to be recorded, and in due time, I hope, I shall hear from you your decision on the momentous things I have outlined.

Faithfully yours,
GUY HOLT

Dumbarton, January 17, 1918

My dear Holt:

You are evidently determined to have your book precisely what you want it. For this volume, you know, you are peculiarly, if not entirely, responsible. You inveigle me into believing that I am the possessor of an exact aesthetic creed, which incidentally you believe to be pernicious, and that my Collected Works proclaim this creed. I am thus led to compose this dizain as an Apologia for my dizain of creative books. That is what it is, a premeditated defence of these ten volumes. And now you propose that the lawyer for the defence say what he had to say upon condition that he make no reference whatever to the defendant. To do this would lend just the crowning touch to my exemplification of human unreason, so that I think your plan is admirable.

Meanwhile you have no notion how colorfully I was developing your ideas. Your contribution proved too short for a separate chapter, so that

I have run it in as the opening portion of Epilogistic. (An eminently suitable word to quarrel with.) Besides, you kept entirely to literature, whereas I aimed in each chapter to have the literary "appreciation" the octave of my sonnet, with some cosmic moral for my sestet. The Arbiter chapter, to divulge a secret, is two octaves run together when I had begun to tire of the book—— Now it will have to be recast. I shall particularly lament the queer pathos I got by putting your derogatory observations as to my books into the mouth of Charteris, where it now figures as the complaint of the marionettes against their creator: and to him also I gave your concluding remarks as to the oblivion which has overtaken the real founders of religion and art, which you will find have suffered a sea-change—— Do you know, you had contrived fine cadences and written a deal of excellent prose in that long letter? You must have known it, though. At all events, I pilfered with avidity.

Now, divers considerations as they occur to me. Anonymity is impossible to preserve with anyone who remembers *The Certain Hour,* or by the wildest improbability *The Cords of Vanity,* since this book simply iterates and embellishes much matter from these volumes. There is thus no reason why the deliverer of these observations should not remain one of my book characters: and I want it to join on to the body of my work explicitly. But now the "creator" business is overboard: Charteris met his well merited doom in the September of 1903: he could thus discourse on current events with no one save his creator. Kennaston had lost the knack of talking. Ergo, this book relates the interview of an unidentified person with Robert Etheridge Townsend.

The "creator" business, I repeat, I will eliminate, and "I" will be anonymous. The Prolegomena (*vide* preceding note) I will revise, with Townsend substituted for Charteris, and endowed with a front garden. The references to my books will simply be removed. Only in one place do I foresee trouble, in the introduction of Mrs. Deland's letter, which is for my purpose quite requisite, but in this place I can equivocate along somehow. Indeed here as elsewhere I can refer, at a pinch, to "a book I recently ran across" or to what "I remember to have read somewhere," without too ostentatious coxcombry— That is what you are driving at, you know. There is the tradition that no author must seem to take his own work seriously, and the tradition is weighty. He may devote his existence to producing books and preserve our respect so long as he proclaims the books are not worth producing. This, I grant you, forces most of us to tell the truth in spite of ourselves, but hardly lessens our enforced hypocrisy. Meanwhile, elimination of the "creator" of course makes for coherency on the part of the main speaker. My dream library I shall preserve, as a flight of Townsend's fancy, for I think well of this

Bibliotheca Abscondita. As I get on I become penurious with ideas, and am loath to squander the tiniest. So many of my short stories impress me as a whole book run through by a spendthrift.

The essays, you will find, are easily separable. Indeed, they were written as separate papers, in the beginning, and their conjunction is purely a matter of chronology. Sometimes there is really no actual connection apart from the camouflage of the introductory sentence or so. Consider, and you will see that my literary texts, after my general exposition, are determined by the year of so-and-so's birth, and the thread of my argument quite superficial. But the *Atlantic*, forsooth! and who is going to bell the cat? Who is going to hypnotise any magazine editor into touching such insidious underminings of his livelihood? I need not say that hypothetical worker of miracles will have my benediction.

Now as to publishing *Beyond Life* anonymously, I think it might well be a good notion. Townsend is utterly forgotten, and the book may be attributed to any number of people, with some result commercially. So suppose we make it anonymous. I cannot quite figure out, though, that you recommend this course in so many words. Do you, or don't you?

Please get together in your mind what minor changes might be advisable, and let me know in proper time. I, in the book, don't want to be a smart Alec: and I consciously endeavored to write—here's the real article in coxcombry—nothing that could not be understandable in 1927. Of course, I probably did not succeed, because it is hard not to be "vital": but I tried, as well as to avoid despair.

Such is the tangled exposition of my concurrence with most of, if not all, your suggestions. So do you formally submit the thing, and capture if you can the Baptist vote. Would it not be judicious flattery to invite suggestions from that quarter, as to the requisite changes, and to appear to fall in with such dicta as just what we wanted and were not bright enough to think of? I have frequently practised this method in other walks in life, and find that it invariably fetches excellent results, whether or not you actually do follow the suggestion. I bar the obvious advice to burn the manuscript.

This done, return the book to me to operate upon, as revision from the just decipherable copy now in my hands is out of the question. And then by March the thing will be complete so far as I come in, and we can talk over the last finishing touches.

Reverting to other matters, the Mérimée essay is in the *Miscellaneous Studies:* substitute for his interest in architecture an interest in genealogy, and you may detect with me a certain similarity. Really, I think you would like Pater now. The *Renaissance,* at least, is consecutive and pleasant going. If I may whisper it, I don't find the "style" so wonderful, for the ungetoverable fact that so many of his sentences need re-arrangement in the order of their constituents.

... I was yesterday surprised to find in the November *Athenaeum* two columns and a half about *The Certain Hour*. I wonder if you also encountered it? You "take" from Luce [Press Clipping Bureau], I believe, who does not, to me, send *Athenaeum* notices, and therefore I inquire. I was vastly flattered and spotted some quite quotable bits, but, alas, the sole copy in Richmond belongs to the State Library. If you can manage to run across this notice, I think its English consideration of respectable worth, although it misses the whole point of "a truthful representation" by ignoring the adjective, as well as the circumstance that my remark was not confined to novelists, but included all creative fiction, from Homer down. Still, it is serious acceptance of the book's aesthetic theories, in quite your personal manner. There is another adjective, mark you, which should not be ignored. For the rest, what writer, after sixteen years of writing, would not rejoice to hear he displays a talent which by-and-by may develop into something?

Yours faithfully,
JAMES BRANCH CABELL

Letters from Chicago gave evidence that some citizens of that Midwestern center seemed early to care for Cabell's work. Galantière was active in the book business, foreshadowing his later interest in translations to which he has given much of his life. He wrote Cabell that he had brought Rascoe into the circle of Cabell admirers. Then of course there was Starrett, the first of the champions of Arthur Machen.

From Arthur Machen

Edward House
Lisson Grove
London, N. W. 1
Sexagesima [February 17], 1918

My dear Cabell

Pray let me thank you most heartily for your curious, singular & enchanting book: *The Cream of the Jest*. I have read it with admiration & delight. It is, indeed, beautifully done; you have all my congratulations.

But I do not know whether you know all that is to be known concerning small mirrors: but of this, silence.

By the way: do you use the word "prelate" in America differently from our English way? Here, "prelate" and "bishop" are synonymous.

If I may be autobiographical for a moment; I may say that I have fallen on evil days: I have been a busy London journalist for more than seven years. Your address: "Dumbarton Grange, Dumbarton, Va." sounds to me very pleasantly: I imagine you, I hope correctly, sipping mint-julep on your piazza. And, speaking of journalism, all of my most moving news in it was to take three American officers—Southerners—over the Tower of London last June. The Yeomen of the Guard saluted as your countrymen went by; it was somehow "too deep for tears."

I remain with most hearty thanks,

Yours

ARTHUR MACHEN

Dumbarton, March 8, 1918

My dear Mr. Machen:

Your letter gave me such huge pleasure that I forthwith seize upon the flimsy pretext of assuring you that, so far as I know, we in America apply the word "prelate" to the higher clergy generally—as indeed seems logical. A cardinal, I would say, is eminently praelatus, and, between us, it was Cardinal Gibbons who "sat" for me—— All this, though, is but an excuse for explaining that the book was sent you in such doubtfulness as to its reception that the escorting letter by no means voiced the greatness in my eyes of Arthur Machen. Now that you have been civil, and far more than civil, I feel a little more at liberty to speak concerning my experience with the writer's books—— Seven years back it was an unfavorable review of *The House of Souls* which led me to purchase that volume, and thus brought me into perfect sympathy with Keats' watcher of the skies, as well as into astonished bewilderment when I discovered this was not a new book and not a generally famous book. Without flattery, the last circumstance remains to me still quite inexplicable. Such of your other volumes as I found obtainable I have since then procured, though even now my collection stays incomplete: and since then also I have preached your excellence on every feasible occasion. I may even boast it was I who told McBride & Company about you, and sent them after *The Terror,* and incidentally furnished them with your portrait, for the catalogue I forwarded you—these facts being cited not as a claim of indebtedness, but as a substantiating proof of some enthusiasm—— And still nobody seemed to be familiar with your work, save here and there a rare phenomenon like Starrett. In passing, I have never met Starrett, and know very little about him: but we were drawn together

across half a continent by our common admiration for this Arthur
Machen—— But nowadays I begin actually to hear talk of Arthur
Machen. It really looks as though you were about to come into your
own—and, I sincerely hope, a Complete Edition. In short, sir, it really
looks as though all our American bookbuyers were not condemned to
eternal idiocy, and as though a spark or two of intelligence were flicker-
ing somewhere among their doddering ranks. So I pray the spark may
spread and serve to kindle a veritable *feu de joie.* Then to how many persons may I say "I told you so."

Meanwhile I have heard something as to *The Secret Glory,* and hope
it may soon, somehow, be revealed in bookform—— And meanwhile too
it is the fact that you should be a busy London journalist of seven years
standing which seems to me beyond weeping, in view of all the books
unwritten during that time, and all this comes to you as rather incoherent but honest fealty. Godspeed to you, sir, and to the oncoming
fame you merit!

Yours faithfully,
JAMES BRANCH CABELL

Before *The Cream of the Jest,* Cabell had already published nine volumes,
which, when listed in the front of *The Jest,* caused young Burton Rascoe in
Chicago to surmise that they were all imaginary. He later admitted that he
quickly looked up the volumes in a public library and wrote to Cabell: "I am
enclosing herewith a review which very feebly records my reactions to your
wholly delightful books. . . . If I seem to gush, it is with the utmost sincerity
that I do so; you are already numbered among my favorites in modern letters—
a select and distinguished crew, with that benign cynic, Anatole France, at the
helm, James Branch Cabell as first mate, James Stephens as chief petty officer,
Leonid Andreyev as steward, and with a small but sturdy set of able seamen
doing duty aft and below. . . . I wish to assure you, Mr. Cabell, that if my humble typewriter can acquire a potency it does not now possess, it shall help to
make your name known among the discerning readers of this genial but in-
genuous republic."

Whereupon there started the most remarkable, as it was certainly the most
rambunctious, of all campaigns in the history of polite letters, with the appearance in the Chicago *Tribune* of an article by Rascoe headed "Here's a Chance
to Own Another First Edition."

Dumbarton, March 2, 1918

My dear Mr. Rascoe:

It grieves me that you did not send me a copy of "On a Certain Condescension in Our Natives," as the clipping bureau might easily have
missed it in collecting actual reviews. But as it happens, the bureau did

not miss it, so that your generosity again overwhelmed me—on Thursday evening, to be exact—and I am thanking you therefor very heartily.

I should like, extremely like, to think you are right in what you say about me: that apart, I know you are right in the remainder of the article. But as a nation we seem from the first to have combined braggadocio with self distrust: and we continue more or less uneasily to request of visiting foreigners their impressions of America. You have only to attempt to imagine the London press devoting columns to what a distinguished tourist thinks about England, to see that this is really a case in point. Besides, American Literature, as endorsed by the textbooks, is in point of fact a depressing exhibit, of moribund reputations kept alive by the oxygen of patriotism. You really cannot well blame anyone who elects to shrug and avert his eyes. No less, the not unnatural result is rather hard on some few persons here and there who approach their typewriters seriously: and for these few you have spoken with admirable force.

Meanwhile, I believe—or hear, at least—that the Folletts are going to do an article on me, some day or other. I only wish I could look forward to receiving their verdict with a quarter of the pleasure yours has given.

Yours faithfully,

JAMES BRANCH CABELL

From Burton Rascoe

The Chicago Tribune

Chicago, March 7, 1918.

My dear Mr. Cabell:

When I got in from New York yesterday morning I found your letter of the 4th on my desk. I did not send you the squid "On a Certain Condescension in Our Natives" for the reasons that I was rushed in getting my work up in advance before leaving for New York and that Guy Holt had promised to send one to you. He also said he would write you about my coming East.

I made an attempt to see you. In fact I came down as far as Baltimore; but there I discovered that train schedules are made up largely for the embarrassment and harassment of passengers. I found that I could call upon you at 10 o'clock in the night or visit with you between 7:15 and 9:45 in the morning. (These may not be the exact hours; but they approximate fact.) Such a venture would hardly argue for my sanity or general regard for the personal comfort of others: and I had to be back in

New York on Monday morning. So I gave up the trip. It was to me a great disappointment. I had gone East with the hope of meeting you as a compensation for the less pleasant business of talking with publishers about their spring output of Pollyanna and detective fiction.

I got a look at the manuscript of *Beyond Life* while Guy and I were at lunch at Mouquin's on Tuesday. I wanted to take it with me, but Guy said he was going to Richmond on Friday to go over the manuscript with you. I am highly pleased that it is to be published and I felt a distinct glow when Guy told me that what I had written had sold enough of your other books, particularly of *The Cream of the Jest* to impress McBride.

I am sorry I could not bring the manuscript of *Beyond Life* back with me—the tastes I had of it were most relishable. I am to have it later. Guy has probably told you that I have asked to use it, or parts of it, serially in The *Tribune*—on a page in the Sunday sections of which I am in charge. Payment for the rights in this will go to you I presume.

I have heralded your name in the place spiritually called Sodom and Egypt and at least three persons in medieval Boston are now engaged in reading *The Cream of the Jest* upon my urgent recommendation. I talked with Mencken and was surprised and disappointed when he said, "I am afraid your man, Cabell, is not *vital* enough." I was, in fact, so stunned I did not answer for some few moments. However I soon impressed him with the fact that it was your very lack of the Dreiserian vitality that made you infinitely superior to Dreiser. A three page letter goes to him this week, summing up some of the more salient features in your work. He has promised to do the article on you which I had suggested.

Stearns of the *Dial* told me tonight that he had received an article from the Folletts [Mr. and Mrs. Wilson] on you as "The Aristophanes of Virginia." I am to see it tomorrow. Meanwhile I shall mention you almost every week and perhaps get a chance to do another bit at an earlier date. . . . And if you possess the manuscript of one of your books and are willing to part with it, you would find nowhere a more grateful recipient than the writer of this hurried and staccato letter.

Most sincerely,
BURTON RASCOE

Dumbarton, March 13, 1918

My dear Mr. Rascoe:

. . . I do not understand about Mr. Mencken—not as regards his opinion I was not "vital" enough, but as to where he is to "do" an article and when. And here again, you see, I owe you thanks. You are . . . quite overwhelmingly munificent: and I hope your generosity may include a sight of that three-page letter, because I am very honestly interested in the more salient features in my work and would like to know what they are. . . .

Let me . . . try my hand at the Tarkington book.[2] Here is a man, I think, of genius, but certainly of vast talent, who has never written a book in any way commensurate with himself, and who to all appearance has quite lost any inclination ever to write that book. That, I much fear, would be my text, despite the fact that I have enjoyed every volume he ever published.

If I possessed the manuscript of any of my books it would be at your service. But I must tell you that as each book was published, and indeed each magazine tale, I have regularly burned the manuscript, just back of the stable. It has become a sort of recognized ceremony. A manuscript, to its writer at any rate, betrays too nakedly the author's poverty of thought and his makeshifts: it constitutes a quite positively indecent exhibit. I am still almost sure all manuscripts ought to be burned—— "Almost," I say, because Holt came to talk with me about this very matter, and with some eloquence presented the other side. He wrung from me a promise to—well, to consider preserval of my manuscripts for the future. I don't think I went further than that. In that event, I promised him the rough copy of *Beyond Life*—typewritten, but with some million alterations and additions—and that will leave me scriptless save for the two books I have in hand. . . . I can only say that if I finally give him *Beyond Life*—and I feel that I ought to—I hereby promise you the manuscript of the next book by me as ever is. As matters stand, I cannot well say more.

Yours faithfully

JAMES BRANCH CABELL

Dumbarton, March 18, 1918

My dear Mr. Rascoe:

This comes as a sort of postscript to my preceding letter, and is in acknowledgment of your suggestion as to Julian, which arrived just after I had posted the long communication you have probably by this received—— Well, as to Julian, I will think about it. Here is a great theme, of course, but after all it has been a deal pawed over. I had read both

[2] Cabell's review of *Booth Tarkington* by Robert Cortes Holliday (Garden City, 1918) appeared in The *Tribune*, April 6, 1918, under the title of "The Tragedy of Mr. Tarkington."

the Ibsen play [3] (which, with *Peer Gynt* and *The Pretenders, is* probably his best, to my thinking also) and the Merejkowski book (some day I mean to read the third volume of that trilogy also, but thus far it stays a labor deferred), as well as Gibbon, who for no unaccountable reasons warms to the Apostate. And there my knowledge ceases—— Meanwhile I have begun a fantastic sort of a something of which, as loosely outlined to him, Holt seems to think rather well. This I hope to finish by autumn.

Beyond Life has gone to him, and ought to be in your hands now at no remote date. Deal tenderly therewith, for it contains quite unjustifiable orgies of "writing." Still, I seemed to find an idea, here and there, which was not yet in print and rather needed expression.

To the Follett article I still look forward. But why, as yet I wonder, Aristophanes? I could contrive a far more plausible libel against Apuleius, or even Lucian, so far as goes my personal view. Meanwhile with some impatience I await the analogue.

Yours faithfully,

JAMES BRANCH CABELL

Within a few days, Rascoe withdrew his suggestion of Julian the Apostate as a subject for Cabell's efforts, adding ". . . I have a notion, now, that possibly what Mencken said to me was in a way an attempt to draw me out about you; that it was not meant seriously. I hope it was not, for I have high admiration for Mencken's judgment, his accomplishments, and his point of view about life. He could write an eminently readable, worth-while article about your work. What is more, it would have effect."

From Arthur Machen

London, April 8, 1918

My dear Mr. Cabell

I am delighted to hear from you again: I hope you will continue to write to me at your leisure moments. You write the cheering word, & I assure you, sir, I have need of it. I go to my work every morning saying with the Psalmist: *Heu mihi, (quia) incolatus meus prolongatus est (habitavi cum) habitatibus Schechem!* or *Kedar,* is it? [Woe is me, that I sojourn in Mesech, that I dwell in the tents of Kedar! Psalm 120—King James Version.]

[3] *Emperor and Galilean.*

By the way, I was envying a man this morning. I was talking to George Moore—in the way of my business—& he told me, quite gravely, that he was the only person in the whole of English Literature who had taken prose fiction seriously; also that [A] *Mummer's Wife* was the only tale in English which would have the slightest significance to Catullus, Horace, or Apuleius! I wish I could feel like that.

I thank you very heartily for your friendly offices with McBride. They will have none of *The Secret Glory:* I am not astonished, for it is not a bit like *The Terror,* & publishers always desire replicas. I remember— 20 years ago—my publisher, Grant Richards, imploring me, quite seriously, not to ruin the small reputation I had gained by *The Three Imposters* by publishing the tedious *Hill of Dreams.*

I have been re-reading your book with very great pleasure. I think that there is a very exquisite skill in your dissolution of the spell, as it were; in your identification of the Seal with the top of a cold cream vase—& yet the truth of the vision remains. It was the fatal & most abominable error of protestantism not to see this, not to see that the art of life is to pass thro' things temporal so that we lose not the things eternal: the eternal things which are hidden under the temporal veils.

Yours

ARTHUR MACHEN

Dumbarton, April 5, 1918

My dear Rascoe:

(For I seem to know you fairly well by this) I am afraid you are almost right as to the garden variety of book reviewers. I don't know why Holt should have sent you the appendix to *Beyond Life*—though I am glad to have it interest you, of course—but I assure you it could have been made much and very much longer. I could have cited quite as uncivil things about the four picture books, but after all the gist of the literary criticism accorded them was that they were "beautifully illustrated by Howard Pyle." Reviews of *The Cords of Vanity,* in particular, would make a handy compendium of Billingsgate: for reasons that I have never quite understood the vast majority of reviewers when dealing with that book seemed to be frothing at the mouth and pawing the air with the left hand all the while they wrote—— But I have become hardened to all kinds of reviews save one—the sort that starts with an intelligent sounding paragraph and then turns word for word into the blurb. These continue to irritate because they raise false hopes—— Some day, when you again turn eastward, my experiences will be at your service. But I am afraid they are not uncommon,—which makes them all the more tragic.

I await your article with the most animated and embarrassed interest. I only hope you may not run it with the Tarkington-book wail of fury, because you are always more than kind, and it would be disastrous thus directly to put side by side the giant painted outside the show-tent and the reality within. . . . Perhaps you do not agree with me about Tarkington? Holt insists that I overrate the Indianian, and privately, I confess that his recent articles on public questions have rather staggered me, as betraying a core of unsuspected puerility. His friends ought to restrain him from doing, or at all events, publishing that kind of blather. But otherwise he delights me, in the bared teeth of my convictions, so that I threw my brick with one hand and with the other removed my hat—— This reminds me that the portraits enumerated in Chapter I of *Beyond Life* are an attempt at honest confession as to my "literary creditors"—— What you have written tempts me to swell the list with Anatole France. I shall sample his books so soon as opportunity serves. I have read only two—*Thaïs* and *Le Livre de mon Ami*—and from neither of these did I consciously acquire anything. Still, one never knows.

I am wondering how much of *Beyond Life* you plan to use, and in what form. Please, in passing, see that these papers and a paper with your article are sent me. I am endeavoring to get them at this end of the line, but the news-dealer, while rich in promise, is not infallible. Then too if you use much of it there is now a new ending to Chapter IX which I would send you for inclusion. . . . And now you have read it, is there not anything you can suggest in the way of change? If so, I very honestly do welcome criticism and suggestion up to the moment the book is electrotyped. Holt has in this respect been perfectly invaluable: and now I am greedily trying to rope you in. Come, now, there must be something in the book you objected to! I had flattered myself there was at least some one thing in this volume nicely calculated to irritate every imaginable sort of reader, and it is really a pity that Holt's marginal comments, many of which were chirographic squeals, cannot well be printed with book—— Now he is bent upon including something—I do not quite understand what—concerning a considerable section of the public, which is pathetically desirous to appreciate literature and yet is not able to recognize it when literature comes their way. And I can only tell him there are no such persons hereabouts—which is the absolute truth—and that in fifteen years of writing, I have detected no sign of them elsewhere. He insists they are everywhere. He is quite wrought up about it. So I am asking him to type his views upon the subject, with a view to their possible inclusion in *Beyond Life*. Meanwhile I adhere to scepticism. . . .

You note I make no reference to "Apuleius and Lucian plus" and all the other outrageous flatteries with which you have submerged me. I am tired of arguing with you. Besides, whatever my opinion of your verdicts as touches their justice, there is no questioning their euphony. So I repudiate and smirk.

Yours faithfully,

JAMES BRANCH CABELL

From Burton Rascoe

Chicago, April 9, 1918

Dear Cabell:

. . . You demand to know if there is anything in *Beyond Life* that irritates me. Looking back I can recall only one thing and that a very inconsequential and piddling one; purely as an unlovely concept, one that brought me up with a jerk; your speaking of a church "adorned with a tall phallic symbol" appealed to me as something I should delete. This repugnance of mine for the use of the word in that connection may be due solely to association—the fact that I have had a violent reaction of repugnance for the facile ability of the psycho-analysts to find a "phallic symbol" in almost everything. "Phallic" in itself is a greasy word; to me it connotes something of the same thing as "ooze." The double "l" and the "phi" or "f" sounds conspire to make the word disagreeable to me. There! As for the rest I would not touch it. In fact, I doubt seriously whether it should have been tampered with even at Holt's no doubt wise suggestions; for after all, a book is a personal expression, the record of moods; and even where it is irritating the result is no more than a clash of temperaments, between reader and author—and the author has the floor, not the reader. At any rate I should like to have a transcript of the original draft and Holt's "squeals." And probably I would not get one intelligent person in fifty to agree with me regarding "phallic." So don't make the change.

No doubt the psycho-analysts could lay some horrible sex charge at my door by reason of my repugnance for "phallic." Did you read Freud's *Leonardo da Vinci?* To me it was unbelievably idiotic. If you haven't read it, get it; it's a revelation of the monstrosity of adductions the so-called scientific mind can build up from a debatable premise.

The references to the war, much as they impressed and delighted me, you know, of course, I cannot run. The new sedition act makes the pragmatic course of avoiding all mention of the war the wise one lest one wind up in Leavenworth prison. It is a frightful concession to make, but you will understand. After the war, when minds have got back to normal—even among the presumably rational—your truths will be accepted; just now rationality hasn't a chance. It would hurt you. That is why it is possible that the book, in its entirety, should not be published until the war is over. Perhaps the emptiest of delusions is that free speech or liberty is possible in America. The things that Maximilian Harden [4] has said in Germany since the beginning of the war would be impossible in America. And, too, perhaps it is for the best— We have been dragged into the war against all reason or rationality but we are in it now to the end; when the casualty lists run into the thousands instead of mothers saying "Why has my son been killed?" they will be saying "Why is my son's death not avenged?" It is the psychology of war, the psychology of the mass: it is beautiful, it is pathetic, it is tragic.

Sincerely,
BURTON RASCOE

Your telling me you have read little of A. France doesn't surprise me. You and he have little resemblance to each other. It is just that he and you stand alone in your generation as ironists. You are not indebted to him, I am fairly sure.

Dumbarton, April 13, 1918

My dear Rascoe:

Very probably you are right, and I stand a detected "realist." I must protest, though, that you have evidently been reading my books in the Intended Edition, rather than in any known to me. . . . The drawback is that when you write such articles about me I am afraid to publish anything thereafter, somewhat as our joint acquaintance Sheridan declared himself afraid to write against the author of *The School for Scandal*, because I comprehend the improbability of my living up to your promises. . . . I am now suspicious that you have been doing what Holt tried to prevent—namely, reading some of my out-and-out "romantic" books? But if so, why the marked omission of *Gallantry*? Ormskirk is still a person whom I regard without disfavor— But truly should you attempt the "romantic" tales, read carefully. You will thus find that the people, putting apart fine talk, are in what they actually *do* and in their actuating mo-

---

[4] German journalist who was an outspoken critic of his Government and of the German High Command.

tives (not always put explicitly, out of deference to the Messrs. Harper) not unpathetically human. At least, I find them so—— Holt says that amounts to making the whole affair a costume ball, and that in fact these tales are nothing more. To which I reply that I like to see human nature tricked out with such splendiferous garb and language because I think it really needs some such enhancement—— Do you remember Thackeray's drawing of Louis XIV?—it epitomizes, I am afraid, my "romantic" formulae—— Yes, now I come to think of it, that drawing is an excellent criticism.

"Phallic"—it is ugly. But then it is perfectly true, and has long seemed to me about the best joke ever contrived by respectability—— The war portions we had gone over quite carefully, and, I thought, had softened into inoffensiveness. (Not for newspaper use, of course: never at any time did I think the *Tribune* would want to run this portion.) But now it seems there still remains some acerbity? Well, I shall again go over the manuscript very carefully, with this in view. . . .

Yours faithfully,
JAMES BRANCH CABELL

Dumbarton, April 18, 1918

My dear Rascoe:

. . . Holt has sent me Mr. [Ben] Hecht's article, with Mr. Sell's [5] offer to permit me to answer it in the *News*. But this I have no intention of doing: there is no need to argue with any one who attacks a book [*The Cream of The Jest*] for containing phrases which are not in it. Still, I resent his remarks as to *The Hill of Dreams*, especially since, as it happens, Machen read and liked my book, and wrote me a letter that I prize, as to this "curious, beautiful and unique volume." [6] I really think that as to this particular point Mr. Machen and I are better judges than Mr. Hecht—— Apropos, "jongleur." If Mr. Follett also employed this word, here is ammunition for you. The jongleur composed nothing and pretended to compose nothing. The troubadour, as later the trouvere, composed the song or the romance, and the jongleur was his attendant who sang or recited it. Later the jongleurs set up in business for themselves, and went through the country singing and reciting the verses of other people, but above all playing upon musical instruments and performing gymnastic tricks and parlor conjuring—were, in fine, jugglers. I indicated quite clearly the functions of a jongleur in *The Soul of Melicent*,

5 Henry B. Sell, Literary Editor of the Chicago *Daily News*, 1916–1920.
6 Actually Machen wrote "your curious, singular, & enchanting book."

if you have ever seen that volume—— So that here again we have the critic glibly employing words of whose meaning he is ignorant. However, your answer was infernally clever and, I think, sufficient.

Faithfully yours,
JAMES BRANCH CABELL

From Burton Rascoe

Chicago, April 20, 1918

My dear Cabell:

I should have been immensely disappointed if you had bothered to answer Hecht . . . but I'll save your dignity, if you permit, by waging the fight single handed. . . .

He reminds me of nothing so much as old Uncle Cabbage, my grandfather's Negro down in Kentucky. Uncle Cabbage used to tell us children about the Bible which he could not read, in the most awe-inspiring senseless words you can possibly imagine. One of them was "miscobobocorration," a blending, I judge, of "mistake" and "corroboration." But after all, Uncle Cabbage was something of an artist: I remember yet the affecting intonation of "I kaint read ner write but I knows the law dat leads to de Hebenly gates. I knows de Bible from beginnin' to end, Genumsis to Rebelations, Alpha, Omega, first and last—and I nebber makes a miscobobocorration."

Thanks for the tip on "jongleur." I knew the correct use of the word; but somehow the point did not occur to me. Any coaching you may offer in my duels will be appreciated.

Sincerely,
BURTON RASCOE

Dumbarton, April 27, 1918

My dear Holt:

Well, here you have another instalment to the serial of revision. Two additions, as you see: and another version of that interminable Tenth Chapter— How does this please you now? It surely starts with a delusive show of lightness; and you will note that for your benefit I have colloquialized at least the opening sentence of the matter ascribed to myself.

Meanwhile I am your very grateful debtor for an early sight of the

Follett article. I liked it. How could I do otherwise when I recognized so much of the stuff that I prepared for that evasive booklet? Even so, it seemed to me charmingly ingenious, if almost too neat in the way it worked out like a mathematical demonstration. "The fatal fault of your theorizing is that it is too complete," as I once observed to Felix Kennaston. Still, it is most complimentary, which shows one of the advantages of preparing the criticisms of yourself—I am presuming *The Dial* uses the article in their current issue, and am asking you in that event to purchase and send me two copies, for newspaper use here.

Rascoe and myself are now corresponding at the rate of some three or four letters a week, and he, I think, is "editing" *Beyond Life* excellently. This should reach you at about the same time as Rupert Hughes' attack on the first extract (of which I have seen a proof), and this, just conceivably, I may answer. The trouble is that the essays themselves will answer him as they appear, and that he in the main says nothing with which the book as a whole will seriously disagree. Two of his points, as to actors' painting their faces and people in contemporary fiction not talking as they actually would talk, I had myself made in the second extract before the appearance of his paper. At any event it is good to discover that Rupert Hughes is interested in, and has theories about, literature— Then, too, I had a letter from Mr. Maule [7] yesterday to congratulate me upon "the tremendous stir your work is making in Chicago, resulting, I am told, in a brisk sale." (Ahem, Mr. Secretary, I shall look with renewed interest for a royalty statement.) And even the *Journal* editor here has noticed the articles (by me) and wants to know if he can reprint some of them. So I begin to think the *Tribune* must be pretty well read.

At all events go ahead with your reading of that poor Tenth Chapter, and when you have finished send me your snarls and fleers and cavils, and objections generally, with suggestion as to what form the next revision had preferably take; and forward the manuscript to Rascoe.

Yours faithfully,
JAMES BRANCH CABELL

7 Harry Edward Maule, editor with Doubleday, Page and Company in 1918.

❦ 3 ❧

BEYOND LIFE

My dear Rascoe:

At the price of vigilance I secured last Sunday's paper at the stand, and make you my compliments upon your editing. You will be hard put to it, though, for titles. Why, for instance, "The Demiurge"? I know, and you know, and Holt would know: but I will wager a reasonable amount that no other reader of the *Tribune* can guess just why the last article should be thus headed—— As for Saturday's evincement of "mania," I found it of more than personal interest. To begin with, I am glad you know *Hieroglyphics,* which I read last summer, in the midst of *Beyond Life,* and so found peculiarly interesting: but then how maddeningly it skips from splendid things to profound inanities! His observations as to Thackeray, for example, are the dicta of an imbecile ward: and, as always, Machen has an irritating trick of hinting at something which is too awful to talk about, when in point of fact he means nothing in particular. But with all that, he is one of my enthusiasms, and I only wish that he were better known. There, sir, is a writer whom you might conscientiously puff.

As for your trinity, how I would like to talk them over with you! Lamb,—well, yes, of course—but, at the same time— That would be about my verdict. There is a sort of worried jocosity about his "style," like a bachelor uncle trying to be agreeable to his small nephews, and I resent it. About Pater you voice one of my personal contentions: that we have here an aesthetic force, rather than a prose model. If you want a personal opinion, Pater wrote badly. He was intrigued by the possibilities of building English sentences in the Greek manner (which really is fascinating: compare the sentences about Millamant in the Candle chapter of *Beyond Life*), but he never, never managed to get his clauses in the best order. Stevenson, of course, is all Gothic architecture: trim and delightful, but so offensively snappy: as for the "tuberose personality," you err upon the side of charitable speech. The Villon essay (and story) is all you assert in the way of prose composition: but Stevenson understood Villon no better than he did, say, aeroplanes; and both the papers are written by the descendant of Scotch Covenanters—— But I am straying into the essay form, where my intentions were epistolary. It is because your article peculiarly interests me. For the personal compliments I have ceased to thank you, having gone into grateful bankruptcy.

The Cords of Vanity has gone to you. I looked it over, and have decided that "convincing" novels of life at twenty five should not be written then, but at about fifty when the author is powerfully aided by forgetfulness—— It is droll to consider that in 1909 this volume was thought shocking: and, indeed, it came too soon, in every way. For the rest, I refer you to the *Tribune* of 7 April 1909: "Probably you will not know quite what to make of it. I frankly confess that I do not."

Holt has sent me a proof of the Follett article, by which I was surprised agreeably. His theory about me works out so neatly that I begin to think there must be something in it: I always liked mathematics. Of course, there is the drawback that the *Rivet* and the *Eagle's Shadow*, and even the *Cords* with any exactitude, decline to fit in with the theory, but over this contretemps Mr. Follett really glides very gracefully, in the way he mentions these books without committing himself to any exact criticism. In fine, I think it is a monstrously clever article: I like it, and far better than I had anticipated—— But even he trips, in denying the existence of Raimbaut de Vaquieras and Riczi. Riczi was a real person, who married Henry IV of England, precisely as is described in "The Navarrese": [1] and Vaquieras, just as he figures in "Belhs Cavaliers," [2] was a well-known Provençal poet, as any book about such gentry will evince. And Alessandro de Medici (of "Balthazar's Daughter") [3] likewise wore flesh and blood to the discomfort of a great many Florentines, as any history-book will prove. And the rest of my "sources"—I need not formally exclude Villon and Petronius—are imaginary, with the surnames of more-or-less noted mediaeval poets but with new Christian names. Here, then, you have the full truth as to the *Hidden Way* volume—though why, indeed, would I be boring you therewith? I do not know. Meanwhile Mr. Follett's mathematical demonstration has stirred me to envy: I shall attempt to complete it, on another sheet. And the word "jongleur" he uses rightly enough.

Yours faithfully,

JAMES BRANCH CABELL

---

1 "Story of the Navarrese," one of the stories in Cabell's *Chivalry*.
2 and 3 Stories in Cabell's *The Certain Hour*.

From Burton Rascoe

Chicago, April 28[?] 1918

My dear Cabell:

. . . What I have written about you has drawn a twelve page un-solicited article against your "historical inaccuracies" out of Rupert Hughes. I am running it Saturday. I shall send you a proof of it tomorrow: it will amuse you immensely. If you are moved to jest with Hughes, by all means do so and I will be highly pleased to print it. I am inclosing a transcript . . . of a letter I have written to Hughes. I could not forbear to kid him ever so gently—I detest his books.

I was at a dinner party last night where Hecht was also a guest. He let drop a remark and I, primed with Bourbon, lit into him. The battle lasted for more than an hour, in which all the venom I have had stored up against the fellow, was poured out with marvelous lack of reticence, tact, and generosity. Present were Sherwood Anderson, Carl Sandburg, Waldo Frank, Llewellyn Jones and Mrs. Anderson. There were fulminations and explosions, highly diverting, they tell me, to the scamps who schemed the debâcle. Poor Frank, expecting probably the deference due a visiting New York novelist, was forced to be content with one utterance: "I did not know that such excitement about literature existed anywhere in the United States."

Would you mind telling me, strictly in confidence, whether the stories you have submitted to Mencken had been offered elsewhere? The reason I ask is this—entirely *entre nous*—that too many stories in the *Smart Set* will help the magazine rather than help you. The magazine has had this merit that it has given a voice to new writers in the past and that it has published much excellent stuff which would have been turned down, I think, in other magazines. But Mencken is a remarkably clever fellow— he is exercising a distinctive force in writing in this country, a force that in some instances has been pernicious, in that men like Louis Untermeyer, Louis Sherwin, Hecht, and others have entirely abandoned self-expression to express themselves à la Mencken; and the tendency I have suspected is for Mencken to mould the younger men into the Menckenian or *Smart Set* mould——This, of course, would never happen to you at all—but I would beg you not ever to revise a story according to his notions. If he wishes to use a story just as it is written, well and good, otherwise get it back, send it elsewhere, if necessary to me, and I'll see that it is published somehow.

Sincerely,

BURTON RASCOE

Cabell answered Rupert Hughes at some length in the Chicago *Tribune,* saying in part: ". . . I have read this article with all that interest which none but feels at seeing himself rebuked in print, as well as with, I trust, appropriate regret that the captain did not in any way approve of my paper on 'Literature and Life.'

"I very honestly deplore this circumstance in accordance with its actual importance. Still, various causes combine to prevent my entering into any serious discussion of Capt. Hughes' literary ideals, either as explained in his article or as exemplified in his books. The latter, as the phrase is, speak for themselves. . . . For it seems more to the point quite humbly to explain that these little essays of mine now being printed in the *Sunday Tribune* are extracts from a volume, to be called *Beyond Life,* which I believe, when published in its entirety, will reveal between Capt. Hughes and myself no difference so wide as to be undesirable. It is merely that Capt. Hughes, in the impetuous way of these bluff military fellows, has seized upon a brick, in part to prove that a building's architecture is all wrong; and incidentally, of course, to heave at the architect's head. . . .

"Meanwhile, his main contention—that literary affairs in America are not very strikingly dissimilar to what they have always been in every land—is one of the contretemps which *Beyond Life* especially laments; and inasmuch as here as elsewhere Capt. Hughes pursues me along lines of argument which I have very lately traveled, with results that are presently to appear in the *Tribune,* this scarcely seems the happiest place wherein to controvert these arguments. For two of his most telling 'points' indeed—as to such dissimilar matters as the employment of grease paints by actors, and of improbable dialogue by novelists—the curious may find that I had actually anticipated, in the second extract from *Beyond Life,* as published a week before the captain was moved to attack me. . . .

"Nor would I willingly omit to express appreciation of the fact that to his presentment of truisms Capt. Hughes has loaned the inestimable ornament of humor. For there can be little doubt that the captain's remarkable display of erudition is a joke that was intentional. In our first bewildered glow of astonishment to discover that Capt. Rupert Hughes is interested in and even has theories about literature, any one of us might pass over his comments upon Greek writers, say, as Gradgrindian stuff quite seriously intended.

"Yet none upon a second reading could fail to perceive that the humor of it all is very fairly describable as Aristophanic, if but in that a footnote is usually required to explain it. Though, indeed, I doubt if for the captain's jokes a footnote is always necessary. His contention, for example, that Greek tragedy ought not to be appraised 'as if Sophocles and Euripides and their contemporaries summed up Greek dramatic art,' but only after comparing all the other Attic dramatists, has certainly a ring so plausible that for the moment one is gulled: yet instantly reflection suggests that the work of these other dramatists has perished a many centuries ago; and you wonder how Capt. Hughes proposes to set about making a study of them, and so perceive that he is voicing his sturdy military humor. . . .

"Thus there seems to be no real conflict between the general contention of Capt. Hughes and the actual trend of that small luckless essay which he has elected very dexterously to assail with his habitual vigor and with his unwontedly clever burlesque of erudition. . . ."

Dumbarton, May 9, 1918

My dear Rascoe:

. . . In the Hughes article I note your editing with entire approval: and even so, the whole thing impresses me as a little underbred (*my* part, I mean). I was irritated, and I showed it, with very little of the auctorial virtue called urbanity. . . . "Dynamic Illusions" came out shorter than I had anticipated, and so has set me figuring. Can you not begin to use more generous extracts? I would like as much as possible of *Beyond Life* to come out in the *Tribune*. It puts the book on a new basis in my own eyes. For some while I have had the uncomfortable suspicion that the only reasons my books were written and published was a certain feeble-mindedness in Holt and myself: but to write articles for the *Tribune* is legitimate business. So I have been counting Sundays up to October, and at the rate we are going now we will nowhere near finish the book in time for publication—— Which brings me, naturally, to the statement that I had this morning a long and delightful letter from Wilson Follett, enclosing a copy of his article. He tells me it was much altered in the *Dial* office, with many deletions which he regrets (did you not see it in its first shape?) and also makes many delightful observations which I would blush to repeat. I am the more pleased—— Now he, too, asks if I know Hergesheimer. And I don't. It is the more embarrassing because Hergesheimer came to Richmond to see me last week, and reduced me to feeble equivocation. Let me know your opinion of him. Ad interim I shall procure *The Three Black Pennys*.

Yours faithfully,

JAMES BRANCH CABELL

From Burton Rascoe

Chicago, May 12, 1918

My dear Cabell:

So Mr. Follett is now interested in Hergesheimer? I am beginning timidly to wonder if my two squibs directed against [his] *Some Modern Novelists* had some effect. H. B. Fuller in the *Dial* backed me up in my contention against that book, although he did not specifically mention

Hergesheimer or any of the American novelists. For Hergesheimer I could not, on the strength of what he has written so far, become so enthusiastic, by far, for instance, as I have for a certain Virginian: it is [a] matter of personal preference in the way in which a book is written and in what is written about. But Hergesheimer is eminently worth reading; he is a conscientious novelist who has somehow got into the *Saturday Evening Post* as a permanent feature; and further, in his metier he performs as excellently, as creditably as any of the young Englishmen who came in for honorable mention in *Some Modern Novelists*. I find the short stories in *Gold and Iron* rather heavy going, just as I found *Tono-Bungay, Clayhanger, W. E. Ford: a Biography, Mendel, The Prussian Officer*, and other books of the current English school rather heavy going. Frank Swinnerton's *Nocturne* of which Holt wrote an excellent review for me on Saturday, and which I read night before last, is, I think, superior to anything done by the young disciples of Wells. This work of Swinnerton's (which you must read) is as perfect as a Zorn etching, as a Brahms concerto; for sheer technical brilliancy it is marvellous: I cannot cease wondering at the effect he gets into the thing, at his economy of method, at his suggestions of tragedy—— But to get back to Hergesheimer, I am going to write an article about his work some time in the near future: it will be expository and I shall not find fault with him, for instance, for not writing *The Cream of the Jest* or *La Rotisserie de la Reine Pedauque. The Three Black Pennys* has some fine qualities, I think, and I would as soon re-read it, say, as anything Wells or Bennett ever wrote, which I have no present intention of doing. . . . You have perhaps by this received a copy of Vincent Starrett's excellent article on you in Saturday's *Herald-Examiner*. It pleased me so much that I wrote him a letter and then called him up at his house and at the office. I was unable to get him, but he came into the *Tribune* about noontime or a little after and we went out together. It was the first time I had met the man, although I had long desired to make his acquaintance—ever since, in fact, I read his article on Arthur Machen in *Reedy's Mirror*. . . . He has promised me an article on Machen. Starrett has a fine collection of first editions of Stephen Crane, Saltus, Bierce, Pollard, Harte, and other American writers. . . .

And now to the Camembert of this epistolic table d'hote: on Friday I received a twelve page, closely typewritten rebuttal from Rupert Hughes. It is one of the most amusing things I have ever read anywhere. I suppose I shall have to use it or parts of it: but to do so will show him up in a more ridiculous light than what you said about him. He tells in it how many books he has read on art and history, recounts the papers he has read before the Modern Language Club, tells his part in the decision on the Rockefeller pseudo-Praxiteles, defends Western Reserve as a fine school where especial attention is paid to the classics, says you weren't honest enough to say that he has also taken an M.A. at Yale, and had contributed to the *Encyclopaedia Britannica,* and that you omitted to mention *The Love Affairs of Musicians* on which he spent many months of research—and he says your writings in the field of history give him "Cabelly-ache." I'll send you a proof tomorrow and you might, I think, write a paragraph to the effect that Captain Hughes's excellent argument is unanswerable inasmuch as it deals entirely with Capt. Hughes with whom you have no personal quarrel and not at all with literature in which you had mistakenly and hastily assumed Capt. Hughes had some ideas. He probably is not such a bad sort personally and I was uncharitable in my letter to you about his military career, inasmuch as it seems that he [was] out of it on account of deafness and bad eyes and is sincerely anxious to throttle the Boche. If he wants to make an ass of himself, let him go ahead. . . . I should much like to have a paragraph or so from you, though, to run at the bottom of his article—if necessary wire it to me at the *Tribune,* day press rates collect. The *Tribune* will pay for it. . . .

As ever,

BURTON RASCOE

TELEGRAM TO BURTON RASCOE
RICHMOND, MAY 17, 1918

AN EPILOGUE BY JAMES BRANCH CABELL PERIOD WITH PARDONABLE GUSTO I HAVE READ EVERY WORD OF CAPTAIN RUPERT HUGHES PAINSTAKING AND ENTHUSIASTIC ARTICLE ABOUT HIMSELF EVER SINCE HE LEFT HIS MOTHERS KNEE AND I CONGRATULATE THE CAPTAIN UPON HIS STRATEGIC REMOVAL TO A TOPIC CONCERNING WHICH HE SPEAKS WITH AUTHORITY PERIOD FOR NOBODY CAN WELL DENY HIS DICTA TO BE UNANSWERABLE NOW THAT CAPTAIN HUGHES CONFINES HIMSELF SO RIGIDLY TO THE ACCOMPLISHMENTS AND EXPLOITS OF CAPTAIN HUGHES AND MEDDLES NOT AT ALL WITH THE MAKERS OF LITERATURE AS TO WHOM I HAD ERRONEOUSLY ASSUMED THE CAPTAIN INTENDED TO FAVOR THE TRIBUNE READERS WITH SOME IDEAS PERIOD INSTEAD IT SEEMS THAT NOTHING OF THE SORT HAS EVER ENTERED HIS HEAD OR ELSE THE CAPTAIN HAS QUITE UNACCOUNTABLY TRANSFERRED THE EXPOSITION OF HIS LITERARY NOTIONS TO THE COSMOPOLITAN MAGAZINE PERIOD WHICHEVER BE THE TRUTH THE CAT OF NATURAL TASTE IS OUT OF THE BAG OF CULTURE AND AT LAST WE HAVE THE CAPTAINS STANDARDS STATED IN GRATIFYING DIRECTNESS PERIOD FOR IN THE JUNE NUMBER OF

THE COSOMOPOLITAN ONE DISCOVERS THAT CAPTAIN HUGHES IDEAL OF A
REALLY QUOTATION BRILLIANT ARTIST QUOTATION IN LITERATURE IS MR
ROBERT W CHAMBERS WHOSE QUOTATION MASTERPIECES QUOTATION AND QUO-
TATION TRIUMPHS OF ART QUOTATION HAVE ROUSED THE CAPTAIN TO A
THREE PAGE OUTBURST OF NAIVE AND TOUCHING REVERENCE BUT LITTLE IN-
FERIOR TO THAT WITH WHICH HE SPEAKS OF THE FRUITAGE OF HIS OWN
FIERCE YEARS OF TOIL.

JAMES BRANCH CABELL

Dumbarton, May 14, 1918

My dear Holt:

But, no! You will have to get the introductory matter and first
chapter from Rascoe (who has no use for them in connection with the
Tribune, anyway), as I have no copy from which any conceivable printer
could set type. In fact, Rascoe could now let you have the second chapter
also, as we have finished that in the paper; and that would make more
than enough for the dummy. . . .

Well, but it turns out that Follett is more than a good sort. I have
now had three letters from him, all quite enthusiastic. Meanwhile, I believe, I am not supposed to know that he saw the outline for the booklet, and find his views uncannily the same as mine. All that apart, he
has for some while now been holding up my books to his pupils as models
of English: one or two of them have written for autographs and book-
plates. So I grow famous. And let me tell you, Mr. Secretary, I have
even had approaches from other publishers, suddenly smitten with al-
truistic desire to see my work obtain the publicity it deserves, and so on.
That I believe is not quite ethical—is it?—but I find it pleasing. At all
events, I replied with perfect truth I would never desert Mr. Micawber,
and explained who, in this case, was really publishing my books, in the
bared teeth of Baptistry. . . .

Lastly I wonder if you saw Starrett's article in the *Examiner-Herald?*
. . . And now if Mencken will only write something! Follett talks of doing
another article, as you perhaps know.

Yours faithfully,

JAMES BRANCH CABELL

Joseph Hergesheimer's first appearance at Dumbarton marked an occasion,
and Cabell soon wrote his reactions to Rascoe.

Dumbarton, May 17, 1918

My dear Rascoe:

. . . I shall certainly read *The Three Black Pennys,* at least—— Between ourselves, Hergesheimer as a person rather disconcerted me. He informed me, for instance, that he and I were the only real artists in America, were kindred souls, and so on—and as yet, 1 don't know whether or no this was a compliment. Then, all the while, I did not dare confess that I had read none of his books, if merely because he assumed, as an affair of course, I had read every one of them. Still, we got on, I believe, fairly well—— His article in the *Sun* was about Ellen Wilkins Tompkins, who wrote *The Egotistical I* and, more recently, *The Enlightenment of Paulina:* and was but flagrant log-rolling, inasmuch as Nellie has written but two chapters of the novel he puffed—— I say "Nellie" because she is my second cousin and told me of all this, though I did not see the article. I wonder if you came across *The Enlightenment of Paulina,* as published by Dutton last autumn? It did not "sell," but I found it surprisingly good—largely, no doubt, because I knew the author and thought well of her as a person—not merely, I assure you, on account of the cousinship. . . . For the rest, you will find me glad to furnish all imaginable data as to myself—quite Hughesianly willing.

Starrett's article impressed me as being surprisingly good, especially as I knew just how many of my books he had not read: though, as I wrote him, that enabled him to stick to *The Cream of the Jest,* and not meander off into pleasant observations about the *Rivet* as my best book—which enrages me almost as much as being told that "The Love-Letters of Falstaff" is my masterpiece—— The latter insult, by the by, I have to endure with surprising frequency. People seem honestly to have liked that story with a cordiality denied to anything I have since done. . . . Starrett should do you a good Machen article. I was gladdened . . . the day before yesterday to receive a second letter from Machen in regard to *The Cream of the Jest.* He had been, he said, re-reading it. . . . It pleased me greatly . . . because I have long believed in Machen's genius —— But he writes like a discouraged man, and I fear that what he has done for posterity is an affair of the past. I cannot understand, quite, how those first books of his have stayed, comparatively, unknown for all of thirty years: and had vaguely intended some day to write for you something in regard to this crime. Meanwhile I am glad to have Starrett do it: and I note with delight that Holt has given you an excellent review, to be followed, I hope, with others. I am always enthusiastic about Holt—having excellent reasons—and now that [the] interminable Tenth Chapter is settled to at least his pretended satisfaction I overflow with tenderness. . . .

My wife informs me it is time to get ready for supper. So I desist.

Yours faithfully,

JAMES BRANCH CABELL

From Guy Holt

New York, May 21, 1918

My dear Cabell:

Mr. McBride returned last Thursday and since then I have read not less than 59 books—if I may call it reading. At any rate my mind is in a whirl and I cannot think and my other work must be done in the meantime. . . . I might give a guess as to the identity of the publishers who wrote you, Knopf probably and Moffat, Yard & Co. perhaps—the latter in the person of Howard Cook. At any rate I shall grin at them knowingly the next time I see them and let their own consciences supply the reason. For it is not quite ethical, although it is generally done. . . .

. . . I have been studying amusedly your passage at arms with Captain Hughes. Behold, Mr. Cabell indulges in some fine fancies about the worthlessness of facts. Captain Hughes admires the fancies and questions the facts. "What, sir, do you bark at me," says Mr. Cabell. Captain Hughes rolls on the ground and protests that he is a good dog and that he studied the classics at his mother's knee. "Ah, well," says Mr. Cabell contentedly. "You are a good dog but do not bark at me again." As a disinterested observer I cannot but feel that Captain Hughes is the real hero of the piece and that I should sympathize with his discomfiture more greatly than I do—— Heaven bless me! I have forty more letters to write, so no more.

Yours,

GUY HOLT

Dumbarton, May 27, 1918

My dear Rascoe:

Freely did I forgive you for the editing of that Epilogue the instant that your letter concerning your amputations had arrived—— You in no way damaged what I wrote: you improved it. So instead of the pardon you asked for, I am sending you thanks. Then too you once requested a manuscript. If you will kindly glance over the enclosed souvenir of an unseemly row, you will readily understand my motives for destroying manuscripts about which I have really taken pains. For I do not, unluckily, find second thoughts to be the best, but have to struggle on toward the ninth or tenth before reaching anything which even to me seems not unprintable: and I shrink from exposing the groan and rattle of my mental machinery. However!

... The *Dial* recently requested me to review the Luce edition of Villon,[4] which I have done on the Economist theory, and trust that they (the Dialers) may not regard as flippant. This, too, will probably be absorbed into that omnivorous *Beyond Life*. ... And I have eventually read *The Three Black Pennys* with high admiration. I hope to write to Hergesheimer this afternoon, and say as much. There is no necessity for talk, explanations, but he, Hergesheimer, after writing this book, this novel, about Howat Penny and what he, Howat, bequeathed, left his descendants, should be watched, observed—something too much of this appositional style I notice, and reproduce for your benefit. But the book is excellent, and shows curiously that he was once a painter. ... I am perfectly willing to let him be the other peak of Teneriffe.

Yours faithfully,

JAMES BRANCH CABELL

Dumbarton, May 27, 1918

My dear Hergesheimer:

But I had no idea you were an attested genius! You see, I make no effort to keep abreast with current fiction: time has its value to me, there is no way of telling what books may be worth while in the welter of blurbs, and so I let the new men pass without bothering about them. For most of them do pass—— So I had read none of your books, although in view of all that I had heard I vaguely meant someday to remedy the omission, not this week exactly, but before very long—you know that fatal state of mind—— All this is my preamble to the statement that I have read *The Three Black Pennys,* and am tendering you thereon my very heartiest congratulations. Somewhat do I congratulate myself likewise, for I did not know that just this sort of work was being done in America—or rather anywhere—and so I look forward to the other three Hergesheimer volumes.

Your conquest of me, too, was made in unfavorable circumstances. For I began with the *Post* story, "Banked Fires": did I but know you better, I could read you a sermon on that story. And then with the book's opening

4 Payne translation with Stevenson essay published by John W. Luce & Co., Boston.

your people of 1750 perplexed me: it is not possible (there was something within me raging) that the man thinks these are Colonists of 1750 either in speech or thought: yet presently I saw the effect at which you were aiming, and presently too I had succumbed. Thereafter all went wonderfully, and as I read I applauded. . . .

I had hoped, since merely as a person you interested me, to have seen you again during your stay in Richmond. But the day after I saw you my wife's sister and her husband descended upon us quite unexpectedly for the week-end: and Monday we were called to Virginia Beach to make arrangements for our summer stay there. I then thought the combination of circumstances to be vexatious: now I regard it with redoubled disfavor. Meanwhile I look to the future.

Yours faithfully,
JAMES BRANCH CABELL

From Burton Rascoe

Chicago, May 29, 1918

My dear Cabell:

. . . By the way, I got a copy of *The Soul of Melicent* from Stokes and I am to run a note Saturday saying that copies of the book are still to be had at the publishers: I have two friends who advertised for and got the book, paying $3 and $3.50 for it. Mr. Morrow of Stokes says he yet has about fifty copies, which, I am sure, will be exhausted shortly after the note is printed. I have now all your books except the genealogies and *The Eagle's Shadow,* which Mr. Follett was unkind to—— I am glad you have sustained Hergesheimer's estimate of himself. Your impression of him delighted me; contrary to exciting my literary animosity, however I might feel about him personally, I was pleased to hear that Hergesheimer considers himself one of the two artists in America—since it is my firm conviction that no writer can produce the best that is in him unless he has a generous amount of that healthy egotism. It is amusing, though, that he coupled you and himself, since you are as far apart as the poles in method and intentions. I was told once of a conversation in which he engaged, during which he said: "I want to write for the people, about things that people can understand, in words that they can understand, reveal to them their own souls, and the best and worst that is in them. Nothing precious, involved, subtle—these I cannot stand." I hope he does not pursue this to its logical conclusion—— Your parody of his appositional style gives me a chuckle. While we are discussing American writers, I here record a pained reaction to Ernest Poole's latest novel, *His Second Wife*. After approaching a certain sublimity in *The Harbor* and *His Family*, he has now written a book which I cannot but regard as trash, badly written, hackneyed in theme, falsely sentimental, practically unreadable. Robert W. Chambers would have written the same story infinitely better, because Chambers has, at least, a sense of prose felicity. Poole is gone, I am afraid, and what is worse is that he cannot even seek residence in the Via Suburba of literature, because the technique of the profession is something he cannot master.

I wish you would write that article for me on Machen. I think it was a matter purely of intention with Starrett, and he is now working for the *Herald-Examiner* literary editor. He has promised me some articles on Bierce, Saltus, and Stephen Crane; but I hardly think he will ever write them. As to Machen I agree with your dicta; and for the life of me I cannot find that resemblance in *The Cream of the Jest* to *The Hill of Dreams*, which has been remarked by Starrett, Hecht (though I think he has read neither book) and Holt. The only thing that I can find that you have in common is that you both have chosen the English language as your medium of expression. Machen's profound, whispered enigma amuses me. . . .

Sincerely,
BURTON RASCOE

From Joseph Hergesheimer

The Dower House
West Chester, Pennsylvania
June 1, 1918

Dear Mr. Cabell:

Many things went through my head as I left you but not that I had been at Dumbarton in the role of the author of "Banked Fires." This was fortunate for me. Indeed I think that particularly your support belongs to me; we have a great many qualities in common.

I wish that I could have seen more of you in Richmond; there is an enormous lot we should talk over; all that you said about your approach to my writing holds true of myself and so I need not repeat it. When I read your tales I thought, "My God, the man is trying to be mediaeval" but I soon forgot that and, as you say, went with you. Old talk, present talk, beauty, was there. I know almost nothing of the intellectual aspects of creative writing; I couldn't tell you what, in your meaning, my intention with

The Three Black Pennys was. I believe I'm a romantic; a quantity of people have explained this to me, each differently and dogmatic. Perhaps.

I am sending you Follett's *Conrad* and with it three stories which, you will remember, were sold to the *Post*. Does it sound impolite to ask you to send the *Conrad* back?

Will you come north; the Virginia summer heat would do for me? I have a lovely old house, a blue-eyed wife and a beautiful sweep of green to enclose the talk we must sometime have.

Very faithfully,

JOSEPH HERGESHEIMER

Beyond Life went to Guy Holt late in 1917, but it was not until after the following summer that the constant revising and rewriting was done. And going yet farther back we find that most remarkable of all letters left in Cabell's files, a part of which is printed below. It is a letter sent him by Holt a year before the book came out. Writing many years later, Cabell said, "*Beyond Life* owes so much to Guy Holt that it could hardly have been dedicated to anybody else. Most of this book was stumbled upon in talk with him, during the . . . years that he was quite fruitlessly endeavoring to sell my books. . . . And the stumbling was done by both of us."

From Guy Holt

New York [date?]

My Dear Cabell:

. . . You asked for it and so here goes. I shall say in my own defense merely that you have so successfully used your own inconsistency that any remark of mine will come as a feeble repetition of something already better stated in this book by you. . . .

So much by way of apology. As for you, sir, I shall say at the outset that not in a long time have I read so fascinating, so ingenious and withal so insincere a book as *Beyond Life*. It is an apology for romance by a man who believes that romance is dead beyond resurrection, and who knows therefore that it is perfectly safe to lament it. It is a tissue of delightful misconceptions—the more delightful because intentional— and has so blandly honest an air that, I protest, upon my first reading I was entirely taken in by it and really fancied its author sitting in honest grief over the lost youth of the world. And the style of it! Greek sentences or no, here is limpid clearness, where often before has been a whirlpool of subtleties and circumlocutions. . . . In this book you wear simplicity with an astounding grace. . . .

Romance, I infer, is the expression of an attitude which views life with a profound distrust as a business of exceeding dulness and of very little worth, and which, therefore, seeks beauty by an abandonment of the facts of living. Living is a drab thing, a concatenation of unimportant events; man is impotent and aimless; and beauty, indeed all the fine things you desiderate in literature and life, are non-existent and impossible. To the problem of living, Romance propounds the only possible answer, which is, not understanding, but escape. And the method of that escape is, you imply, the creation of a pleasing dream which shall somehow engender a reality as lovely. So Romance in literature invents its dynamic illusions (Ibsen called them vital lies, did he not?) of brave men and lovely women, of living as a "uniformly noble transaction," and hopes that in the end mankind will play Peter Ibbetson upon a cosmic scale.

GUY HOLT

On the yellowed pages of the above communication are Cabell's penciled question marks after the words "aimless" and "impossible." So in talk and letters they wrangled over the ultimate truth, until half won over to Cabell's side, Holt wrote: "Think, indeed, of what splendid oblivion has overtaken him who first invented God or Cinderella! Remember how all the creators of religion are become forgotten dust and how only the anthologists—Christ, Buddha, Mohammed and the like—remain. This is the artist's reward that he shall be forgotten and so no longer be inadequate. But his words and the words of many other men will be gathered together until time will discover a new and single maker for them all. And so these men will have become a legendary whole and their work will live on as simple fragments of song or high-hearted thought. They will not be pondered over; but they will be the stuff of which many little dreams are woven. In this they will become witnesses of your own truth; for they shall shape many dynamic illusions and so in time create reality."

Thus in the summer of 1918, reiterating once again his own belief, Cabell ended *Beyond Life* with these words: "And it is this will that stirs in us to have the creatures of earth and the affairs of earth, not as they are, but 'as they ought to be' which we call romance. But when we note how visibly it sways all life we perceive that we are talking about God."

❧ 4 ❧

THE PAWNBROKER BEGINS
HIS JOURNEYING

My dear Rascoe:

It is such an interminable business this being a person—I mean the host of things you have to do because you are a householder or a parent or a church-member or the owner of a typewriter—that I find it interferes vexatiously with my being an author, even of a letter. I am inclined to follow Mr. Follett's suggestion, and become a myth. Meanwhile I have read none of Mr. Poole's books, and begin to think I have now no urgent call to do so. . . . And your dicta as to [R. W.] Chambers, and even more especially as to [Gouverneur] Morris, is appallingly true. I remember when Morris was very near to greatness: and I remember [Chambers'] *The King in Yellow,* as it seemed to me when I first read it, very vividly. And I wonder how these things happen. For it isn't, I think, mere prostitution, not merely the bank-account and the country-home that allures, but the thanklessness of writing your best that appals. The irresistible bribe to any author is to have his work appreciated: and so you "give 'em what they appreciate," not out of avarice, but to stave off the forlorn suspicion that you are wasting time and paper—— At any rate, that theory is tenable.

Galantière, I thought, gave you an excellent paper. Again I "mean to" read France. In fact, I have invested heavily in the Modern Library, and *Bonnard* and *The Red Lily* await my leisure. Then, as always, I read with interest Mr. Cabell's contribution. Do you find that any other people read these papers? For one, I am certain that *Domnei* would have interested me in the author's mental processes, by its bewildering progress from the Roman de Lusignan and love in general to the art of Christopher Marlowe. . . . And for the rest, I am trying, in the intervals between being a person, to write you a book manuscript. It gets on very, very slowly, and has an excellent chance of being suppressed, though whether on the score of salaciousness or blasphemy is not yet determinable. My agreement with Holt was to write the thing as it came to me, and that done, for us to cut out the really impossible portions—— By another ellipsis: you must be making me perceptible upon the horizon, for I am being, actually, besought by publishers, who do not think Mc-Bride is doing enough for me. . . .

Yours faithfully,

JAMES BRANCH CABELL

P.S. . . . a postscript occurs to me. I am writing Starrett a request to do the Machen article for you, if he conveniently can, because for my purpose his article would be better than mine. You see, my nefarious end is just to get Machen puffed in the *Tribune:* and Starrett will sound the trumpet far louder than I could do with an untroubled conscience—— In fact, as I foresee it, I would violently find fault with every book of Machen's except *The House of Souls,* so that my real and great admiration would be obscured. His "whispered enigma" you see, sometimes, on the bare face of it, refers to nothing whatever: and still he whispers. He is as bad as Gordon Craig, who has, I gather, no idea as to what is to be left to drama after those things are gone which he wants eliminated. Or, better still, he shakes his head in very much the style of Sheridan's Lord Burleigh. And then I want to shake him—— In re *The Hill of Dreams,* now, do you not see that, where Lucien trades his corporeal life for dreams, the dreams are not sufficiently indicated for anyone really to believe in them? You are told of an exchange, but there is conveyed to you no sense of an exchange, since you see merely what is given up and not what is acquired, and cannot but suspect the latter element of being non-existent. Then, too, the reader has no conceivable viewpoint: Lucien's is, in the way I have suggested, shut off and obscured, and equally that of the omniscient third person, whereas the viewpoint of Lucien's associates is but occasionally pounced on for derisory purposes. So that you wobble through the book in a gray mist of verbiage—— With more or less modesty, I would suggest that while Kennaston drives a not dissimilar bargain, the bargain is indicated, the dreams are indicated, and you have an actual sense of what he got in exchange. Of course, I could not help it if Mr. Harrowby, also, whispered a few enigmas—— And Starrett and Holt are conscienceless untruthers about their "discoveries." To Starrett I sent the book with a suggestion that it might interest him because it traversed some of the ground covered in *The Hill of Dreams,* which he so much admired. And to Holt I loaned *The Hill of Dreams,* and through repeated pleadings induced him to read it (or say he had read it), so that he could contrast the two. There's gratitude for you!— In all, you perceive, my article on Machen would not be quite untrammeled eulogy. Still, I may write it.

Meanwhile when leisure serves you might compare *The Cream of the Jest* with *The Picture of Dorian Gray,* in at all events the construction.

Dumbarton, June 4, 1918

My dear Starrett:

But your affair is easily arranged, since I had stored away a copy or two of *The Hidden Way,*[1] and of these one now goes forward. Indeed, your request delighted me, because this is my favorite book—on grounds in no way connected with literary merit—and the only one of my books which, I confess, I read over and over again with unfailing zest. I still consider that it was an interesting boy who lived and wrote those verses.— And that any other person should be queer enough to like them I find very grateful hearing.

The book-plate, I regret to say, just now is non-existent. I had one, and discarded it: and have since made a design for another, but, somehow, have never had a plate made from the design. You shall have one of the first lot, however, if ever that lot takes tangible form.— And Le Gallienne is a shrine at which I too have worshipped. But four or five months ago I made the disastrous error of re-reading the *Golden Girl.* For to do that was really an error. Ormus and Kimberley could not combine to bribe me, now, into re-reading *Narcissus:* that much at least I mean to keep in memory just as it never was.

Meantime I hope you are going to do the promised articles for Rascoe. . . . Send me an article occasionally when you can spare a copy, too, for without flattery, I admire your work and Chicago is a long way off.

Yours faithfully,

JAMES BRANCH CABELL

Dumbarton, June 8, 1918

My dear Mr. Hergesheimer:

. . . The Follett book on Conrad I have read with enjoyment, and it returns to you Monday: but your own book I am reading with leisure and careful consideration. . . . Then I shall get to the earlier novels, in full consciousness that it is the unfairest possible proceeding to read any man's books backwards. Yet you, I honestly believe, can stand even so stringent a testing.

Certainly we must arrange for a real talk. We go to Virginia Beach for July, and in August probably to the Virginia mountains, so that the

[1] Cabell's only book of verse, written mainly in his teens.

prospect of my traveling northward is now remote. But in the autumn I hope to see you—— Meanwhile I hope that you have something gorgeous up your literary sleeve? Myself I am now busied in postponing publication of *Beyond Life* (the essay book about I do not know precisely what), so that the Chicago *Tribune* may use as much as possible of it, since their payments are generous where my royalties are problematic. But when it does appear I look to have you give me your opinion of a suitably inscribed copy—— Then too I have an insane story at which I moil daily, for it is yet in that terrible stage of making the first draft, which you read and wonder if your mind has gone irretrievably. At least I do: and find the labor of writing unendurable until one has a whole of sorts, to be revised and made better indefinitely. I am thus candid without solicitation because some day I mean to wring from you a confession as to your "methods."

I desist for the excellent and unusual reason that an eclipse of the sun is beginning, and the children insist that I participate. Meanwhile Mr. Knopf is very flattering, and I appreciate, in any event, the compliment.

Yours faithfully,

JAMES BRANCH CABELL

Dumbarton, June 12, 1918

My dear Mr. Hergesheimer:

So it proves after all a cause for self congratulation that I never read *The Saturday Evening Post* serials (having learned by experience that you invariably miss a number), because otherwise I would have missed, or at the very least impaired, the full effect of those *Gold and Iron* stories—— Yet, since you disclaim any conscious aiming at an "effect," I cannot but marvel how in "Wild Oranges" you so exactly produce the effect of a nightmare, in that fight in the dark, or rather in all that pertains to your infernal Nicholas. Here is writing that rather brutally ravishes and afterward haunts your defenceless reader. Then how vividly do you see, and convey the thing seen—"rendering things—anything, everything, from a chimney-pot to the shoulders of a duchess—as painters render them." But then you were a painter, I remember: and it shows delightfully all through these tales—— About human beings you and I must agree to differ. You will be one of those earnest fellows who deal with humanity with the gravity suited to a weighty and important topic, whereas I, for literary purposes, must elect to take human beings not quite seriously. Thus your iron-master is beyond me, by quires and reams. I see and feel his forcefulness . . . but without any inward stirrings toward emulation: for all this is out of my bailiwick, as is indeed all your *Gold and Iron*. My medium, sir, is filigree—— And thus too your Jason baffled me with the strength of his simplicity. *Meo periculo*, there is a gap in the way Olive Stanes drops out: she would have been in the background of the man's consciousness, as at least a mildly obnoxious feature of the Cottarsport landscape, all through: whereas just once, apparently, does your Jason recollect her existence. I speak of course of the consciousness of such men as I can conceive of: no doubt I do not understand your Titans, and it is you who are in the right. . . . Gold and Iron, now, sums up the "style" exactly—metallic and cool, and bright and strong. . . .

Yours faithfully,
JAMES BRANCH CABELL

From Joseph Hergesheimer

West Chester, June 15, 1918

Dear Mr. Cabell:

I think you must know how pleased I have been by your letters; the pleasure of seeing one's arrows lodge in the gold. I had intended to write you after I had finished your books but some have been difficult to get and I have been interrupted, and that will do for another letter anyhow. I do not, of course, believe that you are for filigree, that's what I first started to make. I know it thoroughly in all its aspects. I no longer care for it, but I do like tremendously *A Certain Hour,* the book I'm latest from.

I look forward to something more than a temporary affair with you and, for that reason, I intend to begin as solidly as possible. The preface, it seemed to me, was hardly more than an ill-tempered and yet amusing one as being in absolute contradiction to what you now say of yourself. I have had a splendid schooling in the general indifference toward creative work other than sentimental flattery and lies. I went to school scarcely two years, painted for a while and then wrote; I suppose I commenced when I was about nineteen and for fourteen years never sold a line, never had the slightest assurance that what I did was not ruck and, worse still and peculiar when one considers the bloody labor, had no special self confidence. I take it that something, at once different and yet very much like, was your own experience and that you found no generous response to what, in your selective and fastidious mind, you knew to be the best of what you had to offer. Indignation, even bitterness, is very natural—God knows I have enough of it; but after all it is the re-

sult of misunderstanding on our part, either misunderstanding or silly
optimism. Why and for whom do we write? For ourselves, of course, or
rather because we can't help it; and secondly, with our hopes set on an
audience with our own sense of beauty and fitness. Certainly there are
almost none of them; if there were the world would be totally different.
A world in which you and myself had our millions of circulation and
Harold Bell Wright his comparative hundreds is simply inconceivable
with the race of man as it is. Resentment is futile, satire I do not conceive to be your position; there remains your work, which should make
you very happy in itself, and the finer quality of your readers. Not only
this but, in the preface, you have an implied objection to other kinds
of creative writing. Everyone has a complete justification to his own
attack and every attack of equal ability is as good as any other.

But *A Certain Hour,* far from filigree, has a basic and poignant beauty.
It is almost a complete expression of perhaps the loveliest known or unknown quality—I suppose it might be called the hunger for the per-
fectibility of love. I think I told you at Dumbarton that there was a
visible literary quality in your writing, a business of floral chapter-
headings and formal pages which, for me, held the attention to surface
and such lesser things. I fly no banner for realism, except in this: that
the more actual one's characters are the more they apparently live, the
sharper the effect of beauty. This is not a criticism since I've just explained my feeling of the necessity for every man to have his manner
unchallenged, and the finality of your effect is, after all, sure and authentic.

I am much less clear about myself: a character spoiled by sickness and
money,—I mean by the indolence of the legitimate child of such parents,
—no education, no practice of industry or admirable motives, with
against that only the labor, a sort of disease of worrying over words, I
have little ground for pretentious formula. Perhaps I might express
something of my work very indirectly—I think the finest creative writers
are skeptics, because they only have the pity for humanity that is the
necessity of great work. That, a little obscurely, is what I mean by efforts
to catch and communicate beauty. It seems impossible not to repeat that
last word to the point of stupidity. One of the first things I tried to write
was about a mother and daughter, luxuriously dressed in a luxurious
hotel, where they were entirely lonely and supported and kept there by
the heroic labor of some gray little American husband in a gray city.
The whole quality, for me, lay in the fact that the man's toil was for a
small vain end. Now I have no other purpose, no other hope, than the
capture and communication of such thrills of realization. It is necessary
for my entire scheme of work that loveliness should be lost: a dream and

a bitter struggle largely hopeless as though it were some earthly ambition on Mars, and a fine surface. These are the materials. All this I mostly see in an age slightly removed from our own, the women in crinoline. Why again I couldn't exactly tell you, except that there I'm freer with nothing extraneously pertinent, either for adventitious assistance or as a danger to the simplicity of purpose.

If your inability to get North stretches out too long, perhaps I shall be South within a reasonable time. You might send me a word of the mountains of which you spoke.

Very faithfully

JOSEPH HERGESHEIMER

From Burton Rascoe

Chicago, June [?] 1918

My dear Cabell:

Now I am in for a job on American writers, described in the catalogue as "designed especially for use in libraries, school rooms, and women's clubs"; and James Branch Cabell is chapter two in this astounding magnum opus, yielding to the venerable [William Dean] Howells by reason of recency only—— This volume, announced for the late fall, will, then, be one in an allied drive to make the world cognizant of Cabell. Mencken, I hear, has at last done the right thing and his article is announced for the August *Smart Set;* and Mr. Follett is to include you in his titularly enticing *Seven Against Realism.* I tremble and I must make haste to get back my manuscript for revision in a race with so well-blooded a stable.

Mr. Follett's utterance is not so cryptic if you remember "On a Certain Condescension in Our Natives" and the editorial immediately following it: they were both directed against *Some Modern Novelists* and in the latter I was perhaps needlessly caustic. But since "A Gossip, etc.," I have regarded him with something akin to warm fraternalism, the more so in that he seems now to contemplate indigenous work and to be less concerned with ephemerae "three thousand miles away." With you as an intermediary I think we might enter upon an *entente cordiale,* and with his kindly move I think I shall write to him this week. . . .

Galantière's paper leaned too heavily on Michaut to be what it might have been had Lewis expressed entirely his own reactions to France's work. Michaut started the onslaught against France and the sceptical tendency in France with his monograph and was, in part, responsible for the present ascendancy of the mystics and Catholics in French literature. If you read the extract from Kettle's book [2] which I published on the highbrow page on Sunday you will see a reflection of what has taken place in France. Kettle, as you probably know, was an eloquent young Irish Catholic, a reactionary and a keen observer, and some time ago he sensed the coming change in France, which has not been due entirely to the war. Lanux, Barrès, Claudel: what they had had to say since the beginning of the war reveals a revival of faith and of the "dynamic illusions." You perhaps have noticed it.

Galantière has a good paper on Claudel in the current *Dial*. He is, as you probably know, now out in Los Angeles, leading an ideal life of camping and tramping in the mountains near the sea. He has made several efforts to get into the service, but has repeatedly been rejected and now he is applying for service with the Canadian army. He wrote me recently that he was going to write an article on you for the Los Angeles *Times* and this I have urged him to do. . . .

I recant herewith what I said some time ago about the *Smart Set*. The last two issues have been very good indeed, somewhat, in fact, reminiscent of that time when the *Smart Set* was the only magazine in this country which was printing real literature in every issue—with Conrad, Beresford, Schnitzler, Walpole, Lawrence, etc. Mencken has, somehow, got hold of James Stephens, and Grant Watson, too, is a man with high talents. And with Jurgen [3] the July number was, all in all, a gratifying product. It seems that Mencken is attempting to break away from the facetiae of sex and print something of more consequence. However, what have you at hand? And have you tried *Harper's* or *Scribner's* with anything recently? And in mentioning them I speak of two possibilities I know nothing whatever about, since I have read neither of them for two years or more. And after all perhaps the *Smart Set* has a more generally intelligent audience. . . .

The Harris book is an astounding thing and it throws a new light upon *De Profundis* inasmuch as the suppressed letter to Douglas is included in it. Wilde did, in fact, find Douglas more intolerant, jealous, and selfish than any woman could possibly be; and it is very adequately revealed that whenever Douglas was anywhere around Wilde wrote absolutely nothing. . . .

Yours

BURTON RASCOE

[2] *Ways of War* by Thomas Michael Kettle, Scribner, 1918.
[3] A short story "Some Ladies and Jurgen," the embryo of the later book.

Dumbarton, June 21, 1918

My dear Rascoe:

. . . My one complaint against your Saturday column is that it continues to tempt me to acquire books for which I have not shelf-room. Thus, after reading *The Gates of Wrath* I formally "swore off" on Bennett: it was manifestly impossible that anyone who of his own volition published such stuff could ever regain the respect of even moderately intelligent persons: but now you make *The Pretty Lady* seem alluring. And Harris's biography of Wilde, also! but really you ought not to tempt us with five dollar books in war-time. I infinitely admire Harris, though: and my only wonder is why nobody has as yet shot him—— And the caption of Hergesheimer's picture was delicious. *Gold and Iron,* in passing, I liked tremendously in spots, but found bewildering incongruities all through. Have you never "done" Hergesheimer? . . .

Yours faithfully,

JAMES BRANCH CABELL

Dumbarton, June 29, 1918

My dear Mr. Hergesheimer:

Et tu, Brute!—that is, then, you also consider the Auctorial Induction (a caption which frenzied the reviewers) to *The Certain Hour* is ill-natured. To the contrary, I insist, it is a quite serious defence of the ephemeral novel as a philanthropic performance, and it perplexes me why people should suspect that screed of irony. What I had to say was, or at least seemed to me, the exact truth, so far as human notions can measure it—— As for popularity, I would like to see my publishers get their money back, and that is really the extent of my aspirations now: were I to publish a book that became really popular, you see, I would be forced to suspect that there was either something wrong with it or else with every one of its predecessors, and either way I would be worried—— And why do we write, forsooth! for the same reason that the coral zoophyte builds his atoll, and for no other. It is the one thing we are good for, it is the thing we were meant to do. So we do it. And I really think you are wrong in saying that we are much spurred by the hope of reaching a congenial audience. Once reached, what good would you get out of it? No, I must qualify that: I delight to receive appreciative (that is, adulatory) letters as to something I have written, but when people talk about it to my face I am uncomfortable and speak mild idiocies—— Nor is there any pleasure to be derived from reading your own stuff once it is a year old—in fact, the process is exasperating. I of course except verse, which the maker can no more judge from literary standpoints than he could his flesh and blood baby— We are thus driven back, I take it, to the zoophyte hypothesis, as the only one conceivable.

You should, I think, stick to the age slightly removed from your own. I wonder if you have done this in *Java Head,* of which I hear proud rumors?— All this is but a prelude, written very hurriedly, to the statement that when this reaches you I shall be typewriterless at Wales Cottage, Virginia Beach, Virginia. Thence I shall probably write you to the detriment of your eyesight, but quite certainly to the provokement of wild guesses. That address holds good for July, all things thereafter remaining unsettled. . . .

I wonder too if you have heard from Mr. Follett, who was delighted by your letter?

Yours faithfully,

JAMES BRANCH CABELL

In the heat of that summer at Virginia Beach, *Jurgen* was being written, perhaps urged on by Holt's criticism that "Nowhere in your writings do I find either that earthiness which makes all men Falstaffs for the moment, or that madness which makes them monsters or saints." Years later Cabell was to write of Holt: "Looking back upon our . . . association, I gratefully recognize that no author was ever more lucky in his publisher . . . [a] person to whom my indebtedness as a writer is paramount."

Sensing this association between Cabell and Holt, Rascoe said in a letter about this time: "Guy Holt, more than any other, enjoys my envy, by reason of his personal relationship with you, his discovery and championing of you in his office, and his peculiar advantage of talking over with you the books you have in process of being."

And during July, Cabell wrote Rascoe from Virginia Beach:

" . . . We have taken a cottage, and are stranded here, I suspect, until September. I have equipped a porch wherein to write, and *Jurgen* has therein fattened prodigiously. He is now a mass of perfectly undecipherable interlineations, from which no human being save myself could possibly wrest any meaning, and even to me the task is gone difficult. A pretty book-manuscript you are to have when all is done, I can assure you. . . . But I talk of *Jurgen.* The Title, actually, is *The Pawnbroker's Shirt: A Comedy of Justice.* Is that an outrageous christening? You see, Jurgen became a pawnbroker: a moment's reflection will show you it is the ideal profession for an elderly poet. And the garment is the shirt of Nessus which Jurgen wears in all save the first and last chapters (without any unpleasantness whatever to him) as he goes prattling of and demanding justice in all sorts of places, and inflicting injustice everywhere. Nowhere of course does he find justice or any particular need of it: and in his travels he touches at the Garden between Dawn and Sunrise (which is at Storisende), at a replevined Wednesday, (spent at Bellegarde), at Glathian (where the father of Guenevere was king), at Cocaigne, at the Island of Leuke, at the Hell of his Fathers, and at his Grandmother's Heaven—making forty-four chapters now in hand, with the last chapter of all untouched. That is to be his interview with Dorothy (Count Emmerich's middle sister—need I say?—the one between Melicent and Ettarre), and all I know of it is that it was The Moment That did not Count—— How interesting all this must be to you! no less, *Jurgen* is either a very fine thing or else it is abject nonsense. But the title?"

Virginia Beach, July 11-12, 1918

My dear Holt:

Great was my delight in the Mencken article when your letter of the third was forwarded me yesterday, after being held up at Dumbarton for several days. I should say that we have here some admirable matter for a booklet: and then there will be Rascoe's stuff and Follett's too to draw on. So I am writing Mr. Mencken very gratefully—— By an ellipsis, you *have* seemed rather out of sorts of late, so far as went epistolary indications, and of the possible explanations you suggest, I infinitely prefer to suspect you of being *enceinte* of a book. You *can* write: witness the paragraphs that I feloniously appropriated for *Beyond Life:* and I have for a long while very earnestly wanted you to write. About this I am profoundly sincere, and so come to it first. You have thoughts, and—incomprehensible being!—you apparently express them easily. What more do you want?—why, what is lacking, I suspect, is the feeblemindedness of taking writing more seriously than anything else—— That reminds me that Mencken delighted me with his divination of the doctrine I once submitted to your violent disapproval, that human ideas are valuable as beautiful playthings but not at all for their truth, since human limitations leave them all false. Certainly I have never expressed that notion—not even here—and therefore I find this Mencken uncanny.

As to the proofs: at Rascoe's suggestion I have been considering the beginning of the Candle chapter, and the ending of the Mountebank chapter in *Beyond Life.* These could—I see the way—be turned to general statements about any war, and the volume be made to contain no reference whatever, anywhere, to the prevailing unpleasantness. Do you and Rascoe foregather as to the worthwhileness of this—— It would not be difficult with the assistance of a typewriter. But in my present destitute condition I find writing a damnable business, and get scant comfort from the reflection that I at least do not have to decipher the result.

Jurgen gets on as well as could be looked for, in these surroundings. We have taken a little house within a hundred feet of the Atlantic Ocean, and, being a large family, dwell therein in appalling promiscuity. But I have retained a porch, rather bigger than a postage stamp, for writing purposes, and so between thunderstorms manage to spoil my share of paper. Meanwhile I must certainly manage likewise to use this idiotic ocean in *Jurgen:* it is a sleek and fat ocean that for ten days has been solemnly spanking the sand, and really the longer you look at it the more futile appears the whole performance— How does the short story title, "Some Ladies and Jurgen," impress you as a name for the otherwise unchristened book—a brown book,[4] I too hope, in course of time.

I particularly look forward to Miss [Dorothy] Scarborough's article since she has confided to me that the Jurgen story was unpleasant and not quite nice. And I am to disfigure the next *Dial* with a few frivolities anent long-suffering Villon. And lastly I am now to accompany my family into the surf of that inane ocean.

Yours faithfully,

JAMES BRANCH CABELL

From Burton Rascoe

Chicago, July 24, 1918

My dear Cabell:

... Books pour from the presses full of unbelievable imbecilities: two books this week crying to the people to wake up to the fact that we are at war, as if the war had not already touched even the hill-billies of the Tennessee mountains. Another book by Poultney Bigelow showing that the Kaiser is the reincarnation of Genseric— But if I should tell you about the books that come to my desk, you would think I was suffering from hallucinations of persecution— I am, frankly, in no fit state of mind to do any writing: the appalling uselessness of it is too apparent. I wish it were possible for me to get into the fight in France: there at least realities are not obscured by clouds of words. ...

I have read Mencken's articles in the *Evening Mail* and the *Smart Set* with great enjoyment and, of course, noted the boost for me, in the former, with gratitude. I haven't seen the new *Dial:* there is some delay in the mails and it has not yet reached Chicago. I have great hopes for *Jurgen* and I think your selection for the title is excellent. The book, as you have briefly outlined it, appeals to me immensely.

John Macy was in town last week. He said he had been to see you in

---

4 This refers to the color of the binding; Cabell's books were published in a uniform edition.

company with the head of a girls' school in Richmond of which he is a non-resident member of the faculty. He was strongly impressed and was sorry that he did not get an opportunity to talk more with you. He had read only *The Rivet*. I got him a copy of *The Cream* and he stayed up until two or three o'clock in the morning reading it. He had it again at breakfast and was over at the office early, much excited. Said he, "What makes me mad is that I had to come all the way out to Chicago to hear about the man. He's a joy. A satirist and an ironist in America, think of it! Another Connecticut Yankee in King Arthur's Court!" He then reminisced of his visit with you, detailed his impressions, and said he was going to write you a letter in the afternoon. I let him read some of the suppressed passages from *Beyond Life* and as he did so, he chuckled and made pleasant comments—— Macy is a great fellow and the author of the only book on American Literature [5] worth reading. I am sorry he has abandoned literature altogether and has become obsessed with the labor question, though I suppose there should be "some to pray all the time for those who do not pray at all."

Yours

BURTON RASCOE

Virginia Beach, August 1, 1918

My dear Rascoe:

So far as I am concerned it is all right about the cutting short of the Sunday articles. I regret, of course, that your managing editor should have taken a dislike to them, even on hearsay: but solely because you seem to think that asperses your judgment and to have grown blue over it: for really I am hardened to people not liking what I write. In the mean time the additions to Chapters IX and X have reached me, and I am looking daily for the manuscript of Part II, which I imagine has been held up somewhere in the express. When it comes I shall forthwith alter the war portions to glittering generalities, and dispatch all to Mc-Bride and Company, who write that the printer waits on my leisure.

Many thanks for *The Pretty Lady*. I read it with interest and pleasure. Yet always I had the feeling that so far was just preliminary to the real drama, and read thus to the end. Mr. Bennett seemed to be leading up to something—I have no notion what—and eventually to decide that, after all, there was not room for it in that book. I could not even think, with Mencken, that Bennett had ever definitely set the problem. No less, I enjoyed the book and prize the inscription—— I prize too your remarks

[5] *The Spirit of American Literature,* Doubleday, 1913.

as to *Ulysses:* [6] and re-voice my wonder that literary criticism as you exemplify it is not more frequently complicated with assault and battery. Mr. Hecht, at all events, can hardly love you with actual cordiality.

I was interested—and pleased—by what you wrote as to Mr. Macy. Upon the only occasion I saw him we were both in a state of repression, induced by serious-minded female company; and all that I know of him was that he had formerly edited the *Youth's Companion* and now corrects the themes which I assist my step-daughters to prepare. Perhaps I was biassed by the circumstance that he never gives me very high marks: still, neither of us had any actual chance to say anything that day: and these fatalities I now regret.

It is excellent news that I may hope to see you at Dumbarton in September. We will remain here for August, not wholly to my joy. There are edible palliations, in the form of soft-shelled crabs and some of the larger fish, but upon the whole an ocean at your doorstep is unbearably tedious. I am tired of the thing's futile noises: and to its fussy irrelevancy is now added a continual reminder of human imbecility, in the shape of transports creeping eastward on the sky-line day after day. So I withdraw to the manuscript of *The Pawnbroker's Shirt,* wherein alone is sanity: and find it, symbolically, an undecipherable tangle of revisions, of which I lack the energy to begin a fair copy. Before long, however, I hope to have the proof sheets of *Beyond Life* to play with.

Well! I hope that by this your book goes forward again? You and Holt are persons whose names I am peculiarly desirous to see upon book covers. We could found a school, you see—— He probably told you of his scheme to make a booklet of the Mencken *Mail* article? I would like to include some of the *Smart Set* paper therewith, for it sounds distinguished, if incomprehensible, to have been a *Minyan* for some years. To me it suggests nothing save vague memories of patent medicine advertisements, and I must certainly find out what is this thing that I have been unwittingly.

Yours faithfully,

JAMES BRANCH CABELL

[6] Installments of the James Joyce work had begun to appear in March 1918 in *The Little Review,* an American monthly edited by Margaret Anderson and Jane Heap.

From Burton Rascoe

Chicago, August 7, 1918

My dear Cabell:

Mencken's *Minyan* is excellent Hebrew, reminiscent of his theological studies. And it was apt in the usage he put it to. It has something of the connotation of quorum, with the added significance of intelligence on the part of the makers of the quorum. A *Minyan* in the Jewish ecclesiastical code was the ten persons of matured and instructed minds required before a public prayer could be offered.

Bennett, no doubt, was conscious of the need for repression when he wrote *The Pretty Lady;* and as it stands it has caused an unearthly howl from critics, clergy, and laymen in England. It seems to me as though he deliberately set himself to get "something out of his system"; and with flashes here and there, I think, he accomplished his purpose admirably. I feel with you that he never definitely set the problem; but I also feel that there was no actual need to do so. As to the issue which Mencken says Bennett shamelessly dodges, I confess to an inability to see why that particular "issue" was not handled rationally and credibly. Hoape was at no time very deeply in love with the girl: he was a prey always of doubts about her, and Bennett was at no little pains to indicate wherein those doubts had very firm foundation. He indicated her tastes, intelligence, sense of propriety, and even her housekeeping as going against the grain with Hoape. Four or five disillusions and then, bang, the discovery that she is a nymphomaniac settled the matter for this very English Englishman. And to quote Mencken, "It never happens? Go to! it happens every day. The papers are forever full of it." A fraternity brother of mine, a graduate student in chemistry, was violently in love with a professional, an attaché of one of Chicago's most notorious dance-halls. He threw up his master's degree on account of her, gave her practically all of his allowance, and one night broke off with her without a word when he discovered that, although he had given her $200 at dinner, she had stolen a two dollar bill from his trousers. And the possibility was that the girl may have been innocent. Mencken is a sentimentalist: he wanted Hoape to marry the girl.

The highbrow page is to be suspended on Sept. 1 for duration of the war in compliance with the new government order which reduces our Sunday paper by forty-eight columns. So your articles anticipate the order by only one week.

I send you herewith some clippings. Any comment you make on the stuff I write will be appreciated. I particularly should like to know whether you share my disparaging estimate of Pound—did I send you my review of his *Lustra?* . . .

Yours sincerely,
BURTON RASCOE

Virginia Beach, August 13, 1918

My dear Rascoe:

Herewith return to you, as you requested, the two clippings, and with them my heartiest thanks. Nietzsche, after all suitable advances toward *Zarathustra* and *Good and Evil,* I seem unable to appreciate: he impresses me, as does the second Samuel Butler, as getting needlesssly worked up over his discovery of Queen Anne's demise. But the Fanfare is delightful, and it is the things you do like this that clamor to be made into a book, of the Economist School of Art. Surely, you must have thought of making such a book? and is there not to be a book this autumn?— With Mr. Mencken I have had some little correspondence of late, particularly in regard to his *Mail* paper "The Sahara of the Bozart" (concerning culture in the South)—a very clever and true performance, though, as I pointed out to him, he is wrong about the F.F.V.'s having emigrated. But it may be you have not seen this production, which in Richmond gave rise to suggestions as to the aptness of tar and feathers for just such cases?

I have daily deferred writing you, in the belief that Part II of *Beyond Life* would surely arrive to-day. Upon the ninth it actually came to hand, so I put in two days revising the war bits into general observations which nowhere refer directly to the prevalent unpleasantness—and while I was about it, left no mention of "romance" as the inspirer of patriotism, but steadily referred thereabouts to "the demiurge." I believe there is now remaining nothing which can offend the sensitive: and I charge my cowardice to the score of urbanity—— So the manuscript went to Holt yesterday.

But you are continually forgetting I am a quite illiterate person! Your Ezra Pound is to me but the shadow of a name, complicated with vague notions of having read somewhere some drivel as to Bertrans de Born signed with this name, in, I believe, your Chicagoan *Poetry.* But certainly you make him, too, sound interesting. . . . I have eventually seen the last *Dial,* and find my Villon parenthesis, to The Economist, was shortened by a line, to the impairment of the grammar—— I shall add this part to the galley-proofs, which I would to heaven could be sent me forthwith at the Beach, as I am now unoccupied. *The Pawn-*

broker's Shirt is put aside until I can make a fair-typed copy of it, and then worry that into illegibility: meanwhile I am vocationless, but have so worked upon my wife's better nature that we are to return home the first of September. . . . There I must turn, first of all, to genealogy, and am committed to a new *magnum opus* in the shape of a Year Book of the S.A.R. in Virginia. I am hoping that about that time, too, you will be calling in person for your *Eagle's Shadow* and *The Majors,* which await you at Dumbarton, with all sorts of welcome. . . .

Yours faithfully,

JAMES BRANCH CABELL

From Burton Rascoe

Chicago, August 17, 1918

My dear Cabell:

. . . I am glad you like the item about Mencken. There is a tremendous personality, living a most interesting life of doing and saying what he pleases, fighting stupidities, lambasting moral uplifters and prohibitionists, showing up charlatans and having a devil of a time doing it. He sees and thinks clearly, goes wrong occasionally (to my thinking) . . . but he is always interesting and provocative reading. I have cause to remember "The Sahara of the Bozart" most distinctly. As soon as I learned that Mencken had contracted with the *Mail,* I wrote the *Mail* syndicate asking that the articles be submitted to me. I ran three and had "The Sahara of the Bozart" set up, an etched head made, and was prepared to use it on the H.B. page when a sudden suspicion came over me that I was endangering my job thereby. I took the proof to the M.E., who read it with many chuckles of delight and then asked me to hold it over until he had conferred with the chief editorial writer. Came next day a note saying that he thought I had better not use it. (The *Tribune* at the time was, and to this day is, anathema in certain parts of the South by reason of a page article I wrote on the Leo Frank case [7] and by reason of several vituperative editorials which followed my article. Letters had been piling in denouncing me and the paper and editorials had appeared in all parts of the South telling us, with reason, that the pot should not call the kettle black and citing our own little East St. Louis

[7] Frank's sentence to hang for the murder of a stationery clerk, Mary Fagan, was commuted to life imprisonment by Governor J. M. Slater of Georgia. A few days after his arrival in prison, Frank's throat was slashed by a fellow inmate serving time for murder. Frank recovered but was lynched by a mob six weeks later.

massacre of the blacks. In both Chattanooga and Memphis I am promised death at sight if I ever set foot in those delightful towns; and an amiable gentleman in Texarkana, Texas, holds the same fate for me as befell the Atlanta Jew if I ever include Texarkana in my itinerary.) The next article from Mencken, "Virtuosi of Virtue," I used without consulting anyone as to the probable consequences and it reaped a deluge of protesting and inflammatory letters. The M.E. wrote asking me if I did not think Mencken was "a little raw" in that last article—and Mencken has henceforth not appeared in our peaceable pages—— That makes three times I have had bad luck in picking contributors for the H.B. page; and, no doubt, to this record I should have added a fourth, had the suspension order not gone through, since I was negotiating with Frank Moore Colby for some articles. Have you ever read Colby? His *Imaginary Obligations* and *Constrained Attitudes* are delightful. You would enjoy them, I think. He has been buried for some time at a desk in the Dodd, Mead & Co. offices as editor-in-chief of the *International Encyclopedia*. A charming fellow with a keen eye for fallacies and hokum and with a delightfully fluid style. He wrote awhile for the *New Republic* youngsters and then omitted to continue so doing when they began to tell him how and what to write. He now writes occasionally for *Vanity Fair,* that imposing periodical for parlour-maids, debutantes, and culturine neophytes.

I am, at times, agreeably astonished and suffused with vanity to find that you, too, regard unfavorably some writer I have been passionless about and for the same reason as you give. I refer to the muchly cried up Samuel Butler, with his everlasting hankering about Handel and his elaborate notations of platitudes not dissimilar from those I recorded in my Journal in my puberty and adolescence. In fact, though I here fail to allow for a due prejudice, I think that the startling heresies I recorded in those days when, through reading Emerson, Darwin, Spencer, Huxley, Schopenhauer, Kant, Hegel, and Fichte, I was shedding Campbellism with early impotence, were couched in better form than the same startling heresies of the *Notebooks*. And Arnold Bennett's "greatest novel ever written" and Shaw's source of all his ideas, or whatever he said it was, I mean *The Way of All Flesh,* I have never been able to plow through or to react to those portions I have read with any of that profundity I am told I should.

Nietzsche, on the other hand, I enjoy to read—not *Zarathustra*, which is mucilaginous and mystic, as windy as Victor Hugo's *Postscriptum de Ma Vie,* the most ominous and stupefying piling up of words about nothing in, I daresay, the history of all literature. But *The Will to Power, Human, All Too Human, The Genealogy of Morals,* and *Beyond Good and Evil* as well as the early diatribes and philological essays I turn to frequently and am always pleasantly occupied and stimulated, even if La Rochefoucauld has said in a paragraph many things that Nietzsche repeats in ten pages. I find myself intrigued by the processes of his mind, the tremendous sweep of his imagination, his criticism and his ill temper, even his obvious puerilities and inanities. No, I grant you II Samuel, but I will not yield on Isaiah and Deuteronomy.

I trust that I did not make Ezra Pound *too* interesting, for I regard him with particular disfavor, as a poseur, a mountebank, and a half-imbecile with some talent. Though I know nothing of Provençal or Early Italian, I suspected that neither did he very much; and I am glad to have your verdict on his Bertrans de Born. In an almost Hughesianly erudite chapter on the troubadours he makes as his one single point in regard to them the overwhelming assertion that they were human beings, "very much like ourselves." And he clenches his argument by quoting a record that "Faidit, a joglar of Uzerche, 'was exceedingly greedy both to drink and to eat, and he became fat beyond measure. And he took to wife a public woman; very fair and well taught she was, but she became as big and fat as he was.'" Pound is as hazy and as ill-informed on the trouvères, I suspect, as he is on many other things about which he discourses with such an air of wasting his time upon the ignorance of the rest of the universe. He says some one is a great artist and another a great philosopher but omits to mention any reasons for his conclusion. Characteristic of him is a reply he wrote to a Chicago poet who asked why he didn't return to America since they apparently appreciated him in England no more than in this country: "Why should I come back to that God-forsaken desert; there is only one intelligent man in the whole United States to talk to—Ben Hecht." Hecht has written some pieces boosting him. . . .

Mencken writes that he expects soon to be shouldering a rifle under the new draft law and that his American language book goes over until after the war.

Macy is back in Boston after a trip through the northwest; him I expect to see at the revered St. Botolph club when I get East. And I have also an invitation (solicited) to drop off in New Haven to visit Mr. Follett. He is now at the Roxbury school, Cheshire, Conn. The roster of his septemvirate is heroic and interesting: I await his book with eagerness.

And now, if you are still extant after all these pages, my wife is ready and I must go to report Miss Illington in *Eyes of Youth*.

Cordially yours,

BURTON RASCOE

Rascoe was drama critic as well as book reviewer on the *Tribune* and followed the theater throughout his life. *The Eyes of Youth* had run for 414 performances in New York, with Marjorie Rambeau in the lead, when Margaret
Illington took it on the road.

Cabell was a great deal isolated from the theater, although in those days
many more road shows went south. His main interest, in spite of a life-long
fondness for the stage, was in books, and he at once reverts to his own ground.

Virginia Beach, August 25, 1918

My dear Rascoe:

Apropos of Pound, my meaning was that you made him seem a person
who had written about interesting topics. I had meant especially to ask
you about the theory—I quote from memory—that ideas (are) (may be)
valuable as ideas rather than as guides of conduct. Here is a notion with
which I had flirted, and lo, you mention it as a notorious truism somewhere in France. It is a continual marvel to me how you appear to
have read everything ever published. . . . I too have managed some reading this summer, in volumes I had long intended to dispose of. First in
personal interest was *Some Modern Novelists,* which I took very leisurely
and with honest enjoyment. I resented from my first glimpse of the
Contents—and still resent—that Phillpotts and Gissing should be in the
book at all: even the Folletts seem annoyed by the fact, which is thus
rendered doubly incomprehensible: but the other interpretations were
delightful. I like their method, which is really as unblushingly "creative"
criticism as anything in *Beyond Life:* take the author as your starting-
point, and go as far as you like in your train of thought: there is the
recipe followed in both volumes. . . . The author dwindles to a metaphor
and to illustrate what you wanted to write about—— But you have
already reviewed the book: and I shall write Mr. Follett as to my enjoyment of it once I am home again. For the rest, I brought with me to the
Beach a considerable part of the Modern Library, as being conveniently
transported: and of these I respectfully protest that *The Red Lily* is an
abominably tedious production. *Bonnard,* of course, I liked: one has
no choice. As to Nietzsche, I accept your dictum: he expresses an apo-
thegm in ten pages: but I am sufficiently Tennysonian to prefer my jewels
five words long—— Now you direct me to Colby, against whom I cherish
a mild grudge because in all his years of opportunity he never mentioned
any of my books. Still, the titles of *Imaginary Obligations* and *Constrained Attitudes* allure me: so I shall give him a fair chance.

All this about reading-matter! but then I have done nothing now
for two months save read, and fatten up the *Pawnbroker,* in hot weather
that has nearly finished me. So the summer has not been wasted entirely.
We plan now to return to Dumbarton September the third. . . .

Eventually, I suppose, you will have to read Tarkington's *The Magnificent Ambersons,* which I have painstakingly followed in the *Metropolitan,* to my bewilderment. It may be due to the omissions in serializing, but I can make nothing of the story, nor guess why anybody should have written it. No, there is not any patent attempt at popularity or "pleasantness": the author seems devoid of any aim whatever. And I submit that as a *dea ex machina* the hero's deceased mother flying beside the window of a Pullman, (with a handkerchief) and keeping nicely abreast of the moving train . . . while she pleads through the window with the better nature of her former suitor, is decidedly precipitous. It is needless to say that such marked perseverance triumphs, so that everything ends well—— But you, I believe, do not take Tarkington as seriously as I.

Yours faithfully,

JAMES BRANCH CABELL

From Burton Rascoe

Chicago, September 1, 1918

My dear Cabell:

You will recall that I solemnly warned you against *The Red Lily* as France's worst book, excepting probably *The Path of Glory;* but you have enjoyed *Bonnard,* a delightful thing which represents another period in France's creative career. I am recurrently heartened by the consoling fact that France did not show signs of actual genius until he was almost forty and that he wrote what must be counted among his best works when he was past seventy. It is curious to reflect that France seems, intellectually at least, to have realized a wish he expressed in *The Garden of Epicurus:* that youth in man, as in certain insects, might be placed at the end of the span of life, that for the last moments before death he might reserve the highest creative function of his life and thus end in a blaze of glory and enjoyment.

Macy told me that your extensive library is made up almost entirely of volumes in French, so it seems strange to me, since I read French only laboriously and infrequently, that you have not encountered in Baudelaire, Anatole France, and Remy de Gourmont, at least, a tendency to regard ideas as playthings of the intellect rather than as bases for action. It is the one outstanding feature back of the sceptical tendency dating from Renan, and it has been followed by France throughout his career:

in *Penguin Island* he ridiculed the side he took in the Dreyfus affair impartially with the side of the anti-Semites; although a professed Socialist and democrat he has written the most devastating satire against the French revolution and launched poisoned arrows at everything Demos reveres and professes. He would no sooner be acclaimed by one side as its leader or most distinguished propagandist and follower than he would turn upon that side and become its most pitiless critic. So thoroughly has his real attitude of tolerance and sublime indifference been misinterpreted that he has alternately been applauded and cordially hated by Royalists and Republicans, Catholics and Socialists, radicals and traditionalists, literary theorists and pedants,—all men of one-tracked minds, consuming prejudices, and strong enthusiasms. Gourmont, his disciple, followed France in this, and insisted that ideas "should not be spoiled by action."

It was my recognition of this point of view as not being merely "flirted with" but embraced by you in *The Cream of the Jest* and in *Beyond Life* that has caused me to liken you to Anatole France, and to regard you as the most unique as well as the most enjoyable event in the English literature of several decades. It is the thing which, to me, sets your satire and irony above that of Mark Twain, for instance. When I wrote Mencken that long letter about your work, I pointed this out to him and told him that such was your scepticism of the urgency of any human idea that you would, no doubt, view with amusement his eternal castigation of the Puritans and the moral uplifters.

As a matter of pure fact the failure of Englishmen and of Americans of too literal minds to appreciate that an idea may exist independent of action has made Puritanism necessary. When you know that yearly a crop of half-baked youths and virgins from Iowa and Pennsylvania spring up in Greenwich Village intent upon acquiring "black Venuses," "living dangerously," "realizing the full life of their egos," inducing fancies by absinthe and otherwise applying literally various catchwords from Baudelaire, Nietzsche, Stirner, Sera, Huysmans, and Wilde, there is cause to be thankful Puritanism puts a check upon the possibility of their example being more generally followed.

As for myself, my favorite philosophers are the Sophists and I lament the loss of Protagoras' "Contradictions" more than the loss of the plays of Apollodorus, assuming that the loss of either is not a matter of the utmost unimportance. Unless I can sustain my theory, involving considerable research in which I occasionally engage, that the Socratic dialogues of Plato are really dramatic satires and that *The Republic* is another *Penguin Island,* I shall always have but mild respect for Plato. I should like to write a paper in defense of the Sophists, who have always been maligned by fanatics. Then I should like to write a paper in defense of the Jesuits and say that the Catholic apologists who are forever denying the traditions about those estimable philosophers are really attempting to erase one of the real glories of the Church. Two trifles with a philological significance. Then I submit as another idea, Master, an irradiation from your own ever delightful work, a paper setting out that Sincerity as people most frequently know the term is the one serious deterrent, if not the actual blighting, of every work of art. Leonardo, whose claim to the rank of artist is not inconsiderable, agrees with me or rather coaches me in this. Paul Verlaine and your own Economy theories sustain me. All these things, no doubt, have been expressed; but I bring to the composition of them my ignorance of the fact that they have, and shall, or ought to, therefore, make them creative. . . .

On the contrary, it is a constant source of worry to me that I have read so little. I have never read your Phillpotts and only *The Private Papers of Henry Ryecroft* of your Gissing, and I somehow avoided the chapters on them in *Modern Novelists,* having somewhere got the idea that Phillpotts was another Bertha M. Clay (whose many works also I have not read) and having been rather obtuse to the Lambsian observations of *Ryecroft.* But I shall read about them in *Some Modern Novelists* if, as you say, the authors and their works are kept sufficiently in the background for the real duologue of the Folletts.

I shall regret the substitution of typed pages for the holographs, since in all my life I have seen nothing that approached the delicate engraving of your handwritten letters. I have derived from them an esthetic reaction scarcely less than from what you have had to say.

Well, I become garrulous whenever I have written "My dear Cabell" and seem to have no inclination to let up. But when you see me you will be greatly surprised: in conversation I always listen.

Sincerely,
BURTON RASCOE

Dumbarton, September 10, 1918

My dear Rascoe:

. . . Since reaching home I have been favored with a visit by Alfred A. Knopf, who spent last Thursday, or six hours thereof at least, with me. He seems determined to publish me. His plan, as I interpret it, is to "corner" and "feature " the work of Hergesheimer, Mencken, Follett and myself, with side-lines in W. H. Hudson and, possibly, E. M. Delafield. Well, but you have met him, I know. And in the upshot we parted amiably but without promises. He impressed me as efficacious and interesting, but after all non-literary. For he asserts it is the great merit of Hergesheimer's books that each has as its background some big American industry: and such dicta trouble me, into the stuttering of pusillanimous assent.

Also since reaching home I have forwarded you *The Eagle's Shadow* and *The Majors,* to complete your set. . . .

. . . And all this written, without a word as to your delightful letter of the first. Your suggestion about the paper on Sincerity I quite honestly like. Earlier it would have worked nicely into *Beyond Life:* now I shall begin to consider the auctorial vices, with Sincerity as the chief. Indeed it is a notion I adumbrated in "A Brown Woman," just in passing. About the Jesuits you are not explicit enough for me to know what practices you would glorify. And your Sophists are to me but names, unless I can count thereunder Lucian and Apuleius, who, I believe, were merely rhetoricians. Plato I simply cannot read: the *Banquet* and the *Republic* confront me as I write, all translated into English and ready for me, as the books have been for some seven or eight years. Not even Pater's *Plato and Platonism* have I ever been able to get really into, however often I re-read all the other books of Pater. And as an Economist, it worries me thus to waste one volume of the set—— And that reminds me: I have written into the first chapter of *Beyond Life* a formal statement that the book develops the theories of the Economist school of literature. So the movement is duly labeled and launched.

Uncannily you detect my feelings about Mencken: not so much in connection with his attacks on puritanism (which will never of course be damaged by or even aware of his onslaughts), as in the violent objection he entertains against anyone's believing in any personal immortality. Lately, I believe, he has left the topic untouched, but for a long while it seemed with him a veritable King Charles's head, cropping out in everything he wrote. For one, I think it pleasant to believe in immortality, say on Tuesdays and Thursdays: but at any rate, there is naivete in indignation over other persons' notions about this particular question. I would say that Montaigne had settled it, with his Peut-etre, and let it go at that—— But as to Mencken, I shall reserve opinions generally until I have seen him.

. . . *The Pawnbroker* I have been re-copying at odd intervals, until a little more than a third is done. But this time I will not be foiled, and will make of the thing a book of noble and majestic proportions, though it involve the squandering of every idea I possess. Besides, there are all sorts of ways to pad it, once the paper shortage is relieved.

Yours faithfully,

JAMES BRANCH CABELL

§ 5 §

JURGEN EMERGES

My dear Holt:

Is there, do you think, any chance of my eventually receiving proofs of a volume to be published this September under the name of *Beyond Life?* and have you of late seen anything of the Secretary of the Robert M. McBride Company, to whom I have recently despatched innumerable queries, pictures of myself, &c., with no response?

Well!—The most important event of the month has been my meeting "in the flesh" with Rascoe, whom you must have encountered since. I shall always regret that his first visit took place in such horribly upset circumstances, but with him I was delighted. Then too, of course, I have since recollected some 709 things I had intended to ask him about and did not: indeed, now I think of it, neither of us talked enough for what ought to be a Historical Occasion. Of you, though, we did talk: and it was unanimously voted that you *could* "write" and ought to be made to do it. *Breakwater* sounds well, but as touches his creation has a finger actually been laid to the typewriter? I doubt it. Well, but granted that we meet once more before Prohibition goes into effect, I will read you the appropriate lecture.—One point, though: you have emotions, ideas, and so on—say, a viewpoint—which if you do not get into writing now you will have relinquished at thirty, say, for a viewpoint not a whit preferable, and which you will not be able to re-capture. I mean: to my finding the viewpoint of thirty is no more or less valuable or rational than the viewpoint of fifteen or sixty: the point is, thriftily to save all of them. That, sir, is a principle of the Economist school, as you will readily perceive: and stuff that I wrote at nineteen or so I still find invaluable. . . . Your twenties are passing: record your impression of them while to do that is possible: and publish when you will—— Thus do I lecture prematurely and dryly. But I really think you have the talent: and I would deplore its wasting.

I still resent your not having come to Richmond this autumn. There is a chance my wife and I may visit New York this October: as yet, I cannot say. . . .

And I forgot. I am thrilled. Mr. O'Brien is going to print the title of *Some Ladies and Jurgen* with * * * in his book for 1918.[1] I feel that I have "arrived."

Yours faithfully,

JAMES BRANCH CABELL

Dumbarton, October 8, 1918

My dear Rascoe:

Well, it was good to have your note, and now you owe me a letter, via the expeditious typewriter, as to your New York experiences—— I am glad you saw and liked Hergesheimer. I don't believe I mentioned that I, too, liked him extremely: to the contrary, as I afterward reflected with compunction, I may have conveyed to you a quite different impression in telling of our meeting. I think him, of course, egregiously conceited: but (*vide Beyond Life*) I also think that a necessity for, if not invariably a guarantee of, the real literary artist. And I stick to it that my Mountebank and his *Bookman* article are largely about the same thing—— The notion of his party appeals to me: and I think that could we stay magnanimously intoxicated the quintad would get on excellently. . . .

Hereabouts the influenza is working havoc, but we trust to escape by staying out of town. Meanwhile all human existence seems unusually precarious nowadays, and I can but recommend the Gallant attitude. . . . It is a real comfort to have met you: as I forewarned you, I am a perfectly hopeless person to meet, and have had no practice at talking about the things that interest me. But the worst is now over for you, and if you did not find that worst quite unendurable, we will talk in January of the several million things I had meant to ask you about, and didn't. . . .

Since seeing you I have finished the galley proofs of *Beyond Life,* and trust that eventually the book will be printed, though at this rate, that happening cannot but be remote. I noted in this revision a peculiar tendency to invent hitherto unheard-of words ending in "al"—such as "displayal" and "maintainal"—which I still think ought to exist, but have deleted, all save one "displayal." And why should not "to oracularize" be a recognized verb? and why (O venerable wail!) why are we not better off in the way of third person pronouns? and why a number of other inadequacies?— At all events, *Beyond Life* has probably reached its final

1 Cabell had refused permission for inclusion of his short story "Some Ladies and Jurgen" in the annual *Best Short Stories* edited by E. J. O'Brien.

form, and I may now turn whole-heartedly to the pursuit of Jurgen's wanderings.

I want to have in that, by January, a very beautiful and not too sala-cious volume. Its actual improprieties I have reduced to double mean-ings, so that it may get by without suppression. But Jurgen—who, accord-ing to Mr. Lewistam's interpretation (*vide* Foreword), symbolizes the re-splendent, journeying, procreative sun—is not the person for a tea-party. . . . I want you to see, and criticize, this gallimaufry before it goes to the publishers formally: for I am haunted by the suspicion that it may be absolute nonsense throughout.

Now, then, but what is the meaning of this very, very flattering letter from Mr. [Howard] Cook, of Moffat, Yard and Company? I ask because he naively ascribes to you his desire to publish my books. . . . And tell me candidly your notion of this publishing question. You know, I think, my position: I had infinitely rather be published by Guy Holt than by anyone else breathing. And I continue to hope that some day he will be able to publish me with tangible results. Do you not think that this is possible? or—well, in fine, what do you think?

Yours faithfully,
JAMES BRANCH CABELL

Dumbarton, October 8, 1918

My dear Starrett:

It is disgraceful that your letter should have remained so long un-acknowledged, but I have been over ears in the proofs of *Beyond Life.* . . .

What you report from Machen did very honestly delight me, as com-mendation from Sir Hubert Stanley. I intend, whenever *Beyond Life* ac-tually appears, to send him a copy, as I, rather bunglingly, inserted therein a "tribute" to him. It really did not "work in" very plausibly, but I was determined while writing about books somehow to express my appreciation of his—and, save the mark, to advertise him so far as lay within my power. . . .

You must certainly send me your brochures, and I will reciprocate with *Beyond Life*—which, I forewarn you, is a stodgy pudding with, I hope, a few plums here and there—— Now I return to those infernal proofs.

Yours faithfully,
JAMES BRANCH CABELL

Dumbarton, October 22, 1918

My dear Holt:

Your last letter brought me the very best possible news—which does not refer to the improbability of my receiving any royalty statements . . . but to your being up and about once more. . . . I am glad that all ends well. Us the influenza has thus far spared, and we continue to stay away from town, where it has worked considerable havoc.

Write me when you can about the possible appearance of *Beyond Life,* and answer some of the million questions previously hurled at your devoted, and I trust no longer hazy, head. I want to get the volume through with, having completely transferred my affections to the egregious Jurgen.

For *The Pawnbroker's Shirt* is finished in every tuck and frill—there are a great many frills: but not many tucks for I have added and expanded until this magnum opus now runs to 295 pages, and is (in my unreliable figures) some 85,000. I am tempted to expand it yet further, into a monumental 100,000: anyhow, for luck, I must go to 300 pages. —— And now I have this white and indecorous elephant on my hands, without knowing exactly what to do with it. I had hoped to chop it up into magazinable short stories, but the thing grew obstinately away from that possibility. Besides, it is too roguish. And not, you may be glad to hear, a single ———— in the whole book. I like to change my style occasionally. And now there are fifty chapters (without any book divisions, though) it ought to pad out into an imposing volume, with a neat scrap of Latinity on the title-page. And this will finish the love-affairs of Count Emmerich's sisters, who were Melicent and Ettarre and Dorothy.

Well, you will see this farrago, if ever I pluck up courage to hammer out a fair copy of it. Meanwhile good luck to you.

Yours faithfully,

JAMES BRANCH CABELL

Dumbarton, October 26, 1918

My dear Rascoe:

But if you really value a book dedication you shall have the next as ever is. Thus, you are more than welcome to Jurgen's dedication page if, after reading his adventures, you want it: that limitation is made for the reason that while I have put things which seemed big to me into this book, I do not know that I have put these things in a form readily accessible to the reader. Many it may impress as merely laborious obscenity, though I am Bowdlerizing the manuscript as thoroughly as my conscience permits—— In time, then, you shall judge.

Meanwhile I have on my hands this completed book (of not much under 90,000 words), without at all knowing what to do with it. So far as I can see there is nothing to be done with it anywhere before next autumn, and such delay seems shiftless. I can cloudily detect two short stories in it which might be worked off on a magazine, like the earlier fragment. I had hoped there would be some ten such stories, but the book developed obstinately away from the connected-short-stories form. —— Meanwhile I foresee exactly what will happen: this *Pawnbroker* will repose in my desk drawer for months, and for months I shall be unable to resist fiddling with it when I might far more profitably be doing something else. Particularly in this instance, as the style is purposely simple and colloquial, (with Neo-Celtic echoes) and so does not need polishing.

. . . I thank you in particular for your digest of the publicatorial question. I shall as soon as may be possible get Holt's ideas for the future, as well as his candid advice in the matter: and then we shall see that which we shall see. For I confess, quite privately, to a sneaking belief that the *Pawnbroker* could be made to "sell" in respectable figures. About *Beyond Life* I cherish no such illusion—— The trouble is, I get no news from Holt since his note of the eighteenth saying he was back at the office but still shaky: and I have not yet had page proofs of *Beyond Life.* So that the Lord only knows when it will be out. And so I await developments, in no patience whatever.

That was an excellent, a colorful, glimpse you gave us of the elder Yeats, and I thank you for my especial copy. In return, you shall certainly have the picture you requested, so soon as I can get the film into town. You conceive, we are still cowering in the bushes while the influenza ravages Richmond: but now "they say" it is abating, however gradually, so that we hope to get back by and by to normal living—— But will that ever really come again?

Yours faithfully,
JAMES BRANCH CABELL

From Burton Rascoe

Chicago, October 29, 1918

My dear Cabell:

If you insist upon promiscuous blotting, out of deference to Mrs. Grundy, I implore you to make the thinnest of possible lines on *my* manuscript, because I should be very sorry to miss any of the original details of Jurgen's excursions. And I am in hopes that the final draft will

not be too innocuous. I am afraid I suggested a bad precedent to you in
my temerity over the war passages, which now, with peace in sight, seem
permissible, especially since the book may be published after the time
when it is expedient to do what your neighbor thinks——

I will be very unhappy if *Jurgen* is not dedicated to me, now that you
have promised it.

I sent the three children I met some books today. Emmett, I think,
will not be altogether disappointed in his, and Ballard at least may have
the fun my boy had in tearing books to pieces, with his; but I send Virginia two books with great trepidation, lest they be not what she likes
to read at all. You see I have no experience in picking out books for
girls——

Don't take any chances with the flu. It's bad business.

Cordially

BURTON RASCOE

Dumbarton, November 5, 1918

My dear Rascoe:

You are, as always, the giddy dook in the matter of munificence, and
the children are deeply your debtors. Emmett is midway in the Indian
book, and Ballard now understands that the three books on the table are
his, and religiously pretends to read so I figure he is amply supplied with
reading-matter for the next year or two. Then Virginia finished the Caro-
lyn Wells book the day it came, and was delighted therewith. She in-
tends to write you at an early date: meanwhile I grieve to confess that
R. W. Chambers is her favorite author, and in the magazines she always
selects the stories "with lots of conversation in them."

. . . You know my opinion . . . of Phelps as well as of [Harrison's]
Queed. . . . Indeed I went out of my way, in *Beyond Life,* to be rude
about the last named, as I confess almost remorsefully. But, but for seven
years my neighbors have been exhorting me to admire (and if possible
to profit by) the marvelous genius of "your gifted cousin Henry [Sydnor]
Harrison." Auctorial flesh and blood declines to be the kinsman of a
famous novelist. *Moi, je suis ancêtre,* and even the worm will turn at
last: and when he does it is with very much the gesture of a rattlesnake.

—— Still in re *Beyond Life:* I believe you will agree with me, eventually,
that the book is really improved by its ostentatious ignoring of the war,
as a matter so lacking in permanent importance as not to be worth talking about. Then too I consciously addressed myself to 1927 (insultingly
explaining all purely contemporary matters with a footnote), and think
how quaint our "reaction" to this war must unavoidably seem then!

What is to be done about the war books? particularly the "after the war" books? I would suggest an official holocaust of some sort, in kindliness to our descendants, to prevent their being haunted by the thought that insanity is often hereditary.

By all means do you let me see, at your convenience, *A Story-Teller's Holiday.* I enjoyed the *Confessions* (not the *Memoirs,* I confess) and lots of the trilogy, especially the third volume. Oh, yes, and *A Drama in Muslin,* in its first version, (the second I have not) is curiously good. But nearly every other one of the man's [George Moore's] books I have tried to read and simply could not. They are about as readable, by me, as R. S. Surtees sporting novels, without being enlivened by the Leech pictures—— As for Jurgen, he is now (I think) not at all apt to raise the blush of shame upon the unlimited cheek of reviewers. I have finally managed to satisfy myself more or less in his address to God, which I was especially anxious to get more simple: and have otherwise flavored the pudding with verbal plums. But, but how will I ever get it copied! I have prefixed to it, provisionally, a bit of doggerel, as thus:

> *Before each tarradiddle,*
> *Uncowed by sciolists,*
> *Robuster persons twiddle*
> *Tremendously big fists.*
>
> *"Our gods are good," they tell us:*
> *"Nor will our gods defer*
> *Remission of rude fellows'*
> *Ability to err."*
>
> *So this, your JURGEN, travels*
> *Content to compromise*
> *Ordainments none unravels*
> *Explicitly ... and sighs.*

The chief merit of these verses lies in the fact that an acrostic is one of the most difficult forms of composition. Meanwhile the last four lines must seem to you rather inexplicable until you have read the book. Your manuscript, of the first or Virginia Beach version, is ready for you, also when you have read the final version, but not before. My one comfort in sending you your version, as confirmed by looking at it yesterday, is that the thing is practically illegible, by reason of its 90 pages being expanded into some 200 and odd by interlineations. So, after all, my "methods" will not lie naked to the casual eye.

Next week we go in town for the winter, so that after the twelfth you may address me at 3 East Franklin Street, Richmond, Va. We are driven to this step, partly to give the girls a little social life, but mainly by the impossibility of getting enough coal to keep us in comfort here.

Yours faithfully,

JAMES BRANCH CABELL

The Cabells journeyed North the first of December, but were soon called home by the news that all the children had influenza. Those who lived through it, or look back over the history of epidemics, will understand that the influenza of the fall of 1918 was nothing to take chances with. Armed with four quarts of whiskey, the Cabells left New York in haste.

3 East Franklin Street
Richmond, December 11, 1918

My dear Holt:

To-day is actually my first free moment and my first lifting of the typewriter cover. A couple of hours after our parting, my wife and I started for home and devoted a pleasant night to discussing how many of the family we would find dead and whether the sentence for violating the Prohibition laws necessarily included a penitentiary sentence—Mrs. Cabell being quite certain we would both be arrested, and that she would not be let out even to bury the children——

Instead, nothing whatever happened, and I brought in my four quarts without any molestation, to a household sadly in need of such stimulant. All the children, with the nurse, were sick abed, save only Grace: the other servants had left in terror: and not a trained nurse was to be procured anywhere in the city. On top of this Ballard was just developing pneumonia, or rather, throughout Sunday and Monday hung on the verge of it, in a condition which, I candidly confess, kept me sick with terror—— So we have been through four hard days.

Now the prospect is altered. The epidemic continues, but within these walls everybody is in various stages of "getting well," and we even have a servant. In consequence, my thoughts have turned again to you and Jurgen. Indeed, bereft of a manuscript to play with, I have already begun to feel lonely. So do you begin returning it, with all imaginable suggestions, as soon as you can. Some of your ideas, of course, I already have in mind. To the idea of a privately printed edition, which will preserve the tale's immoral integrity, I cling in particular. All that is a part of the book's fundamental idea—"the journeying, resplendent and procreative sun." Much can be done by starting off the reader with the honest belief that a sword or a staff is actually being discussed, and then permitting the evil-minded, such as you, to become suspicious. But, but, but, the

more I meditate upon your suggestion that the Cocaigne chapters be re-
written so as to keep Jurgen in a state of vague horror, the more inclined I am to rank it with Allen's suggestion that I re-model *The Rivet*
by omitting the last book and marrying Colonel Musgrave to Anne
Charteris. The whole point of the Cocaigne experience is that after a
week it was very much like being at home with Lisa. So I charitably attribute this whim of yours to the table d'hôte wine: and for the rest,
entreat you to draw up in full all objections to the book as it stands.
But let's be as roguish as the law permits. You know I really thought I
had removed everything really "improper." Even now, I stick to it there
is not an indecent sentence or any shocking word like "whore" or (that
last favorite) "urinal" anywhere in the book. However, you may now at
your convenience unloose your evil-mindedness.

Send me too about a dozen of the *Mr. Cabell of Va.* [by Mencken].
And believe me, that I enjoyed seeing you especially in my invasion of
your home. . . .

Hastily yours,
JAMES BRANCH CABELL

Richmond, December 28, 1918

My dear Rascoe:

. . . On—let me see—the first of December my wife and I paid an ex-
tempore visit to New York, she to do Christmas shopping, and I for no
especial reason except just "to go along." So I bundled up the Jurgen
manuscript as it stood, and dropped in on Holt without any preparation.
Of him I saw a great deal, and we threshed out the matter of the next
book pretty thoroughly. Mencken was not in the city, nor was Hergesheimer: Knopf also was out of town. Cook I met at a Small Fry luncheon, and was by just the glimpse I had of him delightfully impressed.

Well, we had planned to stay on for some two weeks, during which
I was to call at Cook's office, and Knopf was to be back the end of the
week, and on my way home I meant to stop off at Baltimore. But we had
reckoned without the influenza: for on the fifth day of our visit we were
summoned home posthaste by the news that four of the children—including the three you saw—and the nurse were all down with it. The
trip thus ended amidst alarums, and we returned to face a rather terrible week. All the invalids had a hard time of it, as you probably surmise in the light of memory, but Ballard had the closest call of any: for
two days the most the doctor could say was that he did not think the
child had pneumonia yet, but all the while he was gurgling like a tea-
kettle, so that I was both sceptical and uncomfortable. Ultimately,

though, he did not have pneumonia, and the others too recovered. So all ended well.

But it caused me to miss my meeting with the afore-mentioned litterateurs: and the Jurgen manuscript being left with Holt in the flurry of my departure, he naturally expressed it to an incorrect address. This resulted in the manuscript's being lost for some three weeks, so that only yesterday did I replevin it after no little perturbation, since this was my only copy of the last thirty chapters. Now that affliction too ends happily.

. . . In the meanwhile I have received your two books, and have read the *Story Teller's Holiday* quite through, with vast enjoyment—— The Henry Adams book was equally a surprise and a delight. Rightfully the old gentleman should have been my grandfather. He and I would have had a startling number of points of agreement, and he could have explained to me considerable sections of the book which I candidly fail to understand. This is—or ought to be—an enduring book: I rather think it is a marvelous book—— And I am, for the ten thousandth time, your debtor.

. . . Returning to *Jurgen:* Holt seemed pleased with the thing, in its not very readily decipherable shape, but, to my honest surprise, considers its indecency out of all whooping. I am glad he was spared the earlier version, which I believed I had toned down into quite harmless double meanings perceptible solely to the evil-minded. Really I do not think the book as it stands contains a sentence unfit for utterance in any company: in fact, I know it does not. Holt's idea, at all events, is to print some two hundred copies of the book from type, then substitute other matter for the portions he finds "daring," and so make plates for the trade edition: the first lot to be "privately printed." Meanwhile I am to complete my fair copy, of which thirty chapters remain undone, and the volume—probably—is to appear in August. . . .

Yours faithfully,

JAMES BRANCH CABELL

Richmond, January 6, 1919

My dear Mr. Hergesheimer:

But *Java Head* is splendid! Tentatively I had dipped into it here and and there during its serial appearance (with a vague resultant feeling that you have cut out passages which were printed in the *Post:* I lament that my copies went to the soldiers), but the story as a whole remained an anticipated delight. And now I know my anticipations were correct.

The obvious, the unavoidable, first comment must be that you continue to be miraculously superficial—I mean, in your "rendering" of the surface and look of things. Nobody that I know of anywhere is your peer in that respect. You show the world we live in, too, as an unsuspectedly vivid place, and certainly the color and vividness is not withdrawn until the book's last sentence—— Your "style" continues to puzzle me, and heartens me also, by its fine picture-making and—well, say, full body, with so few actual similes and metaphors. Personally, the infernal things do not come naturally to me, and I painfully insert them because they seem to be more or less expected. Now with you, I went through the first four pages of Chapter VI before lighting on one of these devices: you prove that we—or you, at least—can get along without them very nicely: and that of course pleases me. Another technical point I viewed admiringly is your management of time, with the picked moments set in relief against an actual sense of daily life going on in the background: so few of us convey that sense. For one, I cannot do it even to myself.

But you disclaim interest in these technical matters, in the face of your adroit demonstration how they ought to be handled. Well! . . . You ought, in a word, to be very proud of yourself; having actually the uncanny distinction of meriting what the publisher says about you on the "jacket"—— Indeed, though, the "blurb" is the best I remember seeing anywhere. . . .

I am closely following you into print this year, and an advance copy of *Beyond Life* goes to you to-day. There is a little of everything in it, so I hope you may find something to like—— I was in New York in the earlier half of last month, and had looked forward to seeing you there, but learned at Knopf's address that you had returned to West Chester. Life is not always kind.

Yours faithfully,

JAMES BRANCH CABELL

Richmond, January 6, 1919

My dear Holt:

Taking matters in inverse order, the box of blocks arrived about a half-hour ago, and Ballard is at this moment making a most unholy noise therewith. He seems to be utilizing them as cymbals rather than for constructive work—a born Economist—but is plainly enjoying them. So I thank you in his behalf. . . .

Which brings us naturally to Jurgen. What, first, was your idea in retaining the rough copy? I have found time only to type through XXVI: no work gets done in our upset town-living, but the thing will be finished eventually. Your suggested changes, meanwhile, in the first twenty chapters are not such as we need quarrel over. One or two, really, scent out impropriety where none was intended, as in objecting to the statement "no bubble breaks twice" and to the phrase "a hole and corner business": these expressions were employed without any thought of a double meaning being possible—a clear case of subconsciousness. Still, I can see my way, I think upon the hastiest of surveys, to making the book thus far quite suited to Sunday School libraries, with the sole exception of the paragraph, and ensuing talk, as to Jurgen's hands when he conversed with Guenevere. I hate to cut that part: it rings true, and any evil construction put upon it is something the reader can deduce only in the light of experience. It is with grief that I point out this fact to you—— However, the dangerous traveling comes later in the book, and will be settled down when we get to it. I plan now to send Rascoe the first half of the tale, while I am typing out the last half, and get his opinion thereon. Then when I have a fair copy of the whole, I will amend it bit by bit in the light of your criticism, and decide whether so much of it is unprintable in approximately its present shape as to render necessary two editions. I can, I think, make the "sword" and "staff" and "candle" symbolism come in quite naturally—— While I think of it, have you seen the Beardsley book, in the Modern Library? For months I have been intending to inquire of you if these pictures are copyright, for some of them would make admirable illustrations. Look at the "Baron Verdigris," and you have Jurgen in his habit as he lived: and the "Neophyte" is Jurgen in Cocaigne, of course, with Anaïtis and Mother Sereda. Do you look into this.

. . . Your copy I have inscribed, in pencil since the paper receives ink far too hospitably, and it goes forward with the ORIGINAL MANUSCRIPT tomorrow, when I will have wrapping-paper. I have sent Mr. [S. T.] Clover (of the [Richmond] *Journal*) a book, as I told you I would. And one goes to Mencken, another to Follett, another to Machen, another to Hergesheimer, another to Starrett: and one of course to Rascoe. . . . Hergesheimer sent me a *Java Head*, you conceive: It is good, but not Economic: in fact, I am astounded to note how good it is, without ever attaining the whatever-it-is that Hergesheimer's writing lacks. I don't know what this something is: but in reading I desiderate it.

Now then I will permit you to get back to your main business in life, which is to sell as many copies as possible of *Beyond Life*. I will not hold you to the 2,000 whereof you prattled: but pass the 1,000 mark, and I will give you a best-seller in *Jurgen*. And a book so delightfully thick ought to be salable, with its instant suggestion of getting your money's worth—— The book's appearance, now! that reminds me of my delight in the jacket, than which nothing could be better. I make you my heartiest congratulations—— Still, there is a naive give-and-take about it: Mr. Mencken compliments Mr. Cabell on the exterior, and inside Mr. Cabell reciprocates: Mr. Follett and Mr. Cabell make a similar exchange: Mr. Holt and Mr. Cabell likewise swap civilities: so that in the end, Rascoe alone has no quid pro quo. No matter, his impends in the shape of *Jurgen.*

Yours faithfully,
JAMES BRANCH CABELL

From H. L. Mencken

1524 Hollins Street,
Baltimore, January 10 [1919]

Dear Mr. Cabell:

My best thanks for the book and for the alibi that you set up for me. It is capital stuff, and the ancient virgins of the newspapers will tear their hair over it. The excerpts from reviews at the end belong to the history of American literature. I hope to review it in the March *Smart Set,* barring acts of God and the public enemy.

I am hoping that you'll head this way soon again. All forms of stimulant are still on tap, but who knows when the end will come? I have laid in enough to last three years, but immediately the church bells begin to toll I fear that I'll grow so cautious and saving that I'll be afraid to drink any of it.

Sincerely yours
H. L. MENCKEN

Richmond, January 10, 1919

My dear Rascoe:

I at present dislike you intensely. This is due to a letter received yesterday from your Elisha, "George Gordon." He wishes my last four books sent him, as he is "about half through" his volume, and therewith "an autobiographical letter"—"tell me of the house in which you were born, the gardens where you used to play, the country where you live, something of your philosophy, your liking for flowers or dogs or books, something of your reading, and your hopes for American literature." . . . And it is to this compilation I had looked forward, and to occupying a prominent place therein! Was it your plan, sir, before your translation into theatrical spheres, to inform the public as to my floral predilections and the exact spot in which I first was it in blind-man's-buff?—— Well! therefore do I quote the Soliloquy in a Spanish Cloister.

I avenge myself meanwhile by sending you just half of Jurgen's story, upon which I would value your advice. First, as to whether you will accept the dedication, judging this far. Then, as to whether you find the book "improper"—the remainder is much of a muchness in this respect, as later you will see,—and agree with Holt that in its present form it is unprintable: I don't. Finally, I prize, quite honestly prize, all conceivable suggestions and faultfinding at this stage of the book's existence. As you will note, it comes to you uncorrected, even in typographical errors: and the style I find meagre in many places. I shall endeavor to enrich it here and there: for while I aimed at simplicity and yet again simplicity, I seem to have been over-successful—— In fine, your criticism is invited generally.

When I will get the remainder of the manuscript typed is uncertain: I can get nothing done in my infernal civic surroundings.

Your faithfully,

JAMES BRANCH CABELL

From Burton Rascoe

Chicago, February 12, 1919

My dear Cabell:

The work accumulates and I decay. I find that a letter I wrote you the day I arrived in Chicago has remained unmailed amid the debris which litters my desk. . . . The MSS of *Jurgen* went to you some time since by express. There is, without question, one of the most remarkable books ever written, an amazingly beautiful thing by a monstrous clever fellow. Don't, I urge you, make any changes in the limited edition. I don't understand Guy's marks on the margins—they do not refer to changes to be made for the Economists, do they? I wish I might have gone over [the] whole book with you and Guy. Let me have the original manuscript as soon as possible, and that enlarged picture that you promised.

Yours,

BURTON RASCOE

Richmond, February 15, 1919

My dear Rascoe:

By this time, probably, you are the more or less elated owner of the original draft of *Jurgen*. Accept it with my blessing—— But what earthly good are you as a critic, in private life? "That is fine," you invariably tell me, and "and I wouldn't change it." That is a dangerous verdict, because the self-conceit which is at bottom the sustaining force of authors, invariably tempts me to believe you. I begin to think that maybe I *have* written a masterpiece as splendid as to be incapable of betterment, I begin to think all sorts of manifest impossibilities. Whereas Holt overflows with faultfinding, he does not like a word here, he objects to a sentence there, this paragraph is wrong, that chapter reminds him of Marlowe's attempts at comedy, and so it goes: he emulates the conversational style of Dame Lisa: and after dismissing two thirds of his carping as trivial and idiotic, I find the residue invaluable. But you!

Holt lately spent three days with me, to my delight. . . . The manuscript we went into thoroughly, and finally decided against the limited edition, for the reason that just thirty changes were finally approved as necessary, and the majority of these were so unimportant, that the two editions, we found, would not differ appreciably, and beyond doubt not several dollars worth. So I shall get to work upon Jurgen on the fifteenth of March, *deo volente,* when we return to Dumbarton, and will give him final copy, at latest, upon the first of May—— Those marks on the margin were where he scented trouble with Comstockery: but I think that in the upshot, after I have made my thirty changes, you will find the book very little impaired. In fact, I have already made twenty-two of them, with no real loss to literature. . . .

I thought the playlet fine, and shall treasure it.[2] You might have let me say more, though: at present the thing is a monologue, and in consequence sheer "realism"—our luncheon having been in point of fact a monologue. So when you publish your collected works I shall insist upon writing in the most eloquent remarks for my role.

Still to harp upon that now immortalized luncheon, it has since occurred to me why Hergesheimer objected to what I had said regarding *Madame Bovary:* re-read it, as I have done, and you will see that it applies to the way in which Hergesheimer handles his characters, quite as closely as it does to Flaubert's method. I did not think of it then, nor had I ever thought of it before, but it is true: Hergesheimer does now and

[2] Rascoe had published an interview with Cabell and Hergesheimer in the form of a dialogue called "Jim and Joe."

then describe a dromedary viewed from the North Pole, and describes it infernally well. . . .

I have just read Macy's *Spirit of American Literature,* a splendid thing, and with that tremendously amusing. I would never have imagined it was possible to combine his subject with so many evokers of chuckling. Should he acknowledge the copy of *Beyond Life* which I recently sent him, I shall endeavor to express something of the pleasure I have had from this book: and meanwhile I wonder if he has ever written anything else at all like this? I decline to read about Socialism.

Mencken you may note is more than generous to "Jim and Joe" in the March *Smart Set.*

Yours faitfully,

JAMES BRANCH CABELL

Richmond, February 22, 1919

My dear Holt:

Ever since your departure I have been flirting with influenza, not quite attaining the dignity of "a case," but equally without shaking off the cold I took the day we went to church—or a general upsetness. The more I think of it the gladder I am I took you to Emmanuel [Church]: you now perceive the milieu in which I was reared. Season with your glimpse of the Writers' Club, and you will have a very fair notion of our highest cultural standards.

. . . I have had . . . a letter from your friend Smith,[3] of the *Century,* to the effect that they would have been glad to print the essays in *Beyond Life,* and why did I not send them manuscripts? To this I naturally replied with the inquiry why, if they so admired these essays, they should have refused three of them handrunning without the least suggestion of admiration? and why, if they wanted stories from me, they should so recently have sent back two? (I find they did decline that second *Jurgen* chapter.) And he assures me he has never himself seen any of these manuscripts: that the second chapter of *Beyond Life* they would have, in particular, been delighted to use; and please to send him personally those stories if they are still unsold. In view of insanity evidently being abroad in the *Century* office, do you not think we might work off the serialized *Jurgen* upon them? So long as that remains just possible it seems wiser not to re-offer him the unsold short story.

Now then, but what is this wild scheme afoot to reprint *Beyond Life?* The copy I marked was directed and forwarded to the firm of McBride

[3] T. R. Smith, editor of the *Century* Magazine.

& Company. Meanwhile I wonder how many you have sold, that you should prattle of reprinting.

Your news as to the *Dial* is interesting, and I shall look forward to the Follett article. Mencken says . . . Follett . . . is an amiable enough fellow, but has been ruined by associating with New England sophomores. Personally, I do not agree—— I can write nothing here with any faith in its being tolerably good stuff, and even the Bowdlerization of Jurgen seems beyond me. Yet in a fashion I have made the changes demanded by your pruriency, and do not think the book suffers very, very much thereby—— I am making six expurgations, with modest asterisks to mark them, in six of the immaculately proper chapters, and am calling attention thereto in the preface as all that was necessary to conform the book to the standards of the most squeamish. Result, the reader will imagine something very horrible indeed to fill in these lacunae, and will take the really ticklish portions for granted as having passed the censor. Or at least I hope so. Anyhow, nothing now remains that is incapable of some perfectly respectable and plausible interpretation.

I send you herewith a dollar to cover the two *Melicents*. I am sending, too, renewed thanks for your kindness in the Writers' Club matter, for you really gave them a delightful evening. In fine, you did for me precisely the sort of thing I would have done for nobody, as I humbly confess: you carried it off splendidly; and in a word, I am properly grateful.

Yours faithfully,
JAMES BRANCH CABELL

From Carl Van Vechten

151 East Nineteenth Street
New York City
March 11, 1919

Dear Mr. Cabell,

Aside from a bit of prose which Knopf prints on the wrappers of my books, I have, unreasonably, but mistakenly, passed by your house without knocking . . . until recently when, after an unsuccessful encounter with an automobile which left me on my back in bed, Hergesheimer came in and asked me what books I wanted to read. Of course I thought at once of Ella Wheeler Wilcox's autobiography but he thought of *Beyond Life* and sent it in the next day . . . with the Wilcox. I chose you and read through the book with a sort of bewildered awe of your ironic art, and a great delight in your artful irony. You roused my curiosity to such an extent, indeed, that once able to hobble about I sought the old booksellers for *more*–– I have since devoured *The Rivet* and *The Cream* . . . and *Cords of Vanity* and *The Line of Love* are at hand. I am by the way, indeed, of having a Cabell debauch, and my spies have been commanded to bring me in all your books they can lay hands on. . . . If I had known what was in store * I should have reserved the bachanale [*sic*] for July 1. Indeed the *Cream* and the *Rivet* are as intoxicating as anything alcoholic I've ever met. . . . Of course Joe was very naughty to send me *Beyond Life* first. I shall revert to it later with even greater pleasure. Not that it explains but it makes the mystery still more delicate.

And, by the way, I am not sure that Mencken and Follett are any more right about you than those delicious morsels in the back of *Beyond Life*. You ought to write your own reviews.

sincerely,
CARL VAN VECHTEN

*It's too late to stop now!

Dumbarton, March 15, 1919

My dear Holt:

Your manifest incredulity upon the point compels me to reiterate the statement that we have now removed to Dumbarton Grange, Dumbarton, Virginia–– Now about *Jurgen:* on Tuesday, *deo volente,* I shall set to straightening out the final copy for the printer. The book is now finished!!!!!! I have improved it with several hundred tiny touches, just for my own selfish gratification, because nobody else will even note them; and all that remains is to re-type the pages whereon the marginal additions are practically undecipherable. I shall try to get it to you by 1 April–– The difficulty is the first twenty chapters, of which I have only one copy. I falter at the task of doing them all over again: I equally falter at the notion of entrusting the only copy to the express company. Something might happen to it. So I want you to send me back the copy you have, that I may add my changes to that–– Then you may submit to the *Century* your copy when that is received, and we will pray for the best.– But the title! *Jurgen* does not content me, I cannot bring myself to believe it is the book's appropriate name, and upon the customary bended knees I implore you to re-consider the repudiated *Pawnbroker's Shirt.*

Just now I can write no more. I am alone in the house—for we do not sleep here until Monday—and the furnace is refractory and I am chilled through. So I shall go into the yard to get warm. To-day, you comprehend, I am marooned here, to get the library in shape.

Yours faithfully and frigidly,
JAMES BRANCH CABELL

Dumbarton, March 25, 1919

My dear Rascoe:

You must forgive my long silence, for several reasons. During the latter part of our stay in Richmond I gave up practically all typewriting save copying, partly because my disposition was soured by the uncomfortable circumstances in which I was existing—I scorn the more flattering word "living"—and in part because the impossibility of getting a firm table to write on steadily augmented my rage as I saw with every finger stroke the intestines of the machine shaken up a little more hopelessly. Then began the "moving." For a family of eight, when the "moving" is via automobile, the answer to that problem is ten days of unmitigated misery. Lastly, I am putting in all my time on making a fair copy of *Jurgen*, to be ready for the printer on All Fools' Day. For your book is finally finished, unless Holt even now develops qualms over its castrated decorum. He may.

And to be sure, *Jurgen* is vocal with Celtic echoes! You see, I began with a Russian framework, padded it out with pure Kiltartanese, flavored with Graeco-Roman mythological scraps, and just for luck peppered it with a little Buddhistic lore. And do you know, now that *Jurgen* is complete, I think it very good? and not, quite, like anything else with which I am acquainted.

And the *Tyl* review, I grant you, was inadequate. But then, I wrote it against the grain, equally to oblige the *Dial* and Holt, at a time when I did not want to write anything at all. Crowning misfortune, the Dialers re-punctuated it, to my disgust. In its original form the lengthy sentence which you desired "unscrambled" was an excellent sample of, not Jamesian, but Paternal English, and perfectly comprehensible. For the rest, *Tyl* is a delicious book.[4]

Finally, whatever I might say in defense of my review, I can always leave off talking when I hear a master play. The Ibanez and Strachey reviews were excellent, and the Hergesheimer out of all whooping. Particularly do I now insist that when you come to make your book you

---

[4] *The Legend of the Glorious Adventures of Tyl Ulenspiegel* by Charles de Coster, translated from the French by Geoffrey Whitworth, McBride, 1919.

must have a chapter on Hergesheimer, with this as the corner stone. You have gone farther than I, in explaining why he dispenses with similes: I had merely noticed their absence, the more readily, I dare say, because I was economising on them in *Jurgen*. By the way, I am avoiding formal description in *Jurgen*, to the extent of noticing things approximately when and to what extent Jurgen would have observed them, and letting it go at that—— And of course you are wrong about the last chapter of *Java Head*. In the face of such pertinacity I can but stand perturbed and tender my sympathy to Mrs. Rascoe.

Over and above all this, it happened miraculously yesterday morning that the news-stand, for the first time in months, had a Saturday *Tribune*. So seeing that all were licensed, I made bold to read your personal letter with—need I say?—no small delight. I hope that all you say is true: certainly you seem to find in *Beyond Life* a great many things that I tried to put therein. At all events, it is not a defence of romanticism: I do not think it is even precisely, as Mr. James L. Ford [5] acclaimed it, a book whose main object is to defend Dickens. And while I never said that "sin itself is not what it is cracked up to be by the pious," I sincerely wish I had—— "Never mind, Oscar, you will."

To all these kindnesses add another. Give me some notion as to what sort of book I should write now that *Jurgen* is practically off my hands. The request has a droll ring, but I have the feeling that you have created a sort of legend (I omit any illusion to Frankenstein, as pro-German) to which I am in a manner bound to live up. Come tell me, now, about this Cabell of whom you write so delectably: what sort of book would he in your opinion write next? For my mind is just at present To Let Unfurnished—— I mean this.

... I set you a problem: what will Follett make of *Jurgen?*

Yours faithfully,
JAMES BRANCH CABELL

For *The Charnel Rose* [by Conrad Aiken] I am deeply your debtor. I think it is a delightful book, but not profound. Until yesterday my opinion was much higher than that—— That reminds me that you promised to inquire of somebody about a book called *The Cabells of Virginia*. I strongly suspect there is no such volume, since none of the family hereabouts seems ever to have heard of it, but the off-chance interests me.

[5] Author and editor of *The Porcupine*, 1917–18.

Dumbarton, April 8, 1919

My dear Holt:

Yesterday *The Pawnbroker's Shirt* was expressed to you in its (probably) final shape. It would have gone on the first at latest, under any other than the present Administration. But the government is just now undecided as to whether the express office at Richmond or at Glen Allen is nearer Dumbarton. I thus put in a week haunting the Richmond office looking for the manuscript, which, as eventually developed, had been put off at Glen Allen, where I retrieved it last Saturday, just eleven days after you shipped it. And yet you wonder that I criticize the Administration! In any event, make a note of it that my express address is now "Dumbarton, via Richmond, Virginia."

In re the *Shirt:* you will find that every one of your suggestions has been adopted—— Reading the book as a whole, I am naively pleased with it: I begin to think (which previously I did not think) that it is my best long story, and I find it, after all, autobiographical. In particular, I confess to being pleased with the numerous tiny changes made since you last saw the manuscript: and I request you, again, to note the simplicity of the "style"—— There ought to be a colorful "pretty" passage at the very end of XXIII (the most damnably incisive criticism you ever snarled at me, I remark in passing, was in regard to my willingness to accept prettiness in place of beauty; it still rankles),—and probably another when Jurgen sits enthroned in Heaven. But, but I have worked on the thing now, steadily, for fourteen months, and I want to be rid of it.— By the way, what is the name of the book? . . .

Next in order, is to give the *Century* a sight of it. If they are too much shocked thereby, you might try *Hearst's*. Failing that, it would be a good serial for the *Smart Set*. Apropos, do you not think it would be well for you to see Mencken personally—I suggested this before, I believe,—some day when he is in New York?— I really would like (having tasted blood with the *Tribune*) to do something in the periodical way with this book before solemnizing its funeral, in Mr. Pope's phrase, by publication. . . .

I have really begun on the Intended Edition of my complete works, that is, setting aside one copy of each for marginal corrections and improvements, to be made in spare moments. This may be labor wasted, but, either way, no harm is done posterity, and Ballard stands an off-chance to gain thereby——

How came you not to figure in the *Sun* symposium of publishers? and how does your friend Alfred expect us slighted "others" to forgive his announcement that Hergesheimer is "the only real, honest-to-God literary artist that we have—the only man who writes novels in which he both has something to say and has learned absolutely how to say it." I could have used that for a footnote: well, but Alfred may yet furnish one, in the Intended Edition.

Yours faithfully,

JAMES BRANCH CABELL

From Guy Holt

New York, April 11, 1919

Oh Perverse and Wicked Man!

You haven't tamed down our Jurgen at all—merely concealed the more obtrusive parts of him with such foliage as is appropriate. So I do not say, as yet, that this version is the final one, but I have sent it up to Smith and shall wait to see what he thinks of it. Meantime I reserve judgment, but concede that you have been adroit beyond measure in most of your emendations. . . .

Let us, at your leisure, have a list of final corrections for *Beyond Life.* One reviewer takes you to task for spelling divigate with an antepenultimate "a"— and I would humbly point out that of late your spelling is not impeccable. . . .

For the rest, I am out gunning for Alfred! Did I tell you that I met his salesman in Chicago recently? "Tell me," says I, innocently, "is dear Alfred to publish Cabell's next book?" "I-I don't know," was the cautious reply. "I didn't wish to be over-curious" I told the man. "But I understand that Alfred is telling various booksellers that he is to be Cabell's publisher, and it puzzled me. I thought that Alfred *might* have been misinformed, because, you see, I have already signed a contract for the book myself."—This was in a little crowd of bookmen . . . and did him no good. I still have my claws out for him.

. . . Tomorrow I move. New address, Columbia Road and Old Four Corners, Town of Mt. Pleasant, Valhalla, New York. Our house, I have not yet seen as Beth picked it out and says it is satisfactory. Her purpose is to surprise me with it. All I know of it is that we have about two acres of ground on it, with a brook, many trees and a garage (though what we shall do with that God alone knows). ALSO, I am at last to have a study! You who complain of your back porch, think of trying to write on the dining room table, with your wife sewing or reading nearby, and perhaps the baby climbing upon you. Only a French Catholic decadent could do it. But now *Breakwater* impends. I have, too, a short story all worked out, which requires only a few hours at the typewriter to be a reality.

By the way, I hope you have not obliterated the original ms. of *Jurgen*. It is important that this be preserved, for it should be issued *complete* at some time or another.

Yours faithfully,

GUY HOLT

Dumbarton, April 16, 1919

My dear Dame Lisa: [Cabell addresses Holt as the scold in *Jurgen*]

(For unless you do commemorate *Breakwater,* it is as the "original" of that character you will be known to posterity)—you are, I grieve to state, an unwarrantably fickle-minded virago. Here you have been through *The Pawnbroker's Shirt* with a fine-tooth comb, making (to be accurate) seven hundred and eighty-three objections to this and that. I have adopted every one of your suggestions. My reward is your doubtfulness as to whether this version should be the final one. I am thus forced to refer you to the tale's first title, which was Go to the Devil! Or else find me something in this version that does not permit of a rational un-strained and "decent" interpretation.

The title of this book is *The Pawnbroker's Shirt*. My only reason for mentioning the fact, here, is to forewarn you to get the apostrophe right on the book's back, as, I noted last week for the first time, was not done with the *Rivet. . . .*

Pass we to other themes. Your review of [Alexander Macfarlan's] *Mockery* is excellent, though you do not indicate where it is to appear. And I have hopes for the short story now that you have been summoned to Valhalla. But perhaps—come now, let's all be disagreeable together!—perhaps you only think you want to write, after all. I held discourse with Hergesheimer only last week upon this very topic—the man who wants to write and cannot find time. Hergesheimer was eloquent as to the non-existence of any such animal.

[At this point Cabell took a new sheet, and the following appeared at the top of the page.]

sseexxxxxxx fd bmn-zzxeeeeeeeeeeeeeeexxcc-----xaffa fffff adaaxxxg ass But I must break off to explain that the top line was contributed by Ballard. [He was three years old.] I was called to the telephone just as I inserted this sheet, and he got at the machine in my absence. I let it stand, in spite of the hint of rudeness in his last word, because his in-tention, I gather, was to tell you he sent his picture last week to Cicely, at the Nagle Avenue address, and is worrying as to whether or no she received it. That accounts for a certain incoherence in his remarks.

To go back: Hergesheimer stopped over to see me last week, and we put in a pleasurable four days together. We have sworn, upon the whole, eternal amity, and, upon the whole, I like him immensely. We talked of all things: and have decided to be twin emperors reigning upon equal thrones. His next book, from what he tells me of it, will be curious and by far his best. It is not to appear in bookform until next January, though, running first in *Everybody's*. Of *The Pawnbroker's Shirt* I have promised him an early proof, so that he can review it for the *Sun*, and, he believes, one or two other papers. That we will take up later. Meanwhile I arranged, through our friend Clover, to have him interviewed here, in full length, and he declared me the finest prose artist &c. therein. So it goes—And again Hergesheimer pleaded the cause of Knopf: but I got out of it gracefully by explaining that I could not well publish through a man who declared Hergesheimer to be the only honest-to-God literary artist in America. . . .

Yours faithfully,

JAMES BRANCH CABELL

P.S. I welcome all suggestions as to the *Shirt*, but bar considerations of "decency." The shadow is Comstockery: and the shadow is successfully evaded. The Cocaigne chapters I think fairly good in their new key: the trouble is, that as they stand they discount—a little?—the Hell chapters. . . .

Dumbarton, April 24, 1919

My dear Rascoe:

Well, now, but really! However, I will be magnanimous and write you anyway—— To start us, what do you think of having your book called, after all, *The Pawnbroker's Shirt?* I cannot coax my fancy from that title. And all that I can get from Holt is a "Well, if you insist" and dark hints as to courting disaster and the profoundly unsatisfactory suggestion of *Jurgen*. And *Jurgen*, while the inevitable name of my hero, is simply *not* the title of that book—— I have, I think, improved it no little in the (present) "final version," though the Cocaigne chapters are now perhaps a rather scuffling compromise with propriety. But all the rest is quite certainly bettered.

Hergesheimer lately spent three or four days in Richmond, for the most part in my company, and we have sworn to a-certain-degree eternal friendship. He was on his way home from Florida, whither he went to recuperate from his breakdown after finishing *Linda Condon*. He says it is his best, and indeed from what he has told me of it, it is: I reserve judgment until I have seen it, in view of my underlying suspicion that he wrote it too quickly. Even though it is only 58,000 words, two months is not enough—— Here you have gossip for the Literary Page: Hergesheimer came down, after the completion of his masterpiece, with violent and inexplicable bleedings at the nose: I, immediately after finishing *The Pawnbroker's Shirt* was smitten with almost complete blindness which lasted all one cheery morning. The doctor tells me it was "probably eye-strain" and is changing my glasses: meanwhile I can assure you it is a queer sensation not to be able to see the object you are looking at, but only in a vague way the circumjacent things. After an hour or so it gets quite annoying.

Since then I have started an Intended Edition of my Complete Works. That is, I have revised *The Cords of Vanity* all through, and made it, I really think, infernally good. *The Eagle's Shadow* I am submitting to similar treatment, and the result promises to be—well, pretty fair: I do not claim more. And I mean to give *Melicent* also a looking-over, and just to cast a glance or two at the three Harper books. My notion is to get twelve books in which the "style," anyhow, will stand up under criticism. I am rather committed to it by the Economist theories. . . . It was one of the many topics over which I wrangled with Hergesheimer. "Never revise," he insisted. "Your best work will live, and the rest will be forgotten anyway"—and then went home and set about a revised edition of *The Lay Anthony*. So I must have won the debate.

I stop because I find my eyes are still not focusing properly.

JAMES BRANCH CABELL

From Joseph Hergesheimer

West Chester, May 2, 1919

Dear Cabell:

I have been equally, and with far more need, at the point of writing you every day since my return from Virginia. But I found here—after two months—a quantity of mail impossible even to think about. This Glazer, extraordinary variation of the American critic, has no trace of constipation; he is generous, sufficiently sensitive, and, with a gentle urging in the right direction, should give you some pleasure. Such is the whole duty of critics. But your letter, nominally addressed to Glazer, came home only when it reached West Chester. These things are not for the merely inquisitive mind: the warm silver shimmer, tender darkness, is no graspable reward for industry—— Well, the spring here is as lovely as possible, and soon the lower enclosure—ten years ago I'd have written garden-close—of my lawn will be swimming with fireflies; and the valley beyond is filled with the green piping of frogs. All this is an affair of the dusk, which floods over the road and rises in pools, pouring last through my lower windows. Perhaps you can see, set above a rather long, vivid terraced sod, a long low gray house slipping, but for the lamps, into the night. You might even hear voices, distinguish shadowy legs in flannels: grave young tones with a note of authority brought back from the authentic war; Dorothy with a touch of humorous penetration in her contentment; Ann, abrupt, cool and certain; the other you'll know. Now, in the dark, the smoke, two cigars and two cigarettes, will be visibly pallid; and there should be the suppressed bark of an Airedale asleep and dreaming of craven cats—— Thank Mrs. Cabell for her hospitality; while whatever I could say to yourself is already well understood between us.

> *Joe and Jim and none beside*
> *Mark an age that quickly died.*
>
> *Jim and Joe and none between*
> *Keep an age's memory green.*
>
> *Joe and Jim and only they*
> *Knew the spirit from the clay.*
>
> *Jim and Joe forever are*
> *With Linda Condon and Ettarre.*

Literary doggrel of the year two thousand and nineteen

JOSEPH HERGESHEIMER

Dumbarton, May 7, 1919

My dear Hergesheimer:

It was, to go back a while, excellent to see and talk with you, but perturbing. You are aggressive with your ideas, you overwhelmingly produce the effect of being right about them. Well, but here and there they are not, quite, my ideas: besides, I am an Economist, and it is my own notions, whether right or wrong, that I would perpetuate. Writing I take to be a strategic retreat before unconquerable oblivion: we lose in the end, of course, but you and I may have at least—just possible—the fun of giving oblivion a run for his money. Meanwhile we must each dispose of his troops according to their natural resources, and evolve our own tactics.

Putting it another way, I find in you at last somebody who is quite certainly well worth writing against. We are both aiming at the same thing, anyhow, and that thing is magic. I fancy the formulae of the incantations do not matter so that the magic be produced. . . . There is no need of either jealousy or proselitizing between Friar Bungay and Friar Bacon.

Returning by gradations to the things of the sensible world, Follett "did" you rather handsomely. There should have been more, of course, in sheer length: to me he gave the effect of being confined to an allotted space and bothered by his inability to move therein as freely as he wished. I hope—in fact, I have written him to suggest—that in book-form he will considerably augment this paper—— In re critics, I have not heard anything further from Glazer, but look forward to seeing what he can make of the impossible material we gave him. . . .

I wonder what you are doing? For myself, I am at the cheerless period of actually beginning a new book, the one part of writing which I detest quite cordially. You see, those first draughts prove me so conclusively to be an imbecile. So I temporize by trying two short stories that will convert *The Line of Love* into a dizain. Symmetry is an auctorial virtue.

Yours faithfully,

JAMES BRANCH CABELL

From Joseph Hergesheimer

West Chester, May 17, 1919

Dear Cabell:

. . . Your letter was very clear and reasonable; after all we only disagree on the small affairs of our common undertaking; what I beg of you is not to be diverted outside the crystal of that engagement. But then it was Carl Van Vechten who pointed out to me that recombinations of your elements were probably bringing about an even more mature accomplishment. Glazer wants us to embark on a correspondence to be published, with a brief note, by him. An excellent idea in many ways; except that he seems to think it should be carried forward by differences of opinion. . . . Let them dig this out of our books, since it is from our tables that these fellows are fed and sustained.

Faithfully

JOSEPH HERGESHEIMER

From William Rose Benét

May 21, 1919

My dear Mr. Cabell:

You are giving me a perfectly delightful evening with *The Certain Hour*. I have the atrocious habit of writing letters sometimes to people whose books or stories or poems I like. That is, it is very pleasing to me but must be very deadly to them.

You have awakened in me this evening a most real envy. I am avid of the pleasure you must have had in writing that book. I am also avid of other times, other manners—as in Bernard Capes, Merejkowski, Hewlett, and your gracious self—and, of course, Maurice Baring. You have enlarged my acquaintance with true anodynes.

Really you have added a pleasure such as I had when I first read "The Faithful Shepherdess." In a world full of monthly magazines, advertising agencies (in one of which I am employed), and publishers' jackets —which should be dusted. I fear you, for I have to write about a shaving cream tomorrow—and if it is a sunny day I shall have such a terrible desire to roll in a green field or get drunk in a tavern. . . . All on account of your amethystine book.

I wish I could commit it to memory—but my memory is so very bad. I wish you many more of them. I see that you have written more that I have not read—one, *The Rivet in Grandfather's Neck* that I think I once read for The Century Company, and that we rejected. But such rejections are such an old story in a "vital" world. Some stories of yours I have read in *Harper's* and *Beyond Life*, but I love this present book—still new to me—like a brother.

Pardon this ebullition. It is torture to me to think I couldn't have written *The Certain Hour*—so I write you to betray myself.

WM ROSE BENÉT

From Carl Van Vechten

New York City, May [?] 1919

Dear Mr. Cabell,

Since, on the twenty-fifth of February, 1919, Joseph Hergesheimer introduced me to the work of James Branch Cabell, esq., through *Beyond Life*, I have succeeded with a good deal of perserverance and more luck in rounding up a complete collection of the novels, tales, and poems of that delectable author. Unfortunately thoroughness is one of my vices and so I am writing to ask you if the genealogies are procurable, and if so, where. . . . And do not think, sir, that now I am so near the goal I will lose interest in the object of the pursuit; I am looking forward with a curiosity and interest which I make no attempt to control, to his next book, which, legend has it, concerns a shift at the sign of three balls.

very sincerely,
CARL VAN VECHTEN

Dumbarton, May 22, 1919

My dear Mr. Van Vechten:

Your heroism and powers of endurance have moved me to quite honest admiration. As I figure it, you assert yourself to have waded through eleven volumes which I envy (and question) anybody's ability to read en masse—— I am not sure about the grammar of that last clause, but can find nothing wrong with it, anyhow as touches truthfulness.

I shall complete the dozen, therefore, by mailing you to-morrow with my compliments a copy of *The Majors and Their Marriages.* The other two genealogical essays were privately printed, in the most limited quantity, for members of the Branch family who "ordered in advance," and are now, so far as I know, not to be had anywhere. After a sight of the *Majors,* however, you will not have the least desire ever to possess its fellows in dulness. It is quite unreadable: so you must take my word for it that the book is full of solid and valuable information not to be found elsewhere in print.

Jurgen, I hope, you will like better. He is not, I think, the common type of pawnbroker, but will, I trust, even so exact some interest.

Yours faithfully,
JAMES BRANCH CABELL

From Guy Holt

Valhalla, New York, May [?] 1919

My dear Cabell:

Your letter is reassuring . . . but now I have annoying news for you. McBride has returned and absolutely will not consent to the use of *The Pawnbroker's Shirt* as a title—or as part of it. He points out, with entire justice, that a title is a lure for the prospective reader, not a bit of interpretation for him who has read. It is a cocktail, not a liqueur; an invitation, not a "thank-you note." And in this metaphoric capacity, *The Pawnbroker's Shirt* has only so much of merit: that to him who knows the promise of your name on a book's cover, the title is in accord with past performances. To the larger audience, as yet unreached, it will appeal in less measure than did *The Rivet in Grandfather's Neck*—— I, as you know, agree with him. Of late I have been tempted to ignore caution and past experience alike, and have even gone so far as to suggest to one or two booksellers that your new book might be so-called. In all cases the announcement was greeted with uplifted hands. So let us call it *Jurgen* and see if sales will not follow. I really consider it a good title —others agree with me—and for your consolation you may leave the original title upon that yellow manuscript which I hope to receive from you when the last proof has been corrected. (Have I, by the way, asked you to spare the expurgated passages in this edition? As a record it is desirable that some copy of the original version be left—and I had as lief it were in my possession as in any other's.) . . .

And now a storm has come up, the wind is blowing our shutters furiously, and from my study I can look out upon a regiment of black trees, waving against an indigo sky. So I bid you good night, sir, and prepare to admire the night at closer quarters.

BUT I must thank you again for Ballard's photograph. He appears a model of studious application, and Cicely admires him tremendously. "*Mine* baby," she cries, now and again, pointing to him. So I warn you that the young woman has designs upon him, thus early.

Faithfully yours,

GUY HOLT

THE RECEPTION OF *JURGEN*

My dear Hergesheimer:

The weeks roll around, in that infernal oleaginous imperceptible way they acquire after, say, thirty five, and you remain unwritten to. All this in spite of the fact that there are really a many things I would take up with you.

Anyhow I rejoice to hear there is to be a volume of short stories. . . . Upon the beginning of *Linda Condon* (chèr maître) I make you my sincerest compliments. I forget the name of the sick gentleman who, I believe, set the key note—that is, the magazine is downstairs, and I am too lazy to fetch it,—but he was admirably managed, if the tale is to run as I foresee it. But I desist: I am tolerably certain I apprehend your action, yet it would be uncommonly awkward if I made a mistake and complimented you on the wrong thing. I shall read *Linda* as a serial, then as a whole, and judge you afterward. . . .

Do you know anything about writing short stories? I ask, because I recently borrowed Esenwein's book[1] on how to write them, and read the volume with interest, some amusement and an underlying uneasiness. Here I had written, in my time, some sixty sort of somethings I believed to be short stories, and it seems that many of them were nothing of the sort, and that all either violated or ignored the code of correct short story writing. The only thing that ultimately cheered me, somewhat, was a careful perusal of some of the short stories of an Esenwein graduate. . . . But somehow it did turn me, after a six years vacation, to the writing of two short tales, with one of which I am still amusing myself. . . . For instance, have you ever tried composing, in the third person, a tale all told from the viewpoint of one of the characters, and conscientiously including nothing except what that character actually would notice at the

[1] Joseph Berg Esenwein wrote many books on the short story. This reference is probably to *Writing the Short Story*, Hinds, Noble and Eldredge, 1909.

time it, actually, would be noted or thought of? It is rather fun: it shuts
out local color and scenery and so much else that you can hardly get the
story told at all. . . . In any event I am mildly grateful to Dr. Esenwein,
who has spurred me, if by his idiocy, to enlarge *The Line of Love* into
a dizain: the fact that it was not one has worried me for a long while:
and now it is, at all events in my thoughts, so I will not be worried any
more, since these two tales are done. . . .

Yours faithfully,

JAMES BRANCH CABELL

From Joseph Hergesheimer

West Chester, June 20, 1919

Dear Cabell:

Thank you very much for your kind assurance; but indeed you must
like *Linda*. I was very much amused too by your comments on writing
a proper short story. In my time I read a certain number of instructive
books, appreciated more or less their purpose, but was unable to profit
by any such advice. If I write the regulation thing it's by accident. Even
now beginning a story I have little knowledge of its exact form. It has
been said, with ample support of authority, that I can't write a short
story at all— Yesterday talking to Lorimer [2] about a manuscript I just
sent him he asked emphatically, "Yes, but has it a story?" I replied just
as directly, "It has." But damned if I was sure.

As a fact I detest all the cant phrases that are fastened to our art, detest and suspect them. What I like to accomplish is too fluid, elusive, too
buried in mystery and doubt to permit of any such exact phrasing. What
satisfaction I get from my writing comes from the moments when, it
seems to me, I have captured some beauty. But all I know about that is
contained in a warm indiscriminate thrill about the heart.

I am already looking forward with pleasure to being once more in
Richmond and talking to Nellie and yourself. My present affairs are
rather vague: perhaps a novel, if I can afford it, perhaps one of the short
stories I am unable to write.

Faithfully,

JOSEPH HERGESHEIMER

2 George Horace Lorimer, editor-in-chief of the *Saturday Evening Post.*

Meanwhile Rascoe continued to write from Chicago, asking for more and more data on *Jurgen*. "How are you getting on? . . . I am convinced that *Jurgen* is one of the finest pieces of art in all literature—assuredly the most artistic thing I know of in our literature. . . . What have you done about the title? . . . I have been having some more fights on my hands and enjoying them hugely. My first venture between covers probably will be an introduction to a new edition in English of *Madame Bovary:* the copy is now in the hands of the printers. I am editing a series of translations for Knopf. . . . What source books on mythology did you employ in *Jurgen?* I ask because of the variations in names."

Dumbarton, June 21, 1919

My dear Rascoe:

. . . *Jurgen* has kept my time pre-empted, what with the proofs going astray in transit to me, and being replevined from various express offices at which they had no reason for being,—and what with, of course, those maddening miracles of stupidity which printers invariably perform. At last, however, the galley proofs have been corrected in toto, and they went to Holt this morning. So I am really giving you my first free moment.

Jurgen seems to me, as a whole, rather satisfactory. I would like to believe you are having such a wonderful volume dedicated to you as you say: but I cannot hoodwink myself that far. And *Jurgen* it is to be christened, after all: it is not, as you know, my choice for a title, still I do not very, very actively resent it. To name a book after the main character has always seemed to me a dodging of the issue, unless that character is sufficiently interesting and individual—my notion making, for instance, *Don Quixote* a well-named book, and *Martin Chuzzlewit* just the contrary. . . . For source books (mythological) I used as always Lemprière and Tooke's *Pantheon*—the latter, by the way, giving three times the name of the third Fury as *Magaera*, though I can find that spelling nowhere else. But thereafter, during the temporary possession of my uncle's library, I garnered stray bits of erudition from all sorts of rare improper books, not in your manuscript, and shamelessly stuck them in the text. The book is now a jungle of phallic hints and references, which will shock nobody because nobody will understand them. But then I have a great many private jests here and there in my books: and some day may prepare a concordance.

Turning to other books, I am deeply your debtor for the *Della Robbia Heraldry* and *The Royal Government in Virginia*. The first is a beauty, and is the sort of stuff which I find interesting without attempting to defend my notion. The second I had already looked into, at the State

Library, and had admired, so that I am delighted to possess a copy.
—— That reminds me, by a considerable cast back, of the *Jefferson, Cabell
and the University of Virginia:* no, I do not want it, for I have seen it,
long ago, and it concerns only a great-uncle: and I must honestly confess
to being really interested in nobody's ancestors save my own—and lat-
terly Ballard's. . . .

What interests me infinitely more is your package of enchanted cigarettes. I would preach to you, as I do to Holt, that the book you would
write now must be written now or never; two years hence you will be
unable to write that book, and what you may write then, if equally
good, will be quite another story: but you would only reply, as he does,
—quite irrelevantly—"I haven't the time." And I would be tempted to
say a great deal that would sound nonsensical. . . . Anyhow, I shall look
forward to the *Bovary* introduction, though I defy you to rouse me to
enthusiasm about Emma. And what are the series of translations whereof you speak? . . .

Flying off at a tangent, which is (or are) the best of Mencken's books?
You see, I do not know him at all in volume form and want to try
him in that avatar. . . . For the thousandth time I repeat my wail as to
the misery of living in a place where you cannot go into a store, pick up
a book, and see for yourself whether or no you want it.

And while we are on the topic of misery, my eyes continue to give me
the devil. The oculist imputes it to "getting accustomed to new lenses"
but I do not really believe he knows much about it. And of course the
moiling over the *Jurgen* proofs—in quite small type, prompted by an
endeavor to get the whole thing into 300 pages and save paper,—has not
helped matters. I have recently taken to copious weeping without any
provocation, and in company this is embarrassing and suggestive of some
secret sorrow. . . .

Finally whose French is that you inscribed in the front of the heraldry
book? I heartily, as you know, endorse the sentiment, which is the
strongest bond between Mencken and myself: hence the query.

Yours faithfully,

JAMES BRANCH CABELL

From Burton Rascoe

Chicago [date?] 1919

Dear Cabell:

... The quotation is from Remy de Gourmont with whom you have something in common in the matter of subtlety, ironic scepticism, delicious hedonism, sensuousness, and imaginative quality. An excess of gravity is his main defect: he has not a tittle of your humor. He has, on the other hand, a greater range than you have: he has written on etymology, Eusapia Paladina, church mysticism, the Symbolist poets, Renan, the Jesuits, Nietzsche, philology—on practically every subject touching philosophy and literature; and he has produced romance and realism, *romans cérébrals,* drama and poetry—— If you have not read him, I should like to send you one of his books, because I think possibly it might germinate some ideas for your next volume. I should like, for instance, to see you do a novel somewhat in the line of *Les Chevaux de Diomède,* or as Guy Holt suggests a subjective novel in the modern Canna, Beresford, Rolland manner, or better yet, Guy's delightful suggestion "The Adventures of a Sane Man in the Universe"—(the idea is superb, though the title has a[n] antagonizing braggadoccio about it).

But now, have you any scraps of manuscripts of *Jurgen* about, now that you have mauled it out of all resemblance to the marvellous manuscript that I have? If you have, I demand my proprietary rights in them. Guy says that you promised him the printer's copy; but I insist that all scraps relating thereto which were discarded before the printer's copy was finally in form, belong to me. Am I not right?

Mencken's best book, I think, is *A Book of Burlesques,* with his *A Book of Prefaces* well along in the lead. The former is gargantuan fooling from which you will get many good laughs.

My introduction to Bovary, curiously enough, slights Emma in a degree amounting almost to an affront: I center attention upon Homais, who has always been to me the one real and important character in the book—a truly marvellous creation, indigenous to every village. I pointed out some Homaises in a discursive fashion, Robert Ingersoll, Ernst Haeckel, Elbert Hubbard, and a number of others—— Although there have been several whole books and thousands of articles devoted to Emma and Flaubert, I think I managed to say something that has not been said—something wrong, possibly, but at least not the same old stuff.

Knopf has an idea that we may by a gradual publication of standard French classics in unexpurgated translations open up a field of greater literary freedom in our literature. I am, therefore, to select some innocuous ones as "openers," write introductions to them, see that the translations are valid in letter and spirit, and later we are to introduce into the series some more modern works. There will be in the series *Mademoiselle de Maupin*, possibly *The Temptation of St. Anthony*, Rabelais, the work of some Germans and Austrians, some Polish probably, and some Italians. I know neither Polish nor Italian, except enough of the latter to pony through some of Dante; but that fact will not invalidate the series. But more of it later. A more difficult job for me was to write an introduction to *Manon Lescaut* without holding my nose: Knopf insisted that it be the second in the series. Did you ever read that drooling piece?

No wonder I was curious to know your mythological sources. I have never heard of Lemprière or Tooke. Who are they?

Yours,

BURTON RASCOE

Dumbarton, July 8, 1919

My dear Rascoe:

Well, and what is this clash between you and George Gordon? I have only his mention of it in the *Sun* to go on—— Meanwhile I find interesting what you say about Gourmont, who is but a name to me. I shall be glad to know him more intimately by and by. As for writing one of those "subjective" novels—I wonder if it is worth while to tell everything about yourself at such intimidating length. Yonder, for example, is *Youth's Encounter*, which I puchased a good six weeks ago, and continue to look at tentatively. There is so much to it: and I wonder if I really care that much about Mr. Mackenzie's interior workings. Still, I have long foreseen an atmospheric story of John Charteris and one of the women whom he did not marry, for which I shall make notes this summer, to the tune of *Eheu, fugaces!*

. . . As to my sources, I thought everyone used Lemprière's *Classical Dictionary:* anyhow, Keats got all his mythology therefrom, and I perhaps sentimentally affect it because Lemprière was for eighteen years headmaster of the Abingdon School, founded by one of my English ancestors. Tooke's *Pantheon* dates from the seventeenth century, and is more limited in its scope, but I have found it very useful—— I believe I prefer to invent my mythology, though: for when I read, in *Jurgen*, of Anistar and Schlaug and Phorgemon and Miramon Lluagor, for example, I somehow feel there must be interesting legends connected with them.

Hergesheimer is to review *Jurgen* for the [New York] *Sun,* and Miss Dorothy Scarborough is to "do" it for the *Bookman.* She is a person, of not uncertain age, whom I like very much: she did the *Sun* review of *Beyond Life,* if you remember, teaches short-story writing at Columbia, and visits Richmond each spring. . . . Now that I think of it, you cannot yourself very well review *Jurgen,* since praise would seem vainglorious and fault-finding ungrateful. . . . I shall read the *Bovary* all over again after you have re-introduced me thereto: and please when the *Tentation* is brought out include the earlier versions of what upon the whole I like best in Flaubert.

Yours faithfully,

JAMES BRANCH CABELL

From Burton Rascoe

Chicago, July 18, 1919

My dear Cabell:

But (really) I have no quarrel with George ( ) Gordon. His book [3] is (I think) a most interesting literary curiosity—— Gordon's abandonment of the comma in favor of parentheses is fascinating: I found myself (for the most part) skipping the text to count the number of parentheses to the page. . . .

Neither Holt nor I had any thought of your writing a book in emulation of Compton Mackenzie. He is, perhaps, the least eminent of the English writers we had in mind. . . .

Bovary is to be a beautifully printed and bound book, as will be all of the books in the series. Knopf has an unquestioned taste in bindings. . . .

I saw the dummy of *Bovary* when he was here last week and read therein, for the first time, my preface as it appears in type. . . . I had in mind using the first version of the *Tentation* as being better than the definitive edition.

Yours,

BURTON RASCOE

[3] Probably *The Men Who Make Our Novels,* Moffat, Yard, 1919.

Dumbarton, July [?] 1919

My dear Hergesheimer:

... I have spent the last three weeks alone at Dumbarton, save for the baby, while the others went to Virginia Beach. I did not accompany them, for the excellent reason that I went there last year: now all are home again, and we plan to leave here about 30 July, to spend August at the Rockbridge Alum Springs, in the Virginia mountains, where I shall take notes for a vaguely foreseen atmospheric-subjective novel. Meanwhile I disposed of the two short tales, for whose writing as I have confessed to you Dr. Esenwein was largely responsible, to the *Century*. One of them, I gather, they liked very well and the other not one least little bit—it was, of course, the one wherein I had amused myself with invisible subtleties which they found abhorrent. ... I view them both with respectful wonder, not quite believing that I am once more writing short stories: and have half-way promised Mr. Mencken to "do" him another one if I can manage it.

July and August, though, are my mentally gray months, I find— January, February and March are the black ones,—and I foresee that the will to write cannot but drowse until September. Usually I have something laid aside to tinker with in these barren periods. This year there is nothing. But I am cloudily groping, I think, toward another dizain. —— At no time, it is appalling to reflect, will we ever be able to desist absolutely from this magic-seeking until the undertaker has us alone with him and his shiny black bag. And thereafter you at least will find the "local color" of heaven irresistible, and will be clamoring for a typewriter. I have forestalled this fate's befalling me by "doing" both places in advance.

Faithfully yours,

JAMES BRANCH CABELL

For some weeks in the summer of 1919, Burton Rascoe had been writing to Cabell first about Rascoe's *Jurgen* manuscript, then the printer's copy, and finally the book in boards. "I spent most of Sunday reading my new manuscript of *Jurgen* with ever-increasing admiration. ... Could you tell me what was the nucleus of this extraordinary book, what was the initial idea from which it grew, and something about its evolution? I am curious to know."

Rockbridge Alum Springs, Virginia
August 10, 1919

My dear Rascoe:

Well, very cordially do I hope that some day your collection of Jurgeniana will be extremely valuable. I am tempted to augment it, as you request, by a sort of private preface as to the book's evolution, but,

looking back, detect so many tiny tributaries as to defy cataloguing. . . .
Imprimis, it was a year ago last March that I temporarily put aside my
Something about Eve to write for Mencken the short story he requested
and seemed to merit. I evolved then very much the same "Some Ladies
and Jurgen" in imagination as eventually appeared in the *Smart Set:*
wherein the devil offers Jurgen the three symbolic ladies Guenevere
and Cleopatra and Helen, and the poet prefers, upon the whole, his
prosaic wife. But as I wrote it out, I scented possibilities—how much
more effective, for instance, it would be if Jurgen had previously known
and loved and lost these women. Of course, that meant, to me, a dizain,
with four tales already suggested: it would be out of space and time, of
necessity, if Jurgen were to encounter these three who lived centuries
apart. So, with my story still unwritten, I begin to plan the dizain, of
ten short stories to be disposed of severally for much fine gold. Ah, but
the Cleopatra episode! here I foresee myself heading straight for an
imitation of *Aphrodite* and Louÿs' notion of life in Alexandria. Well,
then, let us substitute the goddess herself in place of the Cleopatra who
symbolizes her, and call the goddess—no, not Aphrodite, the Grecianisms
must be reserved for the Helen part. I consider her other names, and
am instantly captivated by the umlaut in Anaïtis. So my second heroine
becomes Anaïtis, a moon goddess. But her lovers are solar legends——
Why, to be sure, for does not Guenevere typify the spring, Anaïtis
summer, and Helen in her Leukê avatar the autumn? I perceive that
Jurgen is a solar legend, and inevitably spends the winter under-ground.
There is the Hell episode postulated, then. So I make out my calendar,
and find it 37 days short, since obviously the year must be rounded out.
Where was Jurgen between 22 March and 30 April? The question
answers itself, and I spy the chance to use that fine idea that has been
in my mind for fifteen years or more, as to how Heaven was created.

I am getting on now, with my dizain lacking only three episodes—
since the half-written magazine story has obviously split into an opening
and an ending of a book. (That is, I thus far think it the ending.) And
now I am wondering if there is not a chance at last for that other fine
idea I could not ever find a place to work into—the going back to a
definite moment in one's past—— For what? — obviously for a woman,
since Jurgen has by this time taken form as a person—— What woman,
though? — why, clearly the woman who in his youth represented the
never quite attainable Helen. And she was Count Emmerich's second
sister, whose existence I had postulated in *The Jest*, with the intention of
using her in due time. I christen her Varvara, in general consonance with
my Russian Koshchei, who I am beginning to perceive must be more
than a mere devil if the book is to ascend—— Yes, he must be the Demiurge, and God his creation—— Then Koshchei must be rather stupid,

and not be bothering himself about Jurgen at all. I need another super-natural agent, some one more near to purely human affairs, to direct Jurgen's wanderings. My mind being already on Russian mythology, and the regaining of a lost day being involved, the Léshy who control the days present themselves, and I select Sereda for Jurgen to wheedle out of, of course, one of the Wednesdays when he was young. Another episode.

But this Varvara (no, nobody will be certain as to the pronunciation of Varvara: call her Dorothy)—will disappoint him, a little anyhow, if he goes back to the actual girl. Really to go back, he must return to the girl as she seemed to him, and himself be young again—— But the point is already in my mind that, while Jurgen is to keep the youth that would come back to him with the replevined Wednesday, so far as his body goes, his mind is to remain middle-aged. So I grope to the ironic scheme of letting him seem to his ideal girl as he actually is, and be to her unrecognizable—— Then he must, somehow, get rid of his false youth before his interview with Koshchei in the cave: that makes me the tenth episode—— No, I still lack the machinery for getting him to the Garden: a centaur appears the handiest method of combining trans-portation and conversation. I think inevitably of Nessus, then of his shirt. Yes, something must be done with that shirt—— And that episode must come first, while Jurgen is still middle-aged.

Well, there you are. That is about how the outline of the book came to me: and at this stage I went back to the *Smart Set* story and actually wrote it. Thereafter I set about writing my ten episodes (and found them resolutely determined not to be short stories, on any terms); and rewrote them; and put in here and there just anything which occurred to me, and changed this and altered that; and groped to that loathsome last chapter as the tale's inevitable ending. And almost last of all, I pivoted the whole thing upon the shadow and the shirt, which were almost the last things of all I thought of—— So, you see, the book virtually wrote it-self for

Yours faithfully,

JAMES BRANCH CABELL

Before the Cabells left for the Rockbridge Alum, a letter from Sinclair Lewis reached Dumbarton.

From Sinclair Lewis

315 South Broad Street
Mankato, Minnesota
July 24 [1919]

Dear Mr. Cabell:

It seems probable that my nearly two-years stay in the Middlewest—broken only by summer on Cape Cod a year ago—is going to end abruptly, because I am suddenly very tired of hearing about motor cars and crops, wearier yet of making inane black marks on paper and calling it writing; and when I am in that mood, I flee to my wife, making loud vyryle remarks about The Great Open, and immediately we start somewhere by car.

I decided to go this noon—she agreed at 12:17—we start a week from today for the East, driving by way of Tennessee and Virginia—questing a place to live next winter along the way, Virginia—Pennsylvania—Connecticut—I know no more about it than the gypsy knows of his next camping place.

But I do feel sure that we shall come creaking into Virginia some time in August, and I wonder if you are discoverable. Since our three or four letters of almost two years ago, I've wanted to see you. I wonder if you could be persuaded to telegraph me here where I am likely to find you about the middle of August? If you were anywhere near Virginia, I might be able to wander in for a day, and say appropriate things about Balzac and prohibition and matters of state. I regret the indecent suggestion of telegraphing instead of writing, but I shall be going so very soon that a letter would scarce reach me.

This last year, I have had a quite bad play[4] on in New York; various essays at the short story here and there; and I have started a long, wearisome, very dull and excellent novel which I shan't be able to finish for a year or so.

May I hear from you? It will be the first time I shall have been near Virginia these three and a half years.

Sincerely yours,
SINCLAIR LEWIS

Soon after their arrival at the Alum, there came to Cabell another letter from Lewis in sprawling longhand, written on stationery of The Good Hotel, Morristown, Tennessee.

---

[4] *Hobohemia* opened February 8, 1919, at Greenwich Village Theatre, Sheridan Square.

From Sinclair Lewis

[No salutation]
Gray with dust—uncertain as to nails—nose of a rich ripe red that would
have edified Swinburne of the roses—I have straggled thus far, accom-
panied by my (more or less—quite steadily less) immaculate wife. Tomorrow will see us beyond Bristol & into Virginia & about Wednesday
or Thursday the Visitation should appear at the Alum.

We have seen gourds, scenery, blue jeans, corn crops & hotel bacon. We
have climbed roads like this

∧ = flint, a sorry sight on a right smart piece of road.

And I think that (till in that miraculous way known to the practical
minds of wives, mine gets out the electric iron) when we arrive we shall
look quite like that road.

Sincerely
SINCLAIR LEWIS

For some days after Lewis's arrival, the two men sat under the trees at the
Rockbridge and read each other's latest writings. A snapshot shows them,
backs against the same tree trunk, deep sunk in manuscripts. Lewis had begun
Main Street, and Cabell had but lately sent off the page proof of *Jurgen.* Lewis
left with his friend a parting verse:

> *Just beneath the misty range,*
> *Always smiling off to sleep,*
> *Musing of the far-off strange*
> *Era of dead psaltery,*
> *Slumberous the Alum lies,*
> *Bowered by the dappled skies.*
> *Round it corn-fields billow deep,*
> *And the fine-drawn, quivering*
> *Nocturnes of the crickets rise,*
> *Calming my "Efficiency."*
> *Here, with winsome Nicolette,*
> *Cabell mocks my northern fret.*
> *Alum-filled, with folded wing,*

> *Beautifully indolent,*
> *Even my ego's rage is spent,*
> *Lulled to something smiling sweet,*
> *Lo! the acrostic is complete!*

A few days after the Lewises had left, Cabell wrote to Holt in regard to photographs that the publishers wanted, and said: "Sinclair Lewis 'visited with me' three days last week and we were kodaked together in various striking poses. If any of these pictures come out well we planned to use them in behalf of both his new book and mine— Let me say, in passing, he has really a future, and a really splendid book partially written—I have read the manuscript— though the forthcoming *Free Air* is not, he confesses, in any way remarkable."

Lewis and his wife continued their journey until they rested for a while with the Hergesheimers in Pennsylvania. From there, several weeks later, he wrote to Cabell, by this time back in Dumbarton.

From Sinclair Lewis

West Chester,
Wednesday [September, 1919]

Dear Cabell:

Through a period of house-hunting, looking at hills, talking to Joe, & correcting proofs, I have written no letters, despite the receipt of your letter with the admirable photographs, & my recurring desire to thank you for discovering to me the Alum & yourself. It was a memorable & happy few days for both of us. . . .

. . . Monday we came into West Chester and, aside from having the re-repaired spring break, going to New York where they wanted $300 a month for six filthy little furnished rooms, & for a while concluding we shouldn't be able to get a house here, we have led a placid existence. We finally did get a house—tho we sha'n't be able to move into it till about September 15th & our address till then (while we hide in some haunted boarding-house) will be more or less in care of Joe.

My greetings to your wife & my eagerness to see you again—

SINCLAIR LEWIS

The Lewises did not, after all, stay in West Chester, but went on to Washington, from where Lewis sent a card to Cabell on September 24th.

> I am not in any wise in West Chester,
> In Washington am I,
> 1814 Sixteenth Street, Washington.
> N. W., D. C.,

And there in a small house furnished and linened,
Leased and the first month's rent paid,
There, with my faithful spouse, I tarry,
Until next June.
Anyway.
And now the question,
When do YOU come to Washington,
And to us?

SINCLAIR LEWIS

Cabell was almost intuitive in his sensing of relationships, and, as later letters show, was convinced at this point of some rub between Hergesheimer and Lewis.

Dumbarton, September 27, 1919

My dear Hergesheimer:

Again I am your debtor, and again Knopf has made you a handsome book. . . . Of the contents I may speak later with more assurance: three of these tales are new to me, but you know, I think, that I almost invariably succumb to your incantations.

Linda goes on triumphantly. The last *Century* is at hand, unread as yet, in the press of doing a Christmas story and a review of Miss Scarborough's new book [*From a Southern Porch*], and striving to do a review of the new Bojer [*The Face of the World*]. A trifle later, as you perhaps know, I am to try my hand at doing one Joseph Hergesheimer for the *Bookman*— All this is complicated with the final minutiae of bringing out *Jurgen*, who, I believe, is really being published to-day. I assume that Holt sent you one of the paper bound copies: my copies have not yet arrived, but when they do, one of them is, I need not say, to be forwarded you with the author's invaluable autograph.

And then I shall write you a letter. This is but a note to express my very hearty gratitude for the sending of *The Happy End:* the book itself demands and shall receive a far more lengthy disquisition.

Yours faithfully,

JAMES BRANCH CABELL

From Joseph Hergesheimer

West Chester, September 30, 1919

Dear Cabell:

I sent you *The Happy End* as a part of my wish for you to have all my books: if there are any you would like a word shall bring them to you. I have a bound copy of *Jurgen,* and, with books so expensive, I'll bring it with me to Richmond for an inscription, rather than have you send me another.

Jurgen is a very strange and very beautiful book: it is courageous, truer than truth, and made to a marvellous extent from your innate being. There are so many delightful things in it that it would be nonsense to attempt to put them on paper while we are able to discuss them. I wrote, as you probably know, an impression of *Jurgen* for the *Sun,* which I hope you'll like. A book review, in the accepted sense, is a stupid impertinence. As I see it, a review should be the expression of wise enthusiasm directed toward spreading the fame of its subject.

All this in spite of the possibility of your doing the *Bookman* paper. Lewis was here when such an article first came up, and, in discussing the possibility of his writing about my work, it was made clear to me how remote I was from general sympathies. Indeed, that aim must be surrendered and those of us who are what we are must stand a little solider together. I am sending you a set of page proofs of *Linda.* I hope you'll like her.

Nellie is staying with us at present—truly a miraculous creature: and having her here brings the strongest possible sense of Dumbarton Grange to West Chester.

Very sincerely

JOSEPH HERGESHEIMER

Dumbarton, October 11 & 13, 1919

My dear Hergesheimer:

You would have heard from me earlier but for the fact that I lighted on, I think, a rather good notion about you and your work, and have been transferring it to paper for, eventually, the *Bookman.* It "explains" you so completely that I know it must be balderdash: things do not fit together so neatly in lived life: still, barring its disregard for your private sentiments and ties, it is a pleasing and stimulating hypothesis. . . .

Turning to graver matters, I need not assure you that *Linda* is a fine and noble triumph: he who could write that book cannot lack wit to appreciate it. Here is . . . your best work: and while I have six reasons for disagreeing with Knopf as to your being "our only honest-to-God good novelist," I reverently and half-vexedly agree that nobody else could have written *Linda.* I must manage later to write a separate "piece" about it, for one of the public prints. . . . As to the other book [*The Happy End*] you ring the bell most resonantly in "The Flower of Spain," which was brand-new to me. . . . Then "Rosemary Roselle," then—well, anyhow, not "Tol'able David": that is a tale I would have you read through very carefully, and then get down upon your artistic knees and pray God to make you a good boy. It is not merely that one questions the third prince's insouciant methods of massacring the evil, but—do you not see?—the tale runs counter to what you tell us everywhere else, that there are no satisfying triumphs in the flesh. This story is not Hergesheimerian, and I particularly resent the circumstance that you have realized it all with such devilish vividness that I have to fight hard to keep myself from proclaiming the story a masterpiece——

Thus far I wrote on Saturday, and had to desist to unveil the Jackson monument, help entertain a cohort of V. M. I. cadets (friends of my stepdaughters), and honor my wife's belief that there is something in the sound of a typewriter which when mingled with the Sabbath air compounds a poison fatal to the young: I resume on Monday, after a sight of your *Jurgen* appreciation. I can say nothing at all adequate: I consider you a fearful liar, a wholly unprincipled exaggerator, and I am unspeakably grateful to you for having thus paraded your vices—— Especially, of course, I thank you for having comprehended what I was driving at: and—though this is apart—I have already told you, I believe, that I meant *Melicent* and the *Jest* and *Jurgen* to loosely constitute the "moral" of the *Melicent* portion. The "moral" of *Jurgen* you have worded to the least i dot.

What is this Nellie tells me as to a planned tour of the Virginian springs, at this time of year? Do you, by all means, wait until next summer, and then join Lewis and me at the Alum. . . . When, in any event, you do come south remember that I want a copy of *The Lay Anthony*, which I made every honest attempt to procure via purchase in the first edition. I shall then again borrow Nellie's copy and have a particularly good time investigating your revisions. . . .

Yours faithfully,

JAMES BRANCH CABELL

Dumbarton, October 17, 1919

Dear Rascoe:

You are an unconscionable liar, and I am grateful to you for having so delectably paraded this frailty in your review of *Jurgen*. The book is not one quarter what you say it is: I only would that it were: at any rate, I re-read your comments, and beam over their convincingness, and incline to an evaluation of one third. . . .

Mencken's new book I have been reading with vast contentment: I hope you review it, and point out its real foundational solidity, under the pranks of the village cut-up. . . . I received with it the new Knopf catalogue, and read therein of your "very capable hands." I trust that particular bit of manual labor is discharged, and that the *Bovary* and the *Manon* are shortly to appear—— Knopf does . . . make handsome books. And I wish Holt could contrive to give me such clear and uniform printing as Knopf sends forth—— You see, I have also Hergesheimer's new *Happy End*, which too I hope to see you appraise. "The Flower of Spain" could hardly be improved, and "Rosemary Roselle" is excellent: the others, at bottom, are very nice magazine stories.

No, I do not carp at Hergesheimer. I have seen the complete *Linda Condon,* and my respect for its writer is too great to permit me to find fault with him in any way without an underlying suspicion that it may be my appreciation rather than his writing which is deficient. You will properly value, I think, the supreme surface beauty of this book and this, really, heartless heroine. The book, within its chosen area, is superb.

My article about Hergesheimer is approximately complete, but not as yet copied out. It is no masterpiece. But, in view of the really beautiful if not generally comprehensible appreciation of *Jurgen* done by him for the *Sun,* I could not well refuse to do the *Bookman* paper. . . . He will probably spend the last week of this month in Richmond—— Anyhow, my wife and I plan to go on to New York on or about 3 November, and I would that you were to be there then.

We plan not more than a week's stay, during which time I hope to discover what is being done about marketing *Jurgen.* So far reports are vague, and reviews infrequent. Holt . . . is back at the office, but has developed an irritating way of ignoring questions.

For the rest, I am appalled by the yawning void which is my mind when I probe thereinto tentatively after the makings of a new book. The last three volumes have been so very cosmical in theme: I cannot go on writing with the universe in general as my topic: so you must prepare for a letting down in scale at least. . . . What to write! I have no notion, and no ideas of any sort. Privately, though, I rather liked the outrageous bit of nonsense just completed for the Christmas *Century* [5]—— In the November number, too, I am to have a tale which you will have to read twice before you comprehend at what I am driving.[6] That is not a fleer at your penetration, but a criticism of the story.

One of my objects in going to New York is to arrange for a re-printing of *The Cords of Vanity.* As my revision stands, the book is honestly good: and Townsend is, I found with surprise, an adumbration of my pawnbroker.

Yours faithfully,
JAMES BRANCH CABELL

[5] "The Feathers of Olrun," which was included later in *Figures of Earth.*
[6] "Porcelain Cups," included later in Cabell's collection, *Line of Love.*

From Burton Rascoe

Chicago, October 20, 1919

Dear Cabell:

Yes, I am a liar about letter-writing and the weight of my sin causes me great discomfort of conscience. But, Lord knows I have been busy! There was a book fair here all last week, whereat I met a great number of anti-temperance leaguers, who, curiously, knew where to get better stuff than I did. They were a jovial bunch of born teamsters who have got into the book-selling business, and I had a great time with them. The *Tribune*, "the incorruptible," refused to print one line about the fair as being held in Marshall Field's, and the while other book page editors were writing a column or so a day, I had nothing to do but shake hands, eat more at lunch than is good for me, and generally ignore my work at the office. Then Galantière . . . followed a telegram into town, and staid at our house three days, leaving yesterday. . . . I actually have not had a minute for addressing the typewriter. I used in an emergency on Saturday a hold-over piece about Mencken which I meant to revise and otherwise better — I am glad, however, that my silence provoked so entertaining a letter from you.

If I can find the passage to which you refer in the new Bojer book, I shall read that much of the novel and no more; for I have read your review of it in the *Sun* and relished the sly way in which you poked fun at it. Crediting irony to such a purposeful volume is almost like crediting irony to Mrs. Eleanor H. Porter or to Billy Sunday.

Now I haven't read *Jenny Gerhardt* since I first read it, several years ago,—a severe criticism in itself probably—but I remember that I was considerably impressed with the novel; and, with the exception of *The Genius* and the volume of short stories called *Free,* I have always honored Dreiser's sincerity, his lumbering efforts at truthful portrayal, his fidelity to his middle-class viewpoint of middle-class life, and his honest reflection of phases of American life. I know well enough that Dreiser can hardly write a decent sentence, that, at times he is grotesquely sentimental, and that he has an absurd idea that he is a philosopher; but with all that he has courage, a valuable ability at documentation, an intellectual honesty, and an inquisitive mind, always seeking to learn everything he can about people, their queer twists, their ideas about life, their reasons for doing this and that. If this aim and intention is praiseworthy in Englishmen and in Frenchmen it is praiseworthy in an American. We haven't a Hardy or a Balzac, a Chekhov, a Mann, a Barbusse, a Bennett, a Charles-Louis Philippe unless we count Dreiser and Sherwood

Anderson. Both of them do somewhat the same thing for America that
these fellows have done for their milieu. So, whatever be the ultimate
value of such intention, it should be appraised, I think, with the intention in mind.

I am due to go East soon. Just when I am not positive. I shall try my
best to be there during the week of your visit. I sincerely hope that I get
a chance to see you, for it is hardly likely that I will get a chance to run
down to Richmond.

The *Bovary* and *Manon* will be out in November, Knopf promises.
They will really be beautiful books in cover design and manufacture.
The translations are old ones with which I have tampered only to the
extent of restoring some slight misapprehensions of the text. My preface
to *Bovary* I take pride in, because of its prose rhythms and because I
have said, I think, two new things about the book. The *Manon* I kidded,
which seemed to delight Knopf.

Jurgen, they tell me here, is selling enormously well. Kroch says he
has sold 250 copies and expects to sell at least 500. His is only a small
store with a special clientèle. McClurg's and Marshall Field's report a
greater sale of the book than of any of the others, and with several salesmen in each interested in the book the chances are good for a heavy sale
in Chicago.

I met Hugh Walpole last Monday. When I was introduced he said,
"Oh, I have heard about you. You are the one to whom Cabell has dedicated his new book, aren't you? I enjoyed his *Cream of the Jest* immensely
and have just purchased *Jurgen.* Cabell is delightful. As soon as I get
back to London I am going to get him an English publisher." He is interested in Hergesheimer, Mencken, Dreiser, and Willa Sibert Cather. . . .
Hecht and I, by the way, have more than patched up our differences,
and have begun to interchange ideas, books, etc. He is an excellent con-
versationalist, and his stories of his observations and experiences in Europe are highly entertaining. . . .

> Yours,
> BURTON RASCOE

From Wilson Follett

Cheshire, Connecticut
October 24, 1919

Dear James Branch Cabell:

Here's the horribly belated letter, dimly threatening . . . to be as long as it is belated, from the man whom you may very properly tell to go to the devil.

Excuses, I suppose, are never really worth formulating: . . . We have been cut off from everything, for a solid year and more, with no company but worries about money and the sense of all the missing things we wanted and couldn't get at. And—we've lost a child. But now, thank goodness, I've pried myself loose from a loathsome job. . . . It is perhaps crazy to imagine that I can keep my grocer pacified with mere writing. If it is, I embrace my own madness. You see, I have been feeding swine— i.e., tutoring rich young wastrels in a tutoring school. May God forgive me for it. . . .

"For Wilson Follett/ if but in appreciation/ of his part therein"— that is what you wrote on the flyleaf of the treasured one of my three copies of *Beyond Life*. At first, catching sight of some old comment reprinted on the jacket over my name, I thought it ought to have been "thereon" instead of "therein"—but no, there was a "part therein" too; a part in which you had dexterously unhinged an argument of mine in order to let Charteris's argument through a wicket gate into the path where its real adventures were to begin. I shall yet make some tolerable acknowledgment of *Beyond Life*—for I think I have never set down a half adequate expression of what the book means to us in this house. But just here I am only thanking you for the fact of the gift. . . .

You said some very polite things, some (if I remember correctly) unnecessarily deferential things, about a book of mine, *The Modern Novel*. . . . Most of it was originally, I remember, lectures to schoolmarms. They lapped it up. Alfred Knopf and I had an idea that the book might find them and their like. I doubt whether it has done so, very numerously. Thank you for wishing to take it seriously. . . .

Here, on the other hand, is a real contention. I plead Conrad to you— and you look askance at such things as *Chance* and *Under Western Eyes* and *Lord Jim*, and then say Conrad is not for you. Now, one proper measure of Conrad is "Heart of Darkness" (in the volume *Youth*), and the other is *Nostromo*. If a man can reject those (only no such artist as yourself *can* reject them—both), then he is entitled to say that Conrad is not for him. But not otherwise. *Nostromo* you might conceivably abandon, because of its fearful complexity and seeming confusion; it is a thing that comes straight only from the outside and as a whole, when you have finished it. But "Heart of Darkness"—I defy you, sir, to get by or round "Heart of Darkness," which you are hereby sentenced to read.

Jurgen I haven't yet. I have appealed to *The Atlantic's* "Bookshelf" for it; but their selections are made, on principles inscrutable to me, by some committee of librarians, and whether I shall succeed goodness only knows. I couldn't, last winter, make the librarians aware of *Beyond Life;* on the other hand, I succeeded with one or two other recommendations, and am hoping to do it with this. I try periodically to fume the librarians out of existence; but, bless me, I might as well try to fume capitalism out of existence.

Well,—I needn't stretch out this bundle of errands quite to infinity. . . .

Sincerely yours,
WILSON FOLLETT

From Sinclair Lewis

Washington,
Saturday [date?]

Dear Cabell:

I adore *Jurgen*. It has extraordinary beauty and a curious subtle enticing beckoning wit of a sort which, so far as I know, could not be imitated by any other writer in any land—and which, of course, could not even faintly be sketched by any other American. I like it better, by far, than anything else of yours I have ever read. Such paragraphs as that in which Guenevere's father muses of Lynette lying abed somewhere in his city, or that in which the hamadryad foretells her future drifting through fields of asphodel, are so beautiful that I read them many times.

I must say that I admire the way in which you get away with the most peaceful and complacent immorality. *Jurgen* should be added to all Y.M.C.A. libraries under the title, "What a Nice Young Man Ought Not to Know." Somehow I fear that when Harry Mencken reads of the Emperor Jurgen in hell, he is going to read frightfully unjustified meanings into simple, moral objects like the emperor's sceptre.

Do we sometime see you in Washington? I hope so.

As ever,
SINCLAIR LEWIS

Presently Cabell received another bulletin from Lewis:

From Sinclair Lewis

Washington,
Tuesday [date?]

Great idea! Anatole France would, most of all celebrated writing persons now living, appreciate *Jurgen*, providing the ancient reads English. Get your Guy Holt to see to it that he receives—and reads—a copy, and, perhaps, that he issues a fervent imprimatur, and use it for publicity. . . .

Slewis

Also from Washington came a letter from William Rose Benét, then with the United States Chamber of Commerce.

From William Rose Benét

Washington [date?]

My dear Mr. Cabell:

And now I have read *Jurgen*. I think I wrote you how much I admired *Beyond Life* when I also exclaimed upon *The Certain Hour*.

You have probably seen the incident of the Broadwayite who advised his friends to "buy a book called *Jurgen*. It gets away with murder!" If not—that may amuse you.

There is nothing else like *Jurgen* in America. That *Jurgen* now is—and is selling so rapidly—even if to certain folk for obvious reasons—is excellent. I remember—it must have been nearly fifteen years ago—reading stories of chivalry and gallantry by you in *Harper's* and always looking for them. I still have a decided taste for such stories.

Fame, you will say—and rightly—is a lugubrious thing but I am glad it has come to you—for it has come to a man hewing steadily to the line of his own best, and usually that is not appreciated in his lifetime.

An old friend of mine, Sinclair Lewis, tells me something of a delightful visit he paid you—and at a lunch in Philadelphia I heard both Hergesheimer and Hugh Walpole sing your praises. I wish there were more writers like you in America—but we are thankful for what we have.

My brother, a poet, is an admirer of some of your poetry and also of

The Cream of the Jest and *The Rivet in Grandfather's Neck* (what gorgeous titles!) but I have the pleasure of reading those still in reserve. He is—Stephen is—spreading your fame in Yale University.

At present I traffick among the merchants with average boredom but opportunity usually knocks when he gets around to it—with all he has to do.

Meanwhile the best fortunes in the New Year to you and gratitude for many delightful hours,

Sincerely,

WILLIAM ROSE BENÉT

I wonder if you have come upon Lytton Strachey's *Eminent Victorians*. It is fascinating, even when malicious. The "Eminent" usually do need "doing"!

You mention books in *Beyond Life* that I want to *read!* How cruel!

From Joseph Hergesheimer

West Chester, October 27, 1919

Dear Cabell:

Thank you very much, and truly from my heart, for your generous opinions. . . . Hugh Walpole has just left me after one of the happiest times of my life; and this was added to by the fact that his discrimination applauded you very liberally. I hope you will make an effort to see Hugh while he is in America, he'll be here some five months more, for I can assure you that it would be pure pleasure. I hear reports of your getting north: dear Cabell you must get to Dower House. My plans for Virginia are still unsettled. Do write me your plans.

Faithfully,

JOSEPH HERGESHEIMER

Cabell did not travel except of necessity, and even then, not often. He was a shy man, with an infinitely keen perception of the foibles and characteristics of others, and perhaps for that reason was unwilling to expose himself to the gaze of the curious. But the curious as usual became more and more curious. In a letter to Glazer who had asked for a description of the man behind the writer, Hergesheimer at this time wrote: "I am rather overcome at the thought of giving you a picture of Cabell . . . he is a solidly built man of middle height, with a smooth immobile face, deep-set impressive eyes and a mouth touched with humor. A very aristocratic individual. His essence is an extraordinary combination of irony and romance—commonly supposed to be destructive one

of the other—the former increasing with his years. . . . Here [*in his books*] is
the romance; the irony, I am frank to say, disturbs me, in that it is concerned
with the world outside him rather than with his individual essence. It carries
him steadily away from his tales to biting comments on actuality—a business, a
world, not worth attention. Not, that is, in proportion to the other, the dream.
Mr. Cabell, having come alive through the stupid and vulgar flood of realismus
lately darkening literature, for a period of, at least, fifteen years, should not now
bother with the lesser concerns of the fat, the fatuous and the flaccid. When you
write him ask how it comes that his stories, laid far back in point of time,
escape the asininity of the historical novel. Both Cabell and myself know that
secret, but accomplish it in quite different ways."

And the visiting Englishman, Hugh Walpole, who was lecturing up and down
the country, sent a requested letter to McBride:

From Hugh Walpole

November 7, 1919

Dear Sir:

I am delighted to say what I think of Cabell's works. I have only as yet
read *Jurgen, Beyond Life,* and *The Cream of the Jest,* but I must confess that it is absolutely astonishing to me that these books have been so
neglected. In the first place Cabell is a writer with style as individual
and alive as Anatole France's. It is flexible, humorous, dramatic—above
all personal. That in itself in these days of sloppy and colourless writing
is enough to make Cabell important: but any man who can plan a book
of *Jurgen's* kind on so extensive a scale and then carry it through without making it laboured and tedious is no small artist. *Jurgen* is surely a
book that should make Americans proud. I am delighted with its deli-
cacy and good-temper and tenderness, its fancy and its wit. If Americans
are looking for a book to show to Europe here it is. I don't think they
have much to be ashamed of when they can produce *Jurgen,* Miss
Cather's *My Antonia* and Hergesheimer's *Linda Condon* in the same
year.

I believe that *Jurgen* and *The Cream of the Jest* would have success
in England. *Beyond Life* is a fine piece of writing too and is stamped
authentic Cabell from cover to cover.

That he will secure his real and lasting fame is only a matter of time:
it will be a great shame if America doesn't see to it that that time is
short.

Yours sincerely,
HUGH WALPOLE

From Burton Rascoe

Chicago, November 12, 1919

My dear Cabell:

It looks as though my trip to New York will again be delayed. I wrote a sneering paragraph about Coningsby Dawson's most recent book, and he considers himself defamed and slandered, and his reputation as a lecturer and novelist damaged to I know not what extent. His lawyers have written to the *Tribune* demanding a retraction under threat of a suit. The editors of the paper liked the paragraphs and do not wish to make a retraction. But they wish also to avoid a lawsuit, because of the expense entailed, although they (and the *Tribune* lawyers) are certain that Dawson cannot recover. It is just that libel suits have been brought against the *Tribune* at the rate of about one a week for some months past, including, of course, the Ford suit.—I have been in daily conference with the lawyers, and have been forced to read all of Dawson's earlier books, in order to mark paragraphs for the law department's convenience. The whole affair is rather a joke in the office—but also it means some work. . . .

Last night I finished *Linda Condon* and I am writing Hergesheimer a note telling him the pleasure I took in it. I kept thinking as I read that the sheer beauty of its texture couldn't last, and at several points I meant to drop the book out of fear of disappointment. It did last amazingly, and a consummate piece of writing it is. I couldn't somehow believe wholeheartedly in the sculptor's deathless devotion, and Linda's insistence that the uncouth sculptured Simon was she intruded for an uncomfortable flash of irreverent humor upon the illusion; but all and all it is a very beautiful piece of work, not with a great deal of body, but in the telling (with the exception "conventional evening-dress") a thing of pure loveliness. George Grey Barnard [7] obviously sat for the portrait of Dodge, in part, at least.

The poetic quality of *Linda Condon* moves me once more to speculate upon the mystic and intangible idealism of Jews. In those of intelligence and power who have lost their religion there always seems a convenient ability to make literature, poetry, or music a religion. I have just recently read Waldo Frank's *Our America* (which I commend to you): critically it is of little importance, although there are flashes here and there of keen critical insight; informationally it is of little importance; in the

[7] American sculptor, 1863–1938. Because of his great interest in medieval art, George Grey Barnard collected pieces of discarded Gothic art in French villages and established his collection near his home in New York City in a building he called the Cloisters.

whole book there is little that can be summed up as a statement or a declaration; but there is much in it that is moving, impelling. It is passionate, almost an Old Testament lamentation, a crushed cry of pathos and yearning and hunger—bitterness, faith, hope in odic quality appear on every page—— It is all somewhat strange and foreign to me: I cannot, through some lack, work up any great concern for my fellow men; I don't much care what happens to most of them; I am happy enough without any special right to be; and I cannot envisage progress as a demonstrable fact. But here is the Jew, Frank, confidently looking forward to a time when this country will fulfill all his expectations of it, as to such details as housing problems, cities beautiful, appreciation of the fine arts, charity and loving-kindness; and here is the Jew, Hergesheimer [8] voicing through his sculptor a belief that the bigoted, sadistic, hypocritical moron Cotton Mather had a "vision" of beauty and splendor, and that an obscure Puritan led the world on to better things. I, who am not fully convinced that Lincoln was right either about the abolition of slavery or the necessity for preserving the union, find all this beyond me, and I confess I am impressed by it. There is possibly something here of Jurgen's wistful wish to recapture his childish belief in God. The one is as impossible as the other; and I begin to wonder to what extent Hergesheimer and Frank are kidding themselves—to what extent their magnanimity is not a subconscious wish fulfillment of their very active personal desire—and lack? So long, though, as it is productive of beauty, it matters not. . . .

This is *not*, precisely, a note.

Sincerely,
BURTON RASCOE

From H. L. Mencken

The Smart Set
25 West 45th Street
New York
November 14, 1919

Dear Mr. Cabell:

I am very sorry that the chance didn't offer for a meeting. Very likely I was leaving Baltimore at the moment you passed through. The printers' strike has kept me jumping for a month past, and the worst of it still

8 Actually Hergesheimer was of Protestant German and Scottish antecedents.

seems to be ahead. We are now printing the magazine in Albany and finding great difficulty in managing it.

I kept *Jurgen* until about ten days ago, seeking clear leisure for reading it. When I finally fell upon it, it gave me a most delightful three hours. It seems to me to be not only the best thing you have ever done yourself, but clearly the finest thing of its sort ever done in America. This is particularly true of the first half. After the middle, the thing falls off a bit and I am strongly of the opinion that it is slightly too long. But even so, it is a capital piece of work and I hope to tell the great masses of the plain people about it in the January *Smart Set*. Some of the earlier chapters are absolutely superb. In this opinion Nathan fully joins.

I wonder if you ever have any ideas for short essays or sketches. We are eager to get something that is not palpably a short story. The length may be as low as 200 or as long as, say, 2500. If you have any ideas that fit into this scheme, why not let me hear of them from time to time? We could agree upon them in advance of the writing. Such things as the chapters in *Beyond Life* are rather too long for us. As for the choice of subject, there is almost no limit. What we seek is the point of view. The obvious thing, of course, must be avoided. If this plan interests you, let me hear a few ideas and we'll gladly come to terms.

I have a suspicion that the gods in Heaven prevent our meeting at this time because of the great scarcity of suitable refreshments. Later on, I believe, there will be a large supply of contraband stuff. I hear of enormous preparations under way in Maryland to brew beer, distill whiskey and squeeze wine.

Sincerely yours,
H. L. MENCKEN

Unfortunately there are no replies from Cabell to Mencken. Mencken's will bequeathed his file of letters from authors to the New York Public Library, with whom he had made an agreement that the file would not be opened until fifteen years after his death. The letters will therefore not be available until January 29, 1971.

Dumbarton, November 22, 1919

My dear Rascoe:

I have no news. All day I pound at the re-copying of *The Cords of Vanity*, alternating this with an attempt to get what's done of the manuscript of my next book into some sort of coherence. My fore-finger has reached the point where it taps automatically while I am asleep.

Walpole, as you have probably seen, has nobly boosted *Jurgen*.

Mencken promised to speak well of it in the January *Smart Set*. Holt, for aught I hear from him, has entered into his long reward: and I know nothing of the prospects for re-printing the book.

To come to the real gist of this note, though, I do most earnestly want you to make a book of your newspaper articles. I know of few things that I desire more. (I take it, in passing, as queer that after I have told you a thing seven hundred and eighty times you should still question it.) I thought of you and gnashed my teeth as I read *Prejudices:* here was a fine and delightful book made up [of] material of which you were keeping a . . . brand interned in your scrapbook—— When I was in New York I talked to Cook about you, and about the possibility of inducing you, anyhow, to wield scissors and paste. He said he had tried his utmost with you; that he wanted the book. . . . I would write this on bended knees if it were possible in that posture to work the typewriter. PLEASE MAKE A BOOK OF YOUR NEWSPAPER ARTICLES.

Do It Now. Obey That Impulse.

Yours faithfully,

JAMES BRANCH CABELL

Let me know, too, about Dawson. If he can get a penny upon such mild aspersion, I am a multi-millionaire.

From H. L. Mencken

Baltimore, November 25, 1919

Dear Mr. Cabell:

An impression is only an impression. Walpole, who was here the other day, told me that he thought the last part of *Jurgen* was by far the best. In any case, there can be no doubt about one thing: that the book as a whole is a very fine piece of work—probably a good deal better than you think. Walpole was full of enthusiasm. He will do some gabbling about it when he gets back to England.

The *Philadelphia Press* article was in the form of an interview with Walpole, covering a rotogravure page. My name was spelled Menchen in the headline—a lovely piece of irony. Apparently the writer of the interview had heard of none of us save Hergesheimer.

I leave you to dredge up some ideas yourself. If I suggested them they'd probably be bad. The stuff need not be long. But don't let it interfere with books. What are you doing next?

Sincerely yours,

H. L. MENCKEN

From Wilson Follett

Cheshire, Connecticut
Thanksgiving Day, 1919

Dear Cabell:

. . . Now, how on earth is a mere well-intentioned person like myself to take hold of a thing like *Jurgen* and handle it as it should be handled? Whether or no, the thing must soon be attempted, at least on a small scale, even if I shirk it in this letter; for the "Bookshelf's" custodian has at last seen the light, and *Jurgen* is a January "selection" (forgive me for alluding to it as if it were the result of a boarding school miss's being besought to play the piano at a party). My huffing and my puffing were not wasted after all: just after I had given up and explicitly guaranteed that I would say no more, the house fell in with a great crash. At least, it was a great crash in the world of the "Bookshelf": for it took the form of a telegraphed permission to choose for myself from the season's fiction. And now that I've got my way, I stand in mortal terror of—well, the responsibility and my own deficiencies, though it sounds forbiddingly conventional, in a moralistic way, when so put.

One thing I can say, knowing it for real criticism as far as it goes— because it is, quite literally and naively, the report of something that happened to me. An opinion is one thing, the report of an experimental discovery is another. If I offered an opinion of *Jurgen* there would be questions about the merits of the evidence adduced for it and about how large a fraction of the evidence had been taken into account. But when I simply produce the adventure of a soul—a sort of soul—with the book (I dodge "masterpiece" for the moment, simply to stick to the adventure and not prejudge the outcome), why, there I have given you a particularly intractable and unbudging fact. Also, I have thrown the onus of final criticism and decision back on you, by compelling you to do all the deciding about the merits and the representativeness of the soul which had the adventure.

The adventure may seem, after all, rather tame to you; and indeed I must confess that it took the form, merely, of the most sweeping and final verification of something I have known well enough all along, and used often enough before as applied knowledge, whenever there was the time. What I verified was—aside from all question of how good reading you are—how gloriously good *re*reading you are. For, if you will believe me, my progress through *Jurgen* cost me a rambling excursion through pretty much your entire Works (I hope this unfortunate hint of collectedness and definitiveness is not going to make you feel as if you were dead). Don't misapprehend me here. I don't suspect myself of being a Ph.D. *manqué;* and my thumbing of the dozen volumes was not prompted largely by the impulse to track down cross-references and locate echoes and motifs—exciting work though that might be and is. No: nor was I ransacking your past for the rather more creditable study of your growth and of how, in the world you inhabit, one thing leads to another. It was just that, when a passage in *Jurgen* reminded me of the person you were two or five or seven years ago, I dug up the premonition out of your pages in pure fondness for the earlier thing, just as it was and is in itself. And, upon my word, those earlier things of yours had taken it upon themselves to grow actually lovelier in the time I had happened not to look at them. One of these days I shall doubtless go back to *Jurgen* and find that it has been playing the same trick. I think I had never before quite understood why Keats added, " . . . its loveliness *increases*" . . . .

As to the scholarship of *Jurgen,* and for that matter of the others too, I want to confess that I am an admirable supplement to Braithwaite. He is so at home everywhere that he knows even the non-existent originals of your inventions; and I am so little at home outside the world immediately succeeding that at which you poke fun on the first page of *The Rivet* that I find myself ignorant of your originals even when, for all I know, they do exist. . . . In fine, you deal with a hopelessly and candidly ignorant person, whom you can fool to the top of your bent. For all I know, you may consider this completely disqualifying to me. Anyway, I hold by your style, your reading of our common humanity, your constant evocation of truth garbed in comeliness, and your creation of persons. These I feel I understand. At any rate I warmly respond to them. And, so long as that is so, I half defiantly maintain that I can't go far wrong in any of the important ways. . . .

I have written myself into to-morrow, and you, probably, into a coma.

Very sincerely and faithfully yours,
WILSON FOLLETT

Dumbarton, December 20, 1919

Dear Rascoe:

. . . I have not even seen your verdict as to *Linda Condon*—that is, the printed verdict. Please send me what you can of what you have written lately. . . . On *Linda,* as no doubt I have written you earlier, I have a few words in the next *Bookman*. This is, however, really a section of the rambling discourse in the current number, fitting in at a point you will readily detect.

Apropos of my recent contributions to periodicals, I yesterday read "Porcelain Cups," misprints and all, with a naive sort of wonder as to what had made the author so peevish. The thing stinks with cold malignity, directed toward every one of the characters—for no reason I know of,—but the texture of its irony is deep, sir, deep!—— I shall do three more short stories when I have finished the revised version of the *Cords* which is to come out this spring. I am having a fine time with Townsend: definitely dating him first of all, from 1898 to 1903—he was born 23 Sept. 1877, to be exact,—and accounting for and realizing him to the point of convincing myself. With the women I am doing what I can, but some of them stay hazy—— There's the mad point of it: in a book you are supposed to render clear and definite ideas of the people, but surely nobody has such cameo-like conceptions of his associates. The most important things I know about most people are the things I don't know about and guess at—if you know what I mean, Hermione. That is one of the many things I like about your *Jurgen*—the rich full background of matters nobody attempts to explain: compare in passing yesterday or the day before, and you will see how "true to life" this is—— But I was nominally prattling of the *Cords*. Suffice it that I think the volume will be, this time, a fairly creditable and credible performance.

That is all about me. Now, for a change, let us have something about and from you.

Yours faithfully,
JAMES BRANCH CABELL

From Joseph Hergesheimer

West Chester, December 22, 1919
Dear Cabell:

You should have had a letter from me long ago but not only was the November-December number of the *Bookman* delayed but, against every intention, I am bang into the middle of another book. While I am writing I am, in my obligations, lower than any angel ever dared to be. You know already how deeply I am in your debt for your paper: it was exact, discerning, and I like to think just. *Linda,* it turns out, was too difficult a child, too remote from predatory fingers, for the majority of men. The base of your paper, too, was quite correct; but whether it sprung from long disappointment or heredity I am unable to say. I have no interest in consummations, no trust in the flesh, and no assurance of anything else. Nevertheless it is the anything else, the furthest of all, that only engages me. I have been lucky, I feel, in a way that Mencken has yet to realize—I know what love can be. But, as quickly as possible in order to avoid any appearance of sentimentality, I think it's a very rare bird and quite useless morally or socially. Rather than cementing everyone together in a paste of Christian charity it isolates the individual from the whole life and religions of men less orderly and sillier than the ant. In other words, I am extraordinarily indebted to you. It is my present plan to go south in, I think, February; and you may be certain that I'll stop off at Richmond.

Very faithfully,

JOSEPH HERGESHEIMER

In mid-December Cabell received a copy of Louis Untermeyer's latest book, *Including Horace,* inscribed:

> "for James Branch Cabell—
> from one who would have given two fingers
> to have written the opening chapters of *Jurgen*
> & his chance at—er—salvation to have conceived
> the scenes in hell."

3201 Monument Avenue
Richmond 21, Virginia
December 20, 1919

Dear Mr. Untermeyer:

For a long while I have known that you write delightfully, but nothing of yours, to date, has give me greater pleasure than the inscription on the fly-leaf of *Including Horace.* I have no choice but to regard it as your masterpiece—in the vein of extravagant romance, no doubt, but with a wonderfully winning style to it. I thank you most heartily.

And the other contents of the book I like—almost—as well. The things you have done to Horace! and then, when you try, how exactly you " get" him! I know him fairly well—him only of the Romans, I fear,—and I have been playing a sort of game with the verses, saying mentally "That's Horace, this is Untermeyer" and then finding my guesses usually quite wrong. The particularity of your additions to the Faune, Nympharum, for example, took me in completely. And then—but I shall not enter upon formal criticism. I merely wanted to thank you for a two-fold pleasure, and to subscribe myself

Yours most gratefully,

JAMES BRANCH CABELL

7

JURGEN IN THE TOILS

But not everyone found *Jurgen* entrancing. Some were of the opinion of the New York *Sun* editor, who was not "quite hard enough hit" to warrant listing it. However, sales larger than usually attended Cabell's books continued. Rascoe wrote from Chicago: "Did you see the reference to you in the New York Evening *Post* by Louis Untermeyer? In his review of the year of American poetry he dragged you in on the strength of *Jurgen,* not as a poet, but apparently merely to record his conviction that *Jurgen* is a masterpiece of literature. I have handed Louis some heavy wallops, but I am relenting toward him now. I think I shall write him a letter, congratulating him on his discernment, and telling him that he really needn't have apologized for mentioning *Jurgen* in a poetical review, since *Jurgen* contains the most beautiful *sirvente* in the English Language. . . . Holt writes me . . . that he has at last got enough of *Jurgen* in stock to supply the demand. By the way, I met Henry Fuller at a tea the other day and he tells me that you haven't your equal in English literature, 'but he does tread dangerous bounds,' and the old gentleman shook his head. Very interesting coming from a man whose last novel deals with homosexuals." [*Bertram Cope's Year.*]

Arthur Machen and Cabell were at one concerning the poetic possibilities of English prose. But as Machen wrote his friend, Tom Horan, there was a great lack of understanding concerning it: "Mr. Cabell is always kind to me. He is no doubt right in his view [that few people in the United States can distinguish good prose from bad prose]; but it applies on our side of the Atlantic as well as on yours. For obvious reasons: in the first place, because it has only occurred to very few people that prose is an instrument of music; & secondly, because this sort of song is by no means popular."

Cabell agreed heartily that few understood these values even when carefully explained. And when Louis Untermeyer took him to task in a letter of December, 1922: "But what is this coyness re poetry? Ironically enough, the intelligentsia of 1990 will point to you as preeminently a poet," Cabell shrugged it off. For what he objected to was not the melody but the fetters of conventional prosody. That Cabell was indisputably a poet, Edmund Wilson and many other critics have since attested. Even so, Cabell himself recognized that the average reader cares very little about poetic prose, and in fact is often really averse to it. It troubled him to see that the things he cared for most in his books were the things that most readers cared about the least.

Dumbarton, January 2, 1920

Dear Rascoe:

Now for *Fanfare* [Rascoe's book in preparation]. . . . The title, of course, is fine, also the notion about the opening with the "Condescension." Thereafter why not, roughly, make it a sort of Present State of American Literature? This is hardly so much a suggestion as an honest question. I mean, to "go light," or perhaps omit, your papers on foreign authors, for this book, and deal with what is good and what is popular and what is significant—three widely differing sections, you observe,— in present day American letters? You could thus range from Professor Sherman to Hergesheimer, embracing Mencken and the Howells chapter (which you wrote, I believe, for the book you abandoned, though I never saw it), and . . . could take in nearly everything American. You could, too, include the American attitude toward foreign authors— Ibanez, pardon me, Blasco Ibanez, for instance,—concerning whom you have done such excellent stuff. Oh, yes, and by all means, "Excuse My Glove," which is first rate, though I would not, personally, commit myself to the statement that *Salammbo* is better than *Aphrodite:* if you do, some day the remark will haunt you—— In fine, why not make Americanism, in both its good and evil aspects, your cornerstone consciously, and whoop up what is good therein until your conscience feels the strain? . . .

You really must, though, omit acerbity in dealing with Follett and Untermeyer, after their noble rallying to the support of your *Jurgen.* I am beginning to be actively fond of Follett: and Untermeyer has written me such ingratiating flatteries that when his name is mentioned I coo. . . .

In re the Hergesheimer paper, I can see your objection to the opening paragraphs—— He, after some deliberation, I suspect, concluded that he liked it— I find that Mencken is with me in regard to *The Happy End,* but does not, I think, do justice to *Linda Condon.* In any event, I have no quarrel with Mencken about anything, after his review of *Jurgen*—Follett's, too, you will have seen in the *Atlantic?* Excellent despite its 'throne,' and very happy in its allusion to Cocaigne 'wherein is the bedchamber of time,'—a quip I voiced without detecting its profundity— Apropos. I was delighted by Nathan's reference, in the current *S.S.* to the bed as a coeducational institution, even more than by his quasi-tribute to me. Van Vechten, also, has his complimentary reference, so that the January issue is a fine Cabell number.

I begin, D.V., on Wednesday the seventh, at 9:30 A.M. to write three short stories for *McClure's* with childlike faith in my subconsciousness, to which I committed the problem a month ago: its depths have cast up nothing yet, but I like to think that the trio of tales in their entirety are submerged down there to be dredged up by and by. On April the first I shall begin a new book. I am a creature of rare firmness and method.— It is with such fairy tales that I regale myself.

In the meantime I must have my tooth fixed and sit for my photograph, so that life is beer-and-skittle-less.

Yours faithfully,

JAMES BRANCH CABELL

From Burton Rascoe

Chicago, January 5, 1920

Dear Cabell:

I haven't seen the January *Smart Set* or the *Atlantic* with Follett's tribute. I shall buy them when I am out to lunch today. Follett, of course, long ago ingratiated himself very firmly with me, and since his disastrous (to himself) article in the *Atlantic* I have felt strongly attached to him in respect and sympathy. You heard about it, didn't you? He wrote an anonymous article exposing the terrible truths about a small town—he was really very soft, restrained, and gentle throughout, I thought; I should have been much hotter, more sarcastic—and the authorship was traced to him by the outraged citizens.

Your mention of Nathan and his happy quip about the bed as a co-educational institution reminds me of another curious slant on human beings, in a way analogous to Henry Fuller's dubiety—— At dinner in New York Nathan and I were discussing you. I had allowed that you and Anatole France were the world's greatest. "But," said Nathan, "France is smoother; France is easier to read. Cabell is a little difficult. He is involved and sometimes a bit heavy. *Jurgen* was rather hard reading." This coming from a man who often writes a sentence covering almost an entire page, with verb so far away from subject that you have to read the sentence through twice or three times to get his meaning, this, I say, coming from such a writer, has its interest. Nathan aims at a very complex and involved style; in manner he is the very opposite of Mencken; and yet his admiration (expressed) is all for lucidity and simplicity. I could only say that I found *Jurgen* very easy reading, and the style a delight at all times.

Curiously, I have had about the same ideas for *Fanfare* as you outline. That is, I had meant it to be, in a way, a survey of present day American literature—— I must take some time and care in disposing of Paul Elmer

More and Stuart Sherman. Did you see Sherman's marvellous assassination of Mencken in the *Times*? It was really an excellent piece of work, even down to his pinking me. I wrote him a letter of congratulation, and told him I was polishing my poniard. Sherman can write. If it weren't for his slavish adoration of the Calvinistic Paul Elmer More and his belief that a critic must take a high moral tone, he would be a great critic. As it is, he believes one thing, I think, and expresses another. My admiration for him since his assault on Mencken is the admiration of any good sportsman for a worthy antagonist. He was Nietzschean, Prussian, unethical, in his determination to draw blood. His defense was wretched and vulnerable, but he prevented notice of it by his brilliant attack. He is an enemy worth having and worth cultivating.

If I but had your firmness and method! If I could but say "On Wednesday the seventh at 9:30 P.M., I will sit down and start putting *Fanfare* in shape." But I haven't. . . . By the way I have promised Lewis Galantière to send you his letter to me, or part of it, about *Jurgen*. You remember I gave him up in disgust so far as his appreciation goes after I had been unable to change his opinion of you. You remember also, I think, the piece I published in the paper in answer to a letter from him —the piece about the trinity, Pater, Lamb, and Stevenson? Well, now comes this: [Here Rascoe inserted a long and laudatory letter from Galantière regarding *Jurgen*.]

There! . . .

Yours as ever,

BURTON RASCOE

By this time Holt was beginning to be troubled by the tone of some of the news items, and wrote Cabell on January 7: "Other quotes multiply with the publication of the January issues of the *Atlantic, Bookman,* and *Smart Set.* BUT—shall we dare advertise at all in the newspapers with that damned fool on the N.Y. *Tribune* doing his best to have the book suppressed? For that must be his purpose."

A few days later Cabell replied: "The *Tribune* free advertising, I note, continues, and if it adheres to last Saturday's vein should do no harm. Only I would much prefer to have it shut off altogether." And then on January 14 the following was issued:

#128990

Court of General Sessions of the Peace
In and for the County of New York
.... x
People of the State of New York
vs
Guy Holt, Robert M. McBride & Co.,
and Robert M. McBride
.... x

THE GRAND JURY OF THE COUNTY OF NEW YORK by this indictment, accuse Guy Holt, Robert M. McBride & Co. and Robert M. McBride of the crime of UNLAWFULLY POSSESSING AN INDECENT BOOK, commited [*sic*] as follows:

The said Guy Holt, Robert M. McBride & Co., a corporation at all times herein mentioned existing under the laws of the State of New York, and Robert M. McBride, acting together and in concert, in the County of New York aforesaid, on the 14th day of January, 1920, and for a considerable time prior thereto, with intent to sell and show, unlawfuly possessed a lewd, lascivious, indecent, obscene and disgusting book entitled JURGEN, a more particular description of which said book would be offensive to this Court and improper to be spread upon the records thereof, wherefore such description is not here given; against the form of the statute in such case made and provided, and against the peace of the people of the State of New York, and their dignity.

EDWARD SWANN
District Attorney

Holt sent down to Richmond, dated January 15, a summary of the affidavit beginning: "John S. Sumner, Agent for New York Society for the Suppression of Vice, being duly sworn says: That on the 6th day of January, 1920 and prior and sworn thereto at the city and county aforesaid Robert M. McBride & Co, a corporation, and Guy Holt, manager of said corporation Book Department did at #31 East 17th Street in the city and county aforesaid, unlawfully print, utter, publish, manufacture and prepare and did unlawfully sell and offer to sell and have in their possession with intent to sell a certain offensive, lewd, lascivious and indecent book in violation of Section 1141 of Penal Law of New York." It went on to list many pages objected to, beginning with 56, and running on to 343.

Dumbarton, January 17, 1920

Dear Holt:

It is a comfort at last to hear from you, as I did only this morning. My wife has probably ere this communicated with you to the effect that I am in all matters at your disposal.

Meanwhile it is a distinct relief that you apparently do not need me for the present. I am working overtime on the *McClure* stuff—— The book, I presume, is to be defended on the ground that is is a piece of literature, even apart from the fact that it contains no improprieties whatever. I look, for example, on 56, the first page cited, and find nothing more than "And he drew the girl close to him." I would like to have that page re-produced in fac-simile as a sample of the lewdness, obscenity, &c—— Well, as literature, the book has been included, I believe, in all the lists of Best Books of 1919: the reviews could not well be better: and would it not be well to get statements from literary persons to the effect that *Jurgen* is something more than an "offensive, lewd, lascivious and indecent book"? . . . It is all very vexatious, but I protest I cannot find a sentence in the book that could not be read aloud in Sunday School. Nor is there any reference *anywhere* to sexual matters, so far as I can detect.

Yours faithfully,

JAMES BRANCH CABELL

From H. L. Mencken

Baltimore, January 19, 1920

Dear Mr. Cabell:

The news from New York does not surprise me. Those swine seem determined to stamp out all decent literature in America. The ideal is a Methodist commonwealth with no room for anything save the works of Henry van Dyke, Coningsby Dawson and Alfred Noyes.

If I can give any aid, honorably or dishonorably, it goes without saying that I'll be delighted. I surely hope Holt goes to the mat for a fight to a finish. All that is needed is one clear victory, with a vigorous damage suit following, to bring the vermin to terms.

Sincerely yours,

H. L. MENCKEN

From Joseph Hergesheimer

West Chester, January 19, 1920

Dear Cabell:

Now I have you to thank for the review of *Linda,* which, it seems to me, is just such a fine detail as might have been lifted by a magnifying glass from the whole pattern of your previous article. . . .

But it is not *Linda* now that is absorbing, rather the suppression of *Jurgen.* I heard this in the Doubleday book-shop at the Pennsylvania Station and was overwhelmed. There are, of course, two attitudes for us, and I'm not sure which you have adopted: you may be totally indifferent except in the savoring of a jest in double cream; you may have expected it and been derisive or even entertained. Then, it's possible that you're fundamentally disturbed. My feeling is the latter, with, perhaps, a rather unpleasant and hopeless mirth. You don't need to be told that *Jurgen* is a fine accomplishment; no one denies that there is sex in it—why should it be denied! Yet, in our pure land love and the bodies of women are held to be serious blemishes on an otherwise noble nature. The innuendoes of the Broadway stage flourish, the stories that our best citizens whisper to each other are still filthy, and we continue to be skillful and shallow liars about the mistaken objects of our greed and hypocrisy. Well, my dear Cabell, you don't stand alone in this, we are all marked together; this outrage to *Jurgen* gets, too, at my freedom, my store of confidence and my sense, never I am afraid very strong, of a possible ultimate dignity for our beautiful, our free, our consecrated America, or in other words God's Country.

Faithfully

JOSEPH HERGESHEIMER

Dumbarton, January 21, 1920

Dear Hergesheimer:

Your letter was good to have and very like you. I do not pretend to answer it in the present confusion, but my gratitude is no less great.

My attitude is that of cold fury toward our own folly in attempting to furnish literature for a land that doesn't want it.

Still, all is not yet over. So, if by any chance you think *Jurgen* has some claim to be considered less as "a certain offensive lewd lascivious indecent book" than as a piece of literature, I would cordially appreciate your sending such a statement to Guy Holt, at R. M. McBride and Company's. We are collecting such statements from judges of literature, and nobody's could be more valuable to me than yours. . . .

Anyhow, the dedicatory verses of *Jurgen* are justified by the outcome. . . . [For the acrostic dedication, see page 93.]

Yours faithfully,

JAMES BRANCH CABELL

With the book suppressed Cabell and Holt spent busy days writing to friends for statements in defense of *Jurgen*. Mencken replied to Cabell: "I'll write to Holt, of course. But certificates of that sort do very little good, and even printed denunciations have no effect. All the decisions run one way: the defense is not permitted to introduce such evidence. The Comstocks know it very well. Thus the more they are denounced, the more vigorously they proceed. Comstock drew up the law under which they operate. It is his masterpiece—and a noble specimen of American legal balderdash. I think the defense should be easy. Simply deny that the passages complained of have the meaning the Comstocks see in them—that is, accuse them of supplying all the indecency themselves. This should be effective with the Court of Special Sessions."

Mencken's letter to Holt emphasized that "[*Jurgen*] is not only not a pornographic work; it is a very fine and delicate piece of writing—perhaps the best thing done in America in a dozen years. It is a pity that a work of art so earnest, so beautifully planned and so competently executed should be exposed to such mistaken attacks. If such things are permitted to go on, then it will be simply impossible to print decent literature in America. The proceeding, like the Dreiser affair, will only cause the English to laugh at us as barbarians. What the French will make of it I hate to think."

Wilson Follett also responded quickly with a letter to Holt, and said of it to Cabell: "It sickens me to perpetrate this solemn cant, but—you will see through it to the purpose behind. Humor and trust are lost on the prosecuting and judging types of mind." Follett's long letter of protest recounted his comments on *Jurgen* when he reviewed it in the *Atlantic Monthly,* and in addition made these observations: "I said that it is an allegory of man's eternal search for the fulfillment of his innate instinct of justice—of that justice, I now add, which this very book is evidently denied by certain accusers. . . .

"But I did *not* say, nor could I with truth have said, either to the readers of the *Atlantic Monthly* or to my own conscience, that *Jurgen* is an offensive or a lewd or a lascivious or an indecent book. For it is not any one of them. Nor can all the accusations of all the self-elected censors in Christendom make it anything except a fine, a brilliant, a noteworthy, an altogether honorable contribution to American letters, for which we ought all to consider ourselves as debtors to Mr. Cabell."

Sinclair Lewis was equally prompt in writing to Holt, pointing out, among other things: "It seems to me incredible that any person of discrimination should not understand that *Jurgen* is a dignified and noble piece of literature, comparable not to cheap novels but to the classics of fiction, and as devoid of indecency as the Bible or the plays of Shakespeare. Like these, it at times deals with deep though normal human passions, but also, like them, it deals with these emotions in a reverent manner, with the cleanness of understanding and knowledge. . . .

"I wonder if any attackers of the book may not have been influenced by the fact that there are and have been lascivious and vile plays running openly, without let or hindrance, in New York and other cities, into supposing that here, in this story of the love of an unhappy and lonely man, there is also such vileness? That the dozen or more dirty farces familiarly known as 'bedroom plays' should be allowed to exhibit, while this noble work of art by a literary man of high and clean reputation is estopped, is alarming, amazing, and filled with all injustice. . . .

"I have read, if I remember, that Hugh Walpole has praised *Jurgen*. That should be impressive testimony to its art and importance. Mr. Walpole is undoubtedly the most brilliant of the younger British literary men, coming now to rank with Bennett, Wells, and Galsworthy; and his praise of the book—precisely because it *does* come from a foreigner and not from an American, who might be prejudiced—indicates the book's extraordinary merit."

As did many other American writers, another "foreigner," in the person of Ernest A. Boyd of Dublin, rushed to the book's defense:

From Ernest A. Boyd

> 18, Upper Fitzwilliam Street,
> Dublin.
> February 10, 1920

Dear Mr. Holt:

Your letter of the 16th January, announcing *Jurgen* as the latest victim of Comstockery amazed me. I have been through the book again in search of passages likely to offend even the most prurient puritan, for on first reading nothing of the kind had struck me. All I can say is that only the logic which would bowdlerize the Bible or classical mythology could take offense at *Jurgen*. It is a delightful fantasia, a charmingly sophisticated fairy tale, but a fairy tale nevertheless. To inject into that world of myth where Mr. Cabell's fancy plays so skilfully, the crude solemnities of Methodist morality is the supreme act of philistinism. I hope that you will be properly supported in an attempt to vindicate the rights of literature, for never was there a clearer case of the issue which must be faced, if art in America is ever to escape the tutelage of the aesthetically blind. *Jurgen* is not even a Dreiserian chaos of contemporary realism, where the pious stenographer might find some incitement to a life of pleasure. Its action lies outside of time and space, far beyond good and evil, obviously so must the morality (if any) which is read into it. It seems to me as ludicrous to criticize Jurgen's actions, as to blush at the perversities of Leda, or to ostracise Pasiphae on the grounds of immorality. Except that the good pawnbroker did not observe the continence alleged to be the ideal of all true presbyterians, there is nothing to be said against him which would not apply to every personage in the legendary lore of most civilised countries. There is no scene which could be described, in my opinion, as deliberately voluptuous, or specifically obscene. These are the counts, I understand, on which certain masterpieces have from time to time been indicted.

With every good wish for your success in the fight which I hope you will make on behalf of Mr. Cabell in particular and the liberty of the artist in general,

I remain
Yours sincerely,
ERNEST A. BOYD

Dumbarton, January 21, 1920

Dear Rascoe:

First of all, I send you this note, then buckle down to the twenty-some letters that lie before me demanding answer— Well, the Philistines are upon us, and the dedicatory verses of *Jurgen* are justified, anyhow in the first two stanzas. I await the outcome in tolerable content, since either way it justifies my preachments. They tell me you had last Saturday a note about the fracas, but this I have not seen.

The *Bovary* and the *Manon* are beautiful books, in which thus far I have read only the prefaces: I make you my compliments thereon, and mean to re-read both volumes in the light of these inductions: and— need I say?—I thank you for the gift. . . .

I thank you, too, for the excerpt from Galantière's letter, which pleased me greatly because he singled out so many tiny things in *Jurgen* that I had privately rather fancied myself. I wish that your other friend, Conrad Aiken, had been equally appreciative, in the *Athenaeum:* an article there in a more generous vein would have been especially valuable just now. Well, we are called on to forgive our enemies only, not condescending patrons of our "boyishness"—which is a hard thing to have flung in your teeth after you have begun to lose them.

This, mark you, is not a letter. It is, rather, an apology for my lack of the ability to write you a letter at this especially hellish time, and a faint indication of my wish that there were a great many more people like you. I look back upon your doings meward during the last two years, and I am grateful: then I sigh, with more or less urbanity, and turn to the twenty-one letters.

Yours faithfully,
JAMES BRANCH CABELL

From Burton Rascoe

Chicago, January 23, 1920

Dear Cabell:

I had begun to wonder whether I had caused you to choke to death over so huge a letter as my last one. I am glad to hear that you are well, and to have even a note in these busy times.

The trial is set for today and I expect to hear from Holt by wire to-night. Nathan also is to give me a report of the doings. I had a piece last week, which I inclose. Fact is I wrote you a note Saturday morning at one o'clock, inclosing the piece and then took the letter home and forgot to mail it. . . .

Aiken's . . . pronouncement about *Jurgen* in the *Athenaeum* made me positively ill. I wrote him a hot letter in which I said so many things that I am sure that I have made an enemy of him for life—and, distress-fully enough for him, I was one of the few who have shown him any sort of courtesy or respect. I repented to him for having, in an unguarded moment, published the obviously fallacious opinion that he was a great critic. I told him that it had evidently gone to his head. . . . In looking through his *Scepticisms* I found that . . . he chose to devote enormous space to poets whose work he doesn't like and a few lines of faint-hearted praise for the men whose work he did care for. . . . I had a row with him in Boston about your work, and especially about *Jurgen*. . . . I must admit that *The Charnel Rose* contains, as I said, some of the most beautiful poetry written in this country since Poe, and Aiken's prose is a carefully perfected thing. But I am going to dress him down . . . as a critic at the earliest convenient opportunity. . . .

Galantière's letter about *Jurgen* delighted me too for precisely the same reason: he singled out so many bits which seemed to me to be par-ticularly delightful, beautiful, and effective, precisely the bits one likes to write about to another reader of the book, or to recall in discussion of the book, or to read to someone else.

But, here I am writing a letter to you when I should be writing my

stuff for tomorrow. It is, though, after all a pleasanter thing to do, and
the audience is more to my liking. Yet, the *Tribune* is paying me a salary,
and I must discharge my part of the obligation.

Yours,

BURTON RASCOE

Holt meanwhile traveled to Richmond to consult with Cabell. Cabell followed him to New York with a letter:

Dumbarton, February 16, 1920

Dear Holt:

. . . Herewith the *Jest* notice. B. F. Glazer writes that the columns
of the *Press* are at our disposal. T. R. Smith advises me that he is writing you. My scrapbook, in need of bringing up to date, is of course at Mr.
McBride's disposal, and I shall forthwith set about pasting in the several
pages of loose clippings: and will forward it on demand.

Meanwhile I have solved the problem of the Lance ceremony, which
is taken from *The Equinox,* Volume III, pp. 250–258. You have this volume, I know: and will note that this part of *Jurgen* derides a philosophy
which is being taught *to-day.* It is also, perhaps, of importance that these
ceremonies were originally printed in a fifteen cent magazine, the *International,* which was never arraigned for lewdness; since fifteen cents is
considerably less than a dollar and seventy-nine.

Very hastily,

JAMES BRANCH CABELL

Dumbarton, February 16, 1920

Dear Rascoe:

O trumpery! O morrice! as Cicero acutely or approximately observed,
and whatever is to become of my correspondence under these afflictions?
Life is just a writing of one "Please protest" after another, diversified
with futile endeavors on the side to concoct some short stories for *Mc-
Clure's*—— Meanwhile, you tell me, you have been even more sorely perse-
cuted, by the influenza, but are—I hope?—all right by this time. Our
household seems, I am glad to report, to have escaped the last epidemic,
which was tolerably severe hereabouts.

Anyhow, Holt was with me last Sunday, and the trial, as you perhaps
know, is set for 8 March. We have fine-toothcombed the book, and it
really looks to me as if we had a rather strong case. Heaven send the
judges intelligence, and we shall come through unhurt. Of course, I wish
it were all over. It is, though, in any event, a great comfort that Mr.

McBride wants to fight the case, and that he has placed *Jurgen* with Heinemann for English publication this spring. Then too Barrett H. Clark and Edward Bierstadt and Sidney Howard are sending out a formal protest, for signature by authors and publishers, of which something may come—— Only nothing ever seems to come of warfare against human stupidity.

Anyhow—while we are on that topic—your Aiken review was a delight. I was not unbiassed, of course, in thinking this, because the *Athenaeum* article appeared to me peculiarly unnecessary and unfair—indeed, mendacious. For one thing, *Hieroglyphics* and *Beyond Life* are not even remotely allied in their main themes, which Mr. Machen and I have been at some pains to state: for ecstasy in literature has very little to do with man's attitude toward the universe. And then—well, in short, I violently resented the article at my first reading of it, and time does not alter the emotion. . . .

Holt is to see you soon. I wish I were.

Yours faithfully,

JAMES BRANCH CABELL

In regard to Machen's own opinion of the influence on Cabell of *Hieroglyphics* and *The Hill of Dreams*, it is interesting to turn to a paragraph in a letter from Machen to Tom Horan: "I know it is said that Mr. Cabell derives from me; but it strikes me that his obligations are slight enough. I told him as much, in answering a very friendly letter, acknowledging his indebtedness. In one of my books, *The Chronicle of Clemendy*, I owe a great deal to Balzac's *Contes Drolatiques*, and I rather gathered from *Jurgen* that Mr. Cabell had also glanced at that delightful work."

In addition to signing the formal protest against the *Jurgen* suppression drawn up by Messrs. Clark, Bierstadt, and Howard, letters were addressed to the members of the Emergency Committee. One such was Theodore Dreiser's:

From Theodore Dreiser

Los Angeles, February 23, 1920

[No salutation]

I have received and signed and forwarded the James Branch Cabell protest. But of what use are kind words to Mr. Cabell? What he needs and what every independent thinker needs in these acute hours is something tangible and substantial in the way of aid. There should be a cash defense fund such as for the last five years I have advocated, which should be devoted to the hiring of competent lawyers and the prosecution of these cattle in every city in which they operate—and they now operate everywhere. Such a lawyer or counsel of defense could use the newspapers, as well as the courts, and make a showing of opposition at least. As it stands we have pale protests from committees who ask authors to sign them.

Incidentally, of what use is the Authors' League if not to aid in such a case as this? Is it solely devoted to the task of discovering where to sell trashy tenth-rate material and to coerce conventional publishers into paying large royalties on best sellers? The spectacle! I sympathize with Mr. Cabell, but I will do more. I will give one hundred dollars toward a defense fund if others as well or better placed than myself will do as much.

THEODORE DREISER

P.S. If such a defense fund can be gotten together it should be urged by all publishers, producing managers, authors and playwrights, as well as book-dealers, that they contribute liberally, as they should. Let the matter of criticism of books, plays, etc., come from the Attorney General at Washington. As it is now, every little tenth-rate squeak of a minister or white slaver can now pass on France, Freud, Andreyeff, Shestov, and who not else. Think of *Noa-Noa* being barred by a mid-western vice society! These cattle must be debarred from indicting the characters and morals of their betters. Their muddy hoofs dishonor the temple. It is not for an artist to defend himself. The state should do it. But pending the awakening of the state let the writers and publishers combine to defend themselves. I will do whatever I can.

Paul Jordan Smith, a lecturer at the University of California, made affidavit that for ten years he had given lectures on the books of James Branch Cabell, and had found them clean and wholesome and stimulating. He further said that *Jurgen* had been read by his class, without criticism: on the contrary it had received the highest praise.

From Robert M. McBride

New York, March 1, 1920

Dear Mr. Cabell:

After considerable inquiry I found the biggest lawyer in the United States on questions such as are involved in the *Jurgen* case. Not only is he an able lawyer, but an intellectual one as well, and his reading has been very extensive. He has acted in several cases such as the one we have on hand and may be considered to be an expert on the subject. Moreover, he is personal counsel for Charlie Murphy, the boss of New York, Thos. F. Ryan and other Irish American celebrities and political leaders. You can see, therefore, that he is equipped from the standpoint of experience, intellectual training and political influence to defend a case of this kind.

Mr. [John] Quinn has read *Jurgen* very carefully and he says that we would be convicted before the Court of Special Sessions, where the case is scheduled to come up, in ten minutes. Mr. Quinn is familiar with your work, has read a great deal of it and likes your essays better than your fiction, which is of course beside the point. He has read Anatole France, Remy de Gourmont, Aleister Crowley and others of the sort and judging from his own reading and from his experience in the courts he thinks your book is an exceedingly questionable one and would have absolutely no chance of winning. He suggests, therefore, the plan of having the case put off on the ground that he has just come into it and has not had time to prepare the case, and then later on will have the case set over until Fall, then the case will very likely be dropped when the Court hears that the book has been stopped and will not be continued to be published. All of these postponements will have to be done through sheer political influence and while the cost of counsel in this case will be considerable yet it is better than having a conviction with a heavy fine and the calamity of having Holt convicted of a misdemeanor, which is not pleasant of course.

Quinn is a fighter and if there was any chance on earth of our winning the case or not losing it he would be disposed to go ahead, but he thinks it is hopeless from the start. You see the law doesn't permit our introducing any evidence. No letters or opinions from literary experts are admissible, nor is it possible to have the author put on the stand to testify as to his purpose in writing the book. The book must be judged clearly on what it says and its influence on the jury. I think, you will agree, that the book will stand no such test. Its references when pointed out by opposing counsel will seem so obvious in their meaning that we cannot hope for leniency.

Under all the circumstances I cannot see anything else to do but to take Mr. Quinn's advice and, of course, immediate action is necessary if a postponement is to be had because the case is called for Monday next. I thought I had better write and ask you whether you were satisfied with this disposal of the case. Generally I am an optimist but see no other way out.

Faithfully yours,
ROBERT M. MCBRIDE

There was nothing for Cabell to do but to agree to the course outlined by Mr. McBride, but soon he was on his way to New York, "drawn thither by the *Jurgen* imbroglio." And while the case dragged on, letters of praise for his work continued to come to Cabell at Dumbarton, from such people in the literary world as Edward Sheldon, Wilbur L. Cross, Editor of the *Yale Review,* and T. R. Smith. However, Cabell managed to get back to some semblance of normal living in time.

Dumbarton, March 15, 1920

Dear Holt:

This morning I had a note from Walpole, asking if we can put him up for the seventh and eighth of April, before he goes to Miss Glasgow on the ninth for the week-end: and I am, of course, answering in the affirmative. It occurs to me that, if you think it worth your while, we would be delighted to have you spend that week-end with us, and I would see that you "met him" thoroughly.

Anyhow, I want posthaste, and for obvious reasons, his *Green Mirror, Golden Scarecrow, Dark Forest,* and *Secret City.* Three of the others I have picked up here—— Like you, I seem to get down to nothing after taking a trip—— Tomorrow I buckle down to the third and last *McClure* story. And in the back of my mind I cloudily consider what sort of book I shall begin on the fifteenth of April. . . .

Think over my suggestion in the first paragraph, anyhow, and believe me

Yours faithfully,
JAMES BRANCH CABELL

Two weeks later Cabell wrote to Holt again: "The last of the Manuel stories for *McClure's* has gone to them. I plan to do two more in April, making six in all. Now if I complete the Manuel book forthwith, and get it to you by August the first, would that not be in ample time for October publication? This would allow the episodes first to appear in the magazines, and would give you, as I understand you wish, a fantastic romance to follow *Jurgen*—— It will not, I think, be improper; but since it is only by resolutely not thinking about the connecting links that I am able to shape the episodes as short stories, I am not sure. Nor—and this is droll—though I have completed four of the stories, I have not yet formed the least notion as to what sort of person Manuel is to be. I lean instinctively to the *Jurgen* type, but logically want a variant. You might suggest: all that is necessary is that he rises from tending swine to be Count of Poictesme.— You might suggest. At least, let me know about the time limit.— And do you certainly come for the second week-end in April if you can. We shall not make company of you, as you know."

The book in the process of making was *Figures of Earth.* And according to schedule, Walpole arrived in Richmond, to make delighted friends of both Ellen Glasgow and Cabell.

From Sinclair Lewis

                                          Washington, Tuesday [date?]
My dear Cabell:
   Greetings and salutations.
   Guy Holt, here yesterday, told me that Walpole may be in Washington the last part of this week. I wonder if you can, and if you would care to, (seal &) send him the enclosed letter inviting him to use my house and my bum old car as much as he can while he is here? You may know his address between you-all's and here.
   Guy and I talked chiefly of a book about a certain Jurgen, a well-known prohibitionist of the old days.
   I have done nothing but *Main Street* for many months. It will be finished by June 1, and be published in the fall.
   Is one ever to see the benign light of your countenance in Washington?

                                          Sincerely yours,
                                          SINCLAIR LEWIS

From Sinclair Lewis

                                          Washington, Thursday [date?]
Dear Cabell:
   Your letter crossed mine. For yours many thanks. Indeed I shall force upon the poor lamb a copy of *The Job*, with a flourish and a little generous advice about writing novels, so that he may be corrected in any erroneous notions he may have gathered from you and Joe. I shall preach to him the Great Kindly Heart of the Common People—— Please omit flowers. Services at Pete Gadger's Mortuary Parlors.
   I called up Mr. De Vries [1] this morning, and I trust I shall be admitted to gaze upon greatness some place between demi tasse and pajamas.

                                          As ever,
                                          SINCLAIR LEWIS

[1] Marion De Vries, Washington lawyer, who was to be Walpole's host.

Dumbarton (*not* Richmond),
April 18, 1920

[No salutation]

This handmade letter, Hugh, is in deference to my wife's queer notion that a typewriter is on Sunday immoral, and apt by its clicking to attract the attention of a deity who, I deduce, can hear but not see through a roof—— Anyway, I grieved not to see you that last afternoon—except for that fleet glimpse of the upper half of you,—but there was a hopeless combination of mishaps, such as a broken car, the need of getting the children back from school, a misfit train schedule, and the dying of my brother's father in law, all in full progress while I was trying to talk to you through our out-of-order telephone, without your being able, I gathered, to hear one word in five.

Well! Joe will tell you that he and I had at least one good talk, wherein I curiously avoided talking of you—though probably he did not notice that feature. He asked me, be it also known, to come on to West Chester with him, but I could not comfortably imagine the three of us together. "It certainly is" a disconcerting, droll, fine personage, whom I trust you will duly lecture upon the unimportance of externals, before leaving West Chester. For example: he was all excitement as to his recent discovery that a girl with blue eyes and red hair appears to have violet-colored eyes, and that seemed to me an excellent instance of his pre-occupation with such superficial "truths." The love for truth is his tiger, to quote another distinguished author.

I am still wondering about that same distinguished author. Meanwhile I have retired into the not at all lonely solitude that he temporarily invaded or dispersed, and have staidly set about a brace of short stories, to be fused later into the book I trust to complete by August.

And, after we have buried my brother's father in law this afternoon, I foresee no break in the horizon's sleek monotony, for some while—— It is with mingled interest and excitement, of course, that I await the *Yale Review* article, wherein I trust you have made me out to be a very fine fellow indeed, and not a mere "pot of geraniums in the window." But I shall thank you for all charitable misrepresentations later, when I am sure as to their nature and extent.

I think obscurely of so much, and set down so little in this letter, which visibly attests little more than my dependency upon the typewriter. And you leave us this week, after, I rather think, an unequaled conquest of affection from coast to coast. For my part, I must leisurely return to a re-reading of your books, finding in them this time your voice and accent and an astounding change—— I hope—I repeat, dear Hugh, that you are not going to be a Shirley or a Massinger among the

Limited. I hope you will cold-bloodedly comprehend that your endowments will be more profitably invested in writing than in friendship. To love and to be loved is at best your avocation, or in somewhat lower terms grist for your mill. Joe understands this—this much anyhow—far better than you. All is grist. Even you, I hazily foresee in the next story but one by a brown glittering river in the wind—— With which confession I none the less subscribe myself

Affectionately
JAMES

From Hugh Walpole

R.M.S. *Mauretania*
April 25, 1920

My dearest James

The sea is calm for a moment so I think that I'd better take advantage to write you, this also being Sunday afternoon, and all the moon-faced people on every side of me are engaged on the same job. It is not I think going to be fine long! (*Me miserium*) I got your letter at Joe's and the Editor of the *Yale* is delighted with my article. Joe to whom I read it also liked it, but *I* don't. It is dry and dull and uninspired; I think I deliberately tried to make it commonplace because the whole point of it was to make ordinary people read you.

It is at least honest, absolutely—not all praise but exactly what I think minus the love I have for you, which it would be neither wise nor right to insert. Which brings me to your letter. When you talk about 'grist' I am with you—but for *my* work my friendships (or as old Fitz [2] said about his: they are more like loves I think) *are* my grist. You have no idea for instance how you and Joe have filled the well with precious waters these last months. I can't help loving people and so it will always be—and I think it is right for me to do so because I shall always write about more ordinary people than will you and Joe. Old maids, clergymen, nurses and widowers are my real métier as my great Cathedral Trilogy shall one day properly reveal. I shall be, with luck, a kind of modern Trollope—Hawthorne with a little dash of real H.W. added. You see I'm not modest but why the hell should I be? I feel my powers growing and growing within me and my real work is only now beginning.

---

[2] Edward FitzGerald, translator of Omar Khayyám. Tennyson dedicated *Tiresias* in some reminiscent verses to his friend "Old Fitz."

I have made four great friends in America, you and Joe are two, and you are outside and beyond all the others. Throw yourself out then to meet it; launch out and come along. You can give yourself up to me and be perfectly safe; look on it as a kind of Jack-in-the-Box spree to be indulged in once a year—and then back into your box you may go. I go on the gospel of taking all we can see— Life's short and experiences are like manure. Treat me as your very best Top-Dressing and see in a year or two the wonderful fruit trees you will have.

Joe is different. I care for him deeply, he is a fine creature, but you I want to protect and help and care for to the end of my days. You may say you don't want protecting— Well, then, you can protect *me*. Anyway let's do our next moves or two in combination. I have written Barrett Clark a screed about *Jurgen*. Write to me—Come over next year and believe me

Your unchanging friend
HUGH

Dumbarton, April 26, 1920

Dear Rascoe:

. . . *Jurgen*, as far as I know, is at a standstill, and I have rather put the matter out of mind to make way for other things. Your Waldo Frank, for example! I liked and lunched him, and invited him out to Dumbarton. He accepted, but backed out at the last moment, because Walpole was then here, and Frank scented a "reception" and was overcome, he said, by his constitutional shyness of crowds.— Yes, I liked him, and he amused me. But, after all, his book is, in the teeth of your admiration thereof, a rather silly performance. Come, let's be sturdy and fearless pioneers, and grow real hair on our chests, and develop our splendid innate qualities without truckling to tradition and effete foreigners, is, after all, an exhortation that was familiar in the heyday of Elijah Pogram and Jefferson Brick: and I don't see that these spiritual descendants of Whitman are really an improvement upon Dickens.

Besides, he did not mention me among the literati, and that of course was unforgivable.

Well, Walpole came, and during his stay we got on incredibly. I am quite seriously glad that I read, anyhow, seven of his books before being exposed to his personal charm, which cannot but prejudice me hopelessly in favor of aught of his I read hereafter. As it was, the two Russian books had left me violently unenthusiastic. Luckily my favorite of the lot was his—*The Green Mirror*—and he pleased me by, generally, ranking my books relatively much as I do, so that auctorial vanities did not trip the progress of our intimacy. At my last sight of him, he had just procured a blank book in which he was to "do" an article about me, for the *Yale Review* and the *Fortnightly,* and according to my last word from him the article has been completed: so I await.

Thereafter came Hergesheimer, just back from Cuba, where a four weeks' sojourn has afforded him the material for two novels, which he proposes to write forthwith. Well, I like Joe, and I have prodigious faith in him, but his ways are not mine. So I reserve judgment till I have seen the books.

Yours faithfully,

JAMES BRANCH CABELL

From Guy Holt

New York, May 6, 1920

Dear Cabell:

. . . I cannot as yet go into details in regard to the hearing before the grand jury. We [have] followed the course which we planned when you were here, and I am to read some sort of thing which Quinn is preparing. I feel, after a conference with that gentleman, like a naughty little boy who has been whipped and threatened with worse punishment if he does not behave in future. It is all very unpleasant and I am more than annoyed about it.

. . . What, by the way, have you decided about a fall book? Are we to republish *Domnei* to complete that "uniform set of Mr. Cabell's earlier books" or do you think you will be able to make anything of Manuel?

Faithfully yours,

GUY HOLT

From Guy Holt

New York, May 8, 1920

Dear Cabell:

. . . I write this on blank paper because I want to emphasize the fact that the balance of the letter is entirely a personal one. Yesterday Q. telephoned us that his negotiations with our friends down town had been unsuccessful and that the matter is to be followed through with vigor and without mercy. It seems that the mention of Heaven and Hell has offended the religious sensibilities of one or two persons in power, and for this reason we are to be given no opportunity to promise to be good children in the future if they will pardon us this time. I am—I confess —glad that this is the outcome. It was to have been my unpleasant task to appear and explain what well meaning persons we are and how we never should have done it had we known, and certainly never, never would do it again. It is a role I did not fancy. Now, the prospect of a fight even with defeat certain is a comforting one and a sop to my rather undeveloped sense of honor. But—

We are back where we were in January, save for this: that Q. is practically certain to drop the affair, considering that he has earned his thousand, and we are now assured of losing, but have no choice save to fight. We can fight in two ways: vigorously, with the aid of a good and expensive lawyer or feebly with the handicap of a poor but cheap one. The outcome may be the same in either case. But if we fight hard, we may, by a miracle, win, or escape with a small fine. Otherwise we shall be under the expense—in addition to Q.'s fee—of another 1,000 or 1500, a possible 2,000 fine and a few hundreds for costs.

It worries me. As you know, I consider this affair my own responsibility, not that of R.M. I don't want to see him put in a hole because of anything I have done, and I think he has acted splendidly through the whole business, for he has never yet even discussed this aspect of the matter with me. For that matter I think he too is pleased at the outcome of affairs, for he likes to cringe as little as I do. No less, here are some pertinent facts. Our actual sales were, roughly, 4100 copies, on which our gross profit was approximately 60¢ per copy. Our plant cost, as I recall it, $750. Deduct this, plus about $400 spent upon advertising, disregard all selling and other overhead expenses, and we have taken in, in excess of actual sums spent on manufacturing costs, at most $1500. Of this Q. gets $1,000. There remains a balance of $500 against potential liabilities of perhaps eight times that amount, if we lose.

You see? What I have been wondering, and it embarrasses me to suggest it, would you be willing to regard, as we do, all time spent upon this book as being well lost, and if need be, let us apply against legal expenses the amount it has earned for you? I don't know what is fair in such a case as this. I don't know how either you or R.M. would feel about such a proposal, and I know that, if he had any such suggestion in his mind, he'd be embarrassed to mention it to me. I'd rather, then, that any suggestion of this sort would come from one of us, but naturally I wish first to find out what you think of it.

I wish I didn't have to give thought to such things at all. I wish we had fifty best sellers on our list and that the loss of several thousands, plus a year's work was a mere nothing to us. It isn't; I'm unfortunately penniless; and I feel that it is up to me to consider every aspect of the situation, no matter how unpleasant. At least, I know, you will understand my motives and will not resent my action whatever you think of my judgment.

I expect to hear any day now that an indictment has been found. It is probable that next week will see us in the toils, but the trial is scarcely likely to come up until Fall. Anything is possible, however. . . . Please let me hear from you about this at your leisure. Meantime I'll keep the scrapbook in our safe.

Faithfully,

G.H.

Dumbarton, May 11, 1920

Dear Holt:

All right, then, you are hereby authorized to tell Mr. McBride that the *Jurgen* royalties now due are to be retained for legal expenses. But many more investments of a thousand dollars for precisely nothing will be disastrous.

Let's see, now: You should by this have the proof as well as the scrapbook, which were shipped together. You should have, also, my letter to Clark, on which I await your opinion.— It is my real attitude toward the affair, and, as affairs now stand, an attitude I can confess without much hurt. In fine, I refuse to defend *Jurgen* on any count: the book must speak for itself: and those who don't like it can go to hell. So I am out with my platform before any of the political parties.

Obviously the fall publication will have to be *Domnei*. There has been a resolute and quite marked combination among the Fates from the first of this year to prevent my getting any writing done. I take it as evincing rare will power that I have managed to get four short stories done during this period. But it is all rather maddening—

Yours faithfully,

JAMES BRANCH CABELL

The letter mentioned by Cabell to Barrett H. Clark, Secretary of the Emergency Committee, said: "As to censorship of our reading matter, I concede this may, in theory, be advisable. In practice, though, I can imagine no persons or class of persons qualified to perform this censorship. *Pace* the Vice Society, there is certainly a difference between pornography and fine literature, if but the difference that everybody enjoys the first where few care one way or the other about the second: and certainly the two should be appraised by diverse and appropriate standards. A work of art should therefore, in theory, be judged entirely as a work of art, by a jury of practitioners of the art concerned."

From Wilson Follett

Cheshire, Connecticut
May 7, 1920

Dear Cabell:

I now perceive that, in my haste, I quite missed making answer to your question about the New York Evening *Post* and its plans. I don't know when *The Seven Against Realism* will begin: I am writing the papers now, and I should say there would be likely to be a beginning in print by a month or six weeks from now. Anyway, their habitat will be the magazine section of the *Post,* which comes weekly on Saturday nights— a folder of general articles wrapped round a book review section, in format like the *Times* (New York) Literary Supplement, but in substance much better. In June, Henry Canby is to begin a sabbatical year and a half by taking charge of this book review section; and by September he will have it running as a sort of independent literary weekly, in a changed format with good paper, the best contributors he can get, and a magazine rather than a newspaper rate of pay for material. Meanwhile, they have put in William Rose Benét to hold down the job and bridge the gap; and already he has bucked up the thing rather wonderfully, considering how little time he has had. . . . Their idea is to break entirely with the journalistic conception of book reviewing by putting in editors, and getting contributors, who simply don't know anything about journalism. A very interesting venture, at least in promise. The way to keep track of it, I suppose, if you are so minded, is to subscribe to the Saturday *Post,* thereby getting the literary supplement within the magazine section within the newspaper—like a set of Chinese eggs. . . . I think, but have no way of making sure quickly, that my contributions began with the issue of May 1; but these contributions have nothing to do with *The Seven.* I will send you a line when those articles begin— you, Benét, and Knopf being the only three persons in America who "look with interest."

By the way, I want you to discover *We Moderns,* by Edwin Muir, in Knopf's Free Lance Series (introductions by H.L.M.). . . .

Yours ever cordially,
WILSON FOLLETT

Dumbarton, May 12, 1920

Dear Rascoe:

The news as to your leaving the *Tribune* troubles me solely with pecuniary apprehensions. If only the monetary side of the change is not too gloomy, it is the best thing that could well happen. I have felt for some while—and, indeed, have mildly voiced the feeling to you, I believe —that you were wasting an invaluable and non-recurrent period of life in doing ephemeralities. Now can you not really "write"?

You see, I have the strongest possible faith in your ability and in the importance of fully using that ability. At this time, and distance, I may confess that, from an Economical standpoint, I have regarded it as more important than Hazel and the two children. Of course, it would not be seemly for you to agree with me—— Anyway, I am selfishly glad that you plan to "write a little, and locate probably in New York"——

For myself, I hammer away at Manuel in every available interval between the countless unimportant things that have to be attended to. All 1920, thus far, has been a succession of endless damnable distractions, with the *Jurgen* case still hanging fire in a rather hopeless atmosphere.— I have reached the stage of rather fretful irritation with both sides. I don't care what they do if they will just let me alone and permit me to utilize my non-returning forty-second year in writing: that, as near as I can phrase it, is my feeling. For the rest, *Jurgen* is now suppressible by its own demerits, but by nothing else whatever. But I desist, because these common-sense ways of looking at things are un-American and probably punishable by deportation. . . .

Yours faithfully,

JAMES BRANCH CABELL

Dumbarton, June 5, 1920

Dear Hugh:

In this world of inexplicable happenings your letter written on the *Mauretania,* dated 25 April, arrived in Dumbarton 28 May, in brand-new condition, stamp uncanceled, no postmark, and with no sign of having passed through the mails. Heaven alone knows the course of its travels, but in the meanwhile I had naturally been wondering over your epistolary taciturnity. Well! that acknowledgment made, now let me acknowledge—but indeed there is much to acknowledge!

Your picture, first: it is excellent, it has real youishness (most of them haven't it), and I love it. So it duly goes into my private gallery of favorite authors, very gratifyingly displacing the booklet picture.

Then came your earlier books, to rouse my gratitude at first, but later to trouble me with questionings. You did not send me a *Prelude*, but I acquired it, so that my set is now complete—— I say these books troubled me, in that I found myself reading them with more interest and delight than I had given your maturer work. Can it be, I fell to wondering, that he has lost something? but I afterward decided it was merely that I was seeing you in these books, as I had not been able to see you in the others, and that your personality was now beguiling me—— Still, there is in the romantic wonder of the *Prelude* and your Morelli just the stuff that appeals to me: indeed, my Jurgen too talked with Morelli. Then, but come now! do you re-read that meeting between Harry Cornish and Mary in the dawn, and consider if you could quite repeat the ecstasy. There I find four pages of the pure magic: it is the sort of thing I love, the sort of thing that, I repeat, beguiles me into blithering and uncritical delight: I purr over, like a stroked cat. It appeals to me in—irrationally—the same way your *Duchess* [*of Wrexe*] appealed. In fine, I like you in the richly romantic vein.

—Which statement I blandly follow with the statement that *The Gods and Mr. Perrin* is your most consummate book. You have done nothing more thoroughly, though there is a queer wobbling at the end, somehow, as though you were trying to delude the reader into believing things would be better next term. Indeed, I look upon this book as your unappreciated masterpiece, because I never, to my recollection, heard anyone speak of it. For God's sake, don't ever write anything else at all resembling it: I detest it, and I yield it loathing vivid admiration.

In the varied manifestations of your auctorial genius, I must protest, though, I most unfeignedly adore you as critic. Man, have you no conscience? don't you know it is wicked to tell stories? and whither do you expect to go when you die? *Advocatus diaboli* will flourish a copy of the *Yale Review* and that will be the end of your paradisial aspirations. You see, Wilbur Cross wrote asking me to contribute something, and in replying I suggested he might send me a proof of your article on the art of a notorious Virginian, and this he kindly did. (Which, by the way, enabled me to correct for you one or two verbal errors, and to re-instate Charteris as the villain of *The Rivet* instead of *The Cream of the Jest*, as the proof had him.) You must know, dear Hugh, there is nothing at all adequate for me to say in acknowledgment of your paper. I am profoundly, abjectly, and unspeakably grateful. If you "deliberately tried to make it commonplace," you failed: and if you, really, think it "dry and dull and uninspired," I don't. I love it, and I love you. I hope you will let us use it as a booklet, for it is ideal for that purpose: will you? You saw for yourself, from my scrapbooks, what importance Americans attached to what Hugh Walpole said about me. And now to have him say-

ing all this! I consider myself already "established" pending publication
of the July *Review*.

Apropos, my establishment in England is once more deferred. Heinemann, four months after accepting the books, writes unperturbedly that
he has decided the publication of *Jurgen* might get him into trouble,
and that it is all off. This is, of course, the result of McBride's unbusi-
ness-like failure to make any formal contract, and the upshot of a
"gentleman's agreement." I am instructing McBride to turn over the
handling of the books to your friend Pinker, and hope something may
come of it. Yet the longer I stay a failure, the less I really mind it. Unknown, I can write books purely for self relief, making art a, more or
less, "sublime excrement." Already I feel hampered by the expectation
of the tiny clique over here that reads me—considering in the act of writing, what (say) will Mencken think of this? or Hergesheimer? Whereas,
confound it, I should have no concern with what even they think or
prefer—— The *Jurgen* case is still unsettled. The outlook is so hopeless
and damnable, whatever settlement be reached, that I have put the entire affair out of mind—— I should have said, at the beginning of this
letter, that the reason your letter has stayed unanswered ten days is that
it came just as I was revising in mad haste *The Soul of Melicent,* which
is to be re-issued this autumn, under the new—or, rather, the original—
title of *Domnei,* and that this revision was not off my hands until to-day.
Presently, too, I shall be sending you a *Cords of Vanity,* which, after incredible printing delays, is finished so far as my share goes.

So much for me and my affairs. I look forward with liquorish delight
to your next book, because, now, I can read it as I do my own just
printed books, but with the added delectation of being concerned with
and guessing at the outcome. Let me pause here, to be disagreeable: your
"Clive Torby" story was a drop from the level—no, I mean the peaks—
of its predecessors. I am jealous for you, Hugh. I want you to do more
than you, or anybody, can achieve. I wish the others of the Limited
abolished, to leave you not only supreme but unsurrounded. As for our
protecting each other! art certainly, and living too, I suspect, must always be a lonely adventure. But one can love, and hope. These, anyhow,
are emotions that I am prodigally investing in you and in your future.

Yours,

JAMES

❧ 8 ❧

INTERIM

Dear Joe:

Rash words are now coming home to roost. Do you still feel like doing gratis a preface to the reissue of *The Soul of Melicent* when we bring it out this fall under the new title *Domnei?* I told you, I think, that Wilson Follett has thus dealt with *The Cords of Vanity:* and while *Domnei* in the light of its past performance (exactly 630 copies sold in all) seems rather a hopeless venture we mean to try it. This is the book I would pre-eminently desire you to herald, as the only other domnei expert: so if you can within the next two months produce something apropos, I would be grateful; whereas if you can't, there is no harm done. The changes I have made are purely in the direction of tidying the English, with one added chapter to link it with *Jurgen.* . . .

You finished, I hope, your story for the August *Century* in time for us to twinkle as twin luminaries? Mine went on schedule, and is all flippancy—— I heard something of you, last week, through a brief talk with Edwin Knopf, who showed me your dummies. Now I can look forward to the complete Meeker history. The cover for the Cuba book, in passing, is vile: I have no notion you will approve it. This Knopf, too, I liked exceedingly, and it was to my real grief he got here when I was over ears in getting my step-daughters graduated from school. You are, I repeat, very lucky in your publishers, and I still hope for a Knopf-Holt combination which will unite us two in business bonds.

I have just heard from Hugh Walpole, via a letter written on shipboard which has been traveling heaven knows whither. You saw, he tells me, his shameless *Yale Review* article, for which I am deeply and unconscientiously grateful. [Walpole] is, I protest, the most lovable creature I have anywhere encountered, and I incline to regard him as the greatest living English novelist quite irrespective of what he writes. You know, I have just finished his earliest books, and have found them—thanks, I hope, to his dear and beguiling personality—more delightful than the later ones which I read before I knew him.

Anyhow, you know you are to visit me at the Alum this summer, and I at least look forward to that with elation.

Yours faithfully,

JAMES BRANCH CABELL

From Joseph Hergesheimer

West Chester, June 15, 1920

Dear James:

It was as nice as possible to have a letter from you and at once I began to think furiously if I had written you since our splendid party in Richmond. Since then, however, I have been lost in *San Cristobal de la Habana*, hurried not so much by Alfred as by devilish delinquent printers. This is the first book I've written outside fiction: in fact it is a reaffirmation of principle, the declaration that I am still a free man, and I hope you'll like it. It is a performance for my friends, for Cabell, Walpole and Company. Hugh's letter to me arrived the day after yours and I have only to repeat all that you so successfully said. He is full of London literary affairs and contacts: things lacking to us, except in the very particular, and which we must most certainly investigate. *San Cristobal* is finished and I am immediately correcting the MS and so I have only this moment for the necessities of our correspondence. I'll be delighted to do *Melicent;* I haven't seen the May *Bookman* and be damned to it— we're well out of that saccharine quarter; and I was obliged to throw over entirely the *Century* story both because of my book and in consequence of illness. The *Melicent* affair, as I see it, should be about 1500 words but on that we must confer. You must, my dear James, indeed you must and with Mrs. Cabell, come to Dower House: the spearmint under the hedge is as green as possible and I'll have for you a good brown whisky. This is an affair for immediate consideration. O yes, I did see the *Yale Review* article and there is nothing shameless in it.

To the most Honorable, the most Noble and Affable Gentleman James Branch Cabell, Esquire, from his Fellow

JOSEPH HERGESHEIMER

Dumbarton, June 22, 1920

Dear Joe:

The invitation to Dower House is alluring, but none the less its acceptance must stay a pleasure deferred. I am now moiling along some two months behind the year's predetermined program, dazedly hoping by and by to "catch up." I have just come to the point where it is possible for me really to buckle down to *The Fairy Time* [*Figures of Earth*], of which I have promised Holt the manuscript by the first of October. Beyond neatly tabulating the forty chapter headings I seem to make no progress: still, the Table of Contents looks eminently business-like, and I re-read it with a sort of half-belief that I have the complete book somewhere.

So I plan now to labor through a month at Dumbarton, and then to carry the results with me to the Alum to see what mountain air can do for the story. And there I hope to see you too.

What you say of *San Cristobal* is most provocative. I shall await its appearance, now, with redoubled interest: so far I knew of this book only from the sight I had of the dummy cover—which puzzled me—— That brings me roundabout to the astounding O. Henry Prize volume (wherein my Marlowe figures with "puzzled" hair, to my not inconsiderable surprise), and to the query if, with this coming on the heels of the O'Brien gallimaufry, it is not time for us to shut up shop or, else, to sample *felo de se?* These books are, I protest, incredible. I decline to accept them as representative of what is really being done in the writing line, but they are representative of the sort of persons that is permitted to set up as judges, and the sort that is more or less listened to instead of being intelligently and instantly lynched. I find in each volume just five stories in which it is possible to detect something to commend: and all the rest is tenth rate imbecility—— But I desist. I know I have not been in a really responsible condition since reading that the O. Henry committee dismissed all stylistic considerations because housekeepers do not bring home their beefsteaks wrapped in silk. I "recommended," by the by, your Meeker stories to the committee—— Well, but we are doomed to skulk about in a madhouse, and can but be satisfied when the other inmates are not actually violent.

Lord, man, but you are a comfort to me. I mean, it is a comfort to reflect that you and Mencken, anyhow, exist. How did we come, in passing, to figure in such "advanced" company, as in the Hardy cablegram? [An eightieth-birthday cablegram to Hardy signed by many Americans] Ah, well, we madcap youngsters! . . .

Yours faithfully,
JAMES BRANCH CABELL

Dumbarton, July 1, 1920

[No salutation]

It was kind and generous and in all respects characteristic of you, dear Joe, to "do" the *Domnei* introduction precisely as you did "do" it. The immoral result is that I am no longer compunctious about having inflicted this task on you, but hold the means to be justified by the end, in this singular and very beautiful performance. I knew, indeed, I could not help knowing, that the author of *Linda Condon* was the unique man for this job: and now my judgment is confirmed, and my vanity is stroked, and my gratitude is magnified. . . .

Well, my excursus into short story writing is happily concluded, and it is rather good to be back at a book. But my methods of composition invariably appal me at the beginning, with a dispiriting conviction that nothing endurable can possibly come of such disconnected drivel, so that I view life gloomily these hot adhesive days. Still, it is all in the cellar of my mind if ever I get it lugged out——piecemeal.

To-day I am putting aside the second instalment of *Steel,* so that I may read the book for the first time in its entirety. I like you better as a banquet than in snacks. . . .

Yours faithfully,

JAMES BRANCH CABELL

Dumbarton, July 4, 1920

Dear Holt:

To begin with Hergesheimer, I hope you may find time to write him an amiable note of appreciation of his doing the *Domnei* introduction. It was really fine of him to volunteer—or, strictly speaking, be prompted to volunteer—to do gratis what Doubleday, Page & Company gave him $250 for doing for the D'Annunzio book—— The paper too is, I think, quite good for our purpose. It was queer how he picked out the palpable and visible furnishings of the book, just as he treats life in his creative writing: queer, too, how Walpole pounced on your contribution to *Beyond Life,* and proclaimed it never to have been my verdict. . . .

De Casseres' article was somewhat a surprise to me, though, you may remember, I invested one of my two new copies of the *Jest* in him, so that this is bread returning on the waters in the shape of cake with highly sugared icing. I wonder if you have ever met him. He has, he tells me, fifteen unpublished books, each numerously rejected, so it is possible he has given you a call—— In the mean time I want you to get for me, from whoever publishes it, that Frazer's *Golden Bough* from which I have been plagiarizing so long. There are about ten volumes, I believe, but evidently I ought to have it, alleviating the acquirement with a "trade discount."

Yours faithfully,

JAMES BRANCH CABELL

From H. L. Mencken

Baltimore, July 12, 1920

Dear Mr. Cabell:

The O'Brien and O'Henry books depressed me so much that I let them pass. I took a hack at O'Brien two or three years ago. His imbecilities approach the sublime. . . .

The *Yale Review* is very bawdy this month. Worse, the *Christian Register* has just printed an editorial saying that I am a worthy fellow, though unfortunately an atheist. I am going to have the thing printed on a wall-card.

The *Madeleine* case [1] shows what McBride might have accomplished by fighting. Your chances of winning were ten times those of Brainard. A pox upon the fellow.

Which recalls the fact that I begin to despair of ever getting you to Baltimore to drink the waters. This leaves all my Cabell books unautographed. Why not sit down some rainy day and embellish your name upon 12 slips of fair white paper, and so let me gum them in? Your name—and perhaps a word of comfort from Holy Writ? I throw out the suggestion.

I am very rocky—in fact, scarcely able to sit up. But I'll be better tomorrow.

Sincerely yours,

H. L. MENCKEN

[1] Harper and Brothers were raided for publishing *Madeleine*, the autobiography of a girl of pleasure, and when the case came to trial, Clinton Brainard, head of the house, was fined $1000 and denounced from the bench.

From H. L. Mencken

Baltimore, July 30, 1920

Dear Mr. Cabell:

... What a hell of a task I put upon you! Well, I dessay a Christian, such as I am now, should be glad to punish a heathen author like you.

It is very curious, but I believe *The Line of Love* is the only book of yours I have never read. I am tempted to write the preface before reading it. The idea is not bad. I have an order in England for some *Jurgens* immediately they come out, and shall assault the pious with them. Very often lately I have heard the theory that it was not the carnality but the harsh words against democracy that brought down the Comstocks. They are very patriotic, and think that the late Morris K. Jesup [2] was a far greater man than Bismarck.

A new Jurgenista is on the job. He is E. A. Boyd, the Irish critic. Dublin got too hot for him, and he is now in New York, working for the Evening *Post*. He is a fine critic and a very good fellow.

I have finished *Prejudices II* and am sweating through accumulated Mss.

Sincerely yours,

H. L. MENCKEN

From Sinclair Lewis

(Till September 1:)
Kennebago Lake House
Kennebago Lake, Maine
August 2 [1920]

My dear Cabell:

Your letter of almost a month ago came to me in Washington at a time when, on the last gasp of completing *Main Street*, I was working daily till midnight or after. It is done, now; it is utterly different from the preliminary effort you saw a year ago; whether it is good or not, certainly it is much the best thing I have ever written. Harcourt seems to like it.

2 A banker who headed many charities; he helped found the YMCA and was a Trustee of the Society for the Prevention of Cruelty to Animals and the Institute for the Deaf and Dumb. He was also President of various cultural groups such as the Museum of Natural History, the Peary Arctic Club, and the Audubon Society of the State of New York.

The dedication is (unless the luckless dedicatees furiously protest) as follows:

TO

JAMES BRANCH CABELL

AND

JOSEPH HERGESHEIMER

The mag op will be out in September and, unless I fall off one of the piney mountains I am energetically and humorlessly climbing, or am fed as bait to a trout, I shall send you a copy.

My meeting with Walpole was altogether agreeable. I drove him about Washington a bit, and drove him from Washington to Baltimore on his way to meeting Joe H. at Wilmington. I like him immensely—and liked his enormous and patently sincere admiration for you. Now—money, short stories, a recovery from the nine months of novelizing during which I have been daily becoming poorer and poorer and
poorer
        and poorer
          and poorer!
I wish we were to see you at the Alum but we have chosen coolness and small fishes.

As ever,
Tho pennilessly,
SINCLAIR LEWIS

Rockbridge Alum Springs,
August 7, 1920

Dear Lewis:

Here then I have been reinstated in the back porch you know of, for now a week, with the same mountains to consider and with nothing in the outlook changed, except that the field of corn which last year served as the background of photographs is now pimpled with less picturesque cut stacks. I had really hoped we might see you here, and my disappointment is honest.

I would, also, be honestly proud of that dedication. I would like it tremendously. The question is if Hergesheimer would like having his honors divided. Now—and this of course is none of my business—I gather that the meeting in West Chester last September did not "come off" perfectly. No, I have had no account of what happened. I do know, though, that Joe last April was "waiting" to see if you would change the dedication. So would it not, in view of everything, be wiser not to change it?

and, if you will, to reserve the next, or some other forthcoming, master-piece for me?—This much said, I leave the affair to you, and will be pleased by whatever solution you devise.

I am "writing" here, in a sort of somnolent fashion, to the extent of patching together, more or less coherently, the various Manuel stories—I don't know if you have encountered any of them—into a book, for appearance some time after Christmas. Then we are reprinting the earlier ones, in a revised and uniform edition, the first in which, *The Cords of Vanity,* should be out before long with a preface . . . by Wilson Follett. . . . *Domnei* (a revision, or rather padding, of *The Soul of Melicent*) is to follow within a month or two, and to this Hergesheimer has done a preface. Then Mencken has promised me a preface for the third one, which probably will be *The Line of Love,* and later I may be calling on you for an unblushing puff of one of the others. So be prepared. I am using my friends, you see, à la Meredith.

Either way, do you let me see *Main Street* the first moment possible —whatever the dedication—and believe me

Yours faithfully,

JAMES BRANCH CABELL

Promptly came a reply from Lewis:

NO, you stay there in that handsome dedication and I shall be proud if you ever call on me for an introduction to one of your reissued books.

SL

Rockbridge Alum Springs, August 12, 1920

Dear Joe:

It is idle guessing as to where you may be just now, but this will, I take it, be forwarded. And "this" is, after all, just a cross-my-heart assurance that *Steel* is quite infernally good. There seemed to be some dubiety on the point, even in your mind, for I remember your telling me you were not sure about this book. Well, then, you are a poor critic. . . . I want it presently in—of course—a steel gray binding. I have meanwhile the six instalments neatly sewed together in an unsatisfactory volume, which—I now regret—I loaned out the other day, for if I had it now in hand I might comment more minutely. For one thing—as you probably know—you have in this book flashes of humor such as I remember in none of the others. . . . I do not say it is an advance upon *Linda* . . . I like *Linda* the best of your books for the adequate reason that I do like it best, without for a moment bothering as to whether or no it is your masterpiece. I do not like *Steel* in the same way, but very heartily do I admire *Steel*. . . . I wanted to tell you so the first possible moment. And this conveys that message alone.

> Yours faithfully,
> JAMES BRANCH CABELL

From Joseph Hergesheimer

West Chester, August 16, 1920

Dear James:

A letter to you was the next thing for accomplishment when yours came from the Alum. I had a number of details, large and small, for your consideration; but they threaten to develop into so many questions, so much 'round about discussion, that, except for hints, I'm putting them off until, well, until you are at Dower House.

In the first place *Linda* has now had her English press, and there is, it seems to me, a decided element of impatience with her: they will not grant me my theme, the premise, really, and persist in treating the whole affair as a record of ascertainable relationships and values. In these, the general voice sounds, I should have, then, produced something far more staggering: the attitude, unusually kind for their self-satisfaction, is that, listening for a full twelve of the clock, they were aware of only eight, or at most nine, strokes of the bell. Walpole writes me at length from his cultivated London to say that my next work must absolutely—well, it must! However, there's this for satisfaction—that Conrad and myself have, for the season, the field. I ought to explain to you that I'm now almost entirely indebted to Henry James, particularly to a late absorbed study of *Maisie*——pages I haven't read for twenty years.

About *Steel* you tremenduously [*sic*] reassure me, especially since I am going to write it entirely over, and make it much much better; and again since it is better in ms. than it was in the *Post*. For example, where in the latter place Charlotte says, "You've no idea how I've dressed at you," in reality she tells Howard, "You've no idea how I've dressed and undressed at you." Here she really appears.

I'm going to take out all the direct war narrative, and Gage's orderly, and amplify his relationship with Charlotte; making his transition from cold remote dissatisfaction to a colder remoter satisfaction, changing the ruthlessness of war to social economic ruthlessness in a simpler balder way. It has all to be far more singular and beautiful and compelling.

—— Every page from now on, I have determined, must glow with a finer and choicer life and fire.

I have hopes—almost the certainty—that you'll find *San Cristobal* more than a grateful interlude; its physical appearance will be lovely—I shan't tell you a word of that—and, hardly more than forty thousand words, members of the vice squads will be required to pay three dollars for it. A story of twelve thousand words, called "Scarlet Ibis" is on the table, finished in long hand, while I'm waiting for a secretary—Wilson Follett read the proofs of *San Cristobal* for me—and I have determined to go back into the past, maybe 1830, for my next book—the one London demands!—and, I think, for all those subsequent.

I am delighted—in spite of your beautiful and delicate porcelains— that you are back at the novel: we both belong there, although the year which saw *Jurgen* and *Linda* was held to be too barren for the award of the yearly Pulitzer prize for American fiction! I saw Tarkington at Kennebunkport—charming man, charming house, charming wife. . . . He said that Riley was a great realist—Tarkington himself, I thought, being by Riley out of William Dean Howells. I wish he could have known us, yes, and we him, long and well. But more for N.B.T., my damned ego insists on that.

Affectionately

JOSEPH HERGESHEIMER

From Eugene Saxton

George H. Doran Company

New York, September 16, 1920

Dear Cabell:

A manuscript went through my hands the other day by Mrs. W. H. Allen dealing with some intimate pages in the life of Mark Twain. He was a great friend of the Allen family and stopped for quite a while at their place in Bermuda.

What caught my eye in the course of the manuscript was this paragraph about a volume of yours entitled *Chivalry*. It ran:

> "He told us that just before he came to us he had read *Chivalry* by James Branch Cabell. He gave the book to Helen, inscribing it: TO HELEN SCHUYLER ALLEN, THESE MASTERPIECES WITH THE LOVE OF S.S.C. The period of the book fascinated Mr. Clemens. He also thought it wonderfully well written. He said the mere lan-

guage was wonderfully beautiful, so strong and direct as to be almost Biblical in its beauty. 'The Story of the Housewife' was his
favorite."

This may be old stuff to you but on the chance that it was news, I
thought I would send it along to you.

Can't we have something from you for the *Bookman?*

Sincerely,
E[UGENE] SAXTON

We can assume Mr. Saxton's letter gave Cabell much pleasure, for he himself
had written on November 1, 1911, to Albert Bigelow Paine, executor and biog-
rapher of Mark Twain: "That which you tell me of Mr. Clemens has awakened
—and I don't care who knows it—a defiant joy. As far back as I can remember I
have loved him, as one among innumerable millions. For twenty years—to be
exact—I have revered and understood that Mark Twain was only incidentally
a maker of jokes."

Dumbarton, September 22, 1920

Dear Joe:

The Cords of Vanity, in its revised form, has gone forward to you. I
do not think you have seen it in the earlier version: either way, you
may take it as my *Lay Anthony,* and must judge it tenderly, misprints
and all.

I begin to look for your two books, and even to hope, aspiringly, that
my own *Figures of Earth* may eventually be completed. Holt and Galantière came through last week, separately, and several million other
things have conspired to hold me back from finishing off the manuscript, but it looks as though October would see it done. We cannot
all write as you do, completing all at one long sitting.

For example, you are not summoned from your writing, as I am now,
to mark the linen for a step-daughter who is going off to school.

Yours faithfully,
JAMES BRANCH CABELL

From H. L. Mencken

Baltimore—September 22 [1920]

Dear Cabell:

My best thanks for *The Cords of Vanity*. It is a sound book, and I am going to read it again.

It was in my mind to send you a small flagon of Spanish red wine by Holt. Two fears dissuaded me:

(a) The fear that Prohibition officers would grab it at the Virginia frontier.

(b) The fear, amounting to certain knowledge, that he would hog it on the way, and then report it grabbed by prohibition officers.

I am over hay-fever, but still show senile debility.

Sincerely yours,

H. L. MENCKEN

From Sinclair Lewis

c/o Harcourt, 1 West 47th, October 1, 1920

[No salutation]

Elevated trains—young Jewish females announcing with silk stockings legs not really worth the proclamation—ill-cooked meals costing sums dismaying to a poor young novelist—a few people who almost make up for part of the quite inhuman discomfort and sense of security—me in New York, obviously, and to make it all serene and splendid, busily trying to write an inferior story to counteract the considerable poverty resultant from a year of work on *Main Street*—a luxury more costly than buying a Rolls-Royce but fortunately not entailing the purchase of quite so much gas after the initial expenditure. The great work appears in a week or so, and a copy goes to you.

Meantime we try to decide where we shall go for a winter of work, and of waiting to go to Europe. We want to go now, but both poverty and the conditions there—lack of fuel in England and France, disorder and possible plague in Italy—forbid, particularly as we think of taking infant and staying for a year.

Cords of Vanity and your letter have come, to my gratification, and *Cords* is to be read with extraordinary attention when I get out of this revolving door—this revolving door attended by a concierge in gold lace and no undergarments.

A cordial letter from Joe Hergesheimer apropos of the double dedication of *Main Street*.

Tommy Smith, editor of the *Century*, says that Mencken asserts that if McBride really fights the *Jurgen* case through, he will win it. Why in hell isn't he doing it?

Chaotically—
SINCLAIR LEWIS

From Burton Rascoe

Seminole, Okla.,
October 5, 1920

Dear Cabell

It was thoughtful of you to send me the Bookfellows' edition of the *Judging of Jurgen*. [A skit written by Cabell telling of Jurgen before a court of Tumble-bugs.] My gratitude is no less for the fact that I had scraped together enough pennies to make a dollar and was on the point of becoming a Bookfellow in order to get the item. I should have been sorry to be without it, especially since I have the original newspaper clipping and *Jurgen and the Censor*. [A bound copy of the letter of protest circulated for signatures, together with many of the individual letters of protest sent to the publishers.] My dollars, though, are disintegrating and disappearing through a conscientious acquisition of the first (magazine) editions of a certain prosperous pseudo-litterateur. I, who never before bought fiction magazines, now after every trip to town lug home an armload of *Adventures, Centuries,* and *McClure's,* having previously run my finger through the contents tables of a dozen more. If this Morgan of literature publishes in *Snappy Stories* or the *Unpopular Review,* the *Ellenikon Aster* or the *Nouvelle Revue Française,* the *Pagan* or the *Ladies' Home Journal* which do not reach the Seminole Drug Store counter, I hope he sends me a clipping. I wonder what he does with all his money. I have fancied that he has a typewriter set with diamonds and lapis lazuli, a private moving picture palace, and a trusted valet who insures him against herring and mutton. If the work of counting gold becomes onerous an erstwhile literary editor might learn the duties of financial secretary and apply for the job.

I was pleased and grateful too over the inscribed copy of the revised *Cords of Vanity,* a book which I have read leisurely and unremittingly and with the closest attention, delighting in it, being occasionally exasperated by its ellipses, and finding it not a revised edition at all but a new book entirely. I am glad that I possess both versions, for this is suave and smooth and reasoned and full of a mellow beauty whereas the former was sprightly and exuberant and spontaneous. I would still, though, put it sixth down in the list of your accomplishments, at all events so far as my preferences go. . . .

But these magazine stories are the things, curiously, (I say "curiously" because they are so many thousands of miles above the typical magazine story that it seems curious that any sensible magazine editor would buy them) that are making it more and more evident to me that you are the greatest prose artist living. "The Designs of Miramon," "The Hour of Freydis," "The Hair of Melicent" etc. are all wonderful, unique, powerful,—any of the superlatives one might wish to employ. They are, in a way, the very unhappiest sort of reading for me, because they are unsurpassable perfection in stories I should like to have written; and, of course, it is disaster for a writer to admit that some one else writes better than he. Still, if you continue to write my stories for me and do the job well enough I see no reason why I should not become an Oklahoma oil or stock man and read.

When I got *Jurgen and the Censor* I was alternately angry and despondent for two days. The exhibit is pitiable, and from its nakedness I can see no hope for this country. . . . As I wrote Clark, I can have no intellectual respect for any of the persons who signed the second, conditional list, for, whoever signed it, is guilty of mental dishonesty, cowardice and hypocrisy. One is either for or against the censorship, and for one to make a reservation that he "has not read the book and therefore cannot commit himself on that," is idiotic. From such a reservation we are to suppose that, had they read the book and not liked it, they would be for the censorship exercised by the S.S.V. Whereas an honest man would sign without hesitation upon the presentation of a petition of disinterested persons (on the theory that any case flagrant enough to arouse a protest on the part of writing men merited his interest) and, even had he read the book and thoroughly disapproved of it, he would have signed it with no more hesitation—for the simple reason that he is against the suppression of literary expression and the free exchange of ideas. That is why I can respect the firm refusal of Brander Matthews to sign the petition (as an old guard conservative, more Victorian than the Victorians): and cannot respect the attitude of . . . the rest.

The whole booklet, indeed, is depressing, for the letters (excepting Hergesheimer's) of all of us Americans are shoddy and impotent beside the letters of men like Colum, Ervine, Walpole, and Prince Troubetskoy. I, for one, would be rather ashamed for the booklet to stray overseas.

"What a provincial, barbarian race they are!" cannot but be the deepened impression of Europeans.

We had planned to go to New York in September; but so pleasant had been our summer that, instead, we took a place on my father's farm, bought a piano (for we had left our piano in our Chicago apartment which we rented furnished) and now plan to stay here all winter. I have gained nearly twenty pounds in weight, the health of the family is excellent, and I shall have leisure to continue the writing I have begun. The expense is slight. After a nervous, constrained city existence the bucolic life is a rest and a pleasure. And a year in the country should not only prove profitable in a writing way, but put me in shape for any emergencies thereafter.

By the way, have you read Arlington Robinson's *Lancelot?* It is the first long narrative poem I have read in a good while, and I read it without effort. I wish you would write me your opinion of it.

Have you in your library a good volume on the Greek writers of the ultimate decadence? I mean upon that Musaeus, whom J. A. Symonds lauds so extravagantly, Straton, Meleager, Heliodorus, Longus, Lucian, and Apuleius? I have Browne, and Symonds, and Whibley. And I have the Greek Anthology (two editions), the Loeb texts and translations, and the Bohn translations. I am working on an interesting paper which I want you to see before I send it anywhere.

I am sending you a copy of *Maupin,* edited by the very capable hands of Burton Rascoe.

Yours,

BURTON RASCOE

Jurgen and the Censor, which Rascoe found depressing, on the other hand prompted Benjamin De Casseres to write later in *Judge:* "In a hundred years from now the time we live in may be called 'The Era of Suppression,' just as we have an era called 'The Era of Good Feeling' and 'The Times of Old Hickory.'

"The Evil Eye of the New Witchcraft is especially gimletted on books, as of yore, eld and whilom. Wasn't it Victor Hugo who said the alphabet makes books, books create ideas and ideas are powder trains that lead to the rathskeller under a throne—or words to that effect?

"There is (or was) *Jurgen,* the greatest piece of fantastic literature yet produced by an American. We ought to take our hats off to ourselves before our mirrors that we live in the same land with the man who wrote this great satire, one James Branch Cabell. Instead, the flatfoots of the New Witchcraft have expunged it from the bookstalls. It treats—lightly enough—of something we are all interested in—sex. While the Broadway brothel shows and pig-pen 'comedies' are running wide open! Well, you can't account for the lack of taste.

"Here is the report of the Emergency Committee Organized to Protest Against the Suppression of *Jurgen.* It is a protest signed by all the great writers of the English-speaking world. There are a preface by Mr. Cabell that is a superb piece of irony and a letter from Mr. Sumner which means just what it says—and it says nothing.

"The suppression of *Jurgen* may be the seed of something. Stick around!"

From Joseph Hergesheimer

West Chester, October 12, 1920

Dear James:

I have now three things for which, directly and indirectly, you must be thanked: *Tumble-buggery, Jurgen and the Censor,* and *The Cords of Vanity.* Of these the latter is infinitely the more important. I haven't read it yet, the reason for which will soon emerge; and the other two I found the cause of profound melancholy. I have read nothing serious for the reason that, at last, I am caught in the machinery of moving pictures. Or at least I am implicated to this extent—that there is a possibility of Griffith doing from one to three on my own artistic terms. The money involved is at once gratifying and unimportant. This has taken me often and most distastefully to New York and to the Griffith Studios at Mamaroneck, and cut sharply into my ordinary routine: my ordinary routine is now two-fold—a thirty thousand word story called "The Bright Shawl" and the complete rewriting of *Steel:* I propose, perhaps, to eliminate both Sophie and Moreland, bring Howard back from the wars unmarried and involve him more fundamentally with Charlotte. I should like to add a married couple with the man in the uneasy forties destroyed, as if by a glimpse of Diana, by Charlotte's charm. But this I must discuss with you and when the moving picture situation is simplified into either understanding or nothingness, I'll come to Richmond. This should see me there in about ten days or two weeks.

Faithfully,

JOSEPH HERGESHEIMER

Dumbarton, October 16, 1920

Dear Joe:

Herewith I devote a line to the superfluous, in saying it will be a delight to see you in Richmond. I wish I could offer to put you up. But we have not had a servant in the house since last spring, there is no dark face upon the horizon even now, and you would not be comfortable. I must manage, though, to "entertain" in your honor.

At first glance, your ideas as to the re-modeling of *Steel*—I mean, the last batch of ideas: the first were excellent,—seem almost entirely wrong, and out of the question. I shall, though, consult my "limited edition" of the book with these in mind, and be better up in the matter when you come. I, however, shall probably be babbling of my *Figures of Earth,* which I am being allowed to play with until November, so you should come with at least a faint apprehension of conducting your visit in dumb show.

I am two-thirds through *Main Street.* I incline to believe that Lewis has really and deeply honored us. . . .

Yours faithfully,

JAMES BRANCH CABELL

Dumbarton, October 18, 1920

My dear Lewis:

It is abominable that I can foresee no chance of communicating my profound and high enthusiasm about *Main Street* but by thumping at typewriter keys, but do you take my word for it that such enthusiasm exists. You have done an eminently solid and fine thing, you have gone miles beyond the Lewis of yesterday.

I finished the book last night, at the third sitting—beginning with dubiety as I saw how, or rather that, your admirable first plan had been altered. (I apologize for that doubting now: the final form is the better.) But I ended with nothing save admiration. I mildly regret that you did not permit Carol to be seduced by Eric, and somehow feel that Bea has been badly treated in being denied the career you formerly planned for her. You have made all the necessary points, however, with Vida—more, probably, for nothing could be better than Chapter XXI. . . .

. . . Your people are emphatically all there. You have followed, even if you forgot, my advice of not tendering any panacea. In fine, you harrow, and delight—for instance, if you wish to cultivate insufferable self-conceit you have only to re-read that long bedroom talk in Chapter XIV—— But I shall not pick out the plums for you who inserted them. It is much simpler and more sensible simply to cry bravo!

I am very proud that this book should have my name upon the dedication page. I am also proud, in that I have been foretelling to everybody how good it was going to be, to have my repute as prophet thus prodigally bolstered. I do hope that the public recognizes at least a tenth of

the charm and merit of the book, and so transfers the author at once
from Main to Easy Street. And for the rest, I am, as always, but now much
more than ever,

Yours very gratefully and admiringly,
JAMES BRANCH CABELL

From Sinclair Lewis

1639 Nineteenth Street, N. W.
Washington, D. C.
October 21, 1920

Dear James:

I'm very proud of your letter—very glad that you find the book worthy
of the names on the dedication page.

After six weeks in the murkiness of New York, and a desire to go
abroad frustrated by a state of pennilessness after the long siege of writing the book, behold us just come here, for six months at least, and again
becoming human, (now that the elevated is out of our ears) able to sit
quietly, and even to conceive reading—particularly a book called *Cords
of Vanity*, the first chapters of which, unlocked in New York, threw a
golden net over us—

Afmo.

SINCLAIR LEWIS

I, too, wanted Eric to seduce Carol, but she would none of it—for all
her aspirations to rebellion she was timorous; she was bound; she would
never have endured it.

From H. L. Mencken

Baltimore, October 29 [1920]

Dear Cabell:

. . . The Lewis book, between ourselves, amazed me mightily. I always
had a notion that Lewis was a talker—that he planned good books but
always wrote bad ones. But *Main Street* is full of genuinely distinguished stuff. The specimens of everday American in the dialogue, in
the extracts from the town paper, in the sermon of the Methodist dervish
and in the speech of the boomer are all superb. I agree with you that

the girl should have yielded up her person, but I incline to think that the lawyer should have flounced her, rather than the Swede. The episode would have given a final touch of irony to the book. As you say, nothing would have happened. But even as it stands, the story is extraordinarily good. I suspect that you preached it into Lewis.

Walpole şeems to have a curious distaste for *The Gods and Mr. Perrin.* I wonder why. It seems to me that his later stuff is not to be compared to it. We are printing one of his early sketches, by the way, in the December *Smart Set.* Nathan unearthed it from an old file of the *Saturday Review,* and we bought the American rights.

Thanks for the booklet. When you come to Baltimore at last to drink and be merry you must autograph it for me; also the *Jurgen* Protest book. The whole *Jurgen* episode has been of enormous value to you. I await *Figures of Earth* with eagerness.

For some reason or other I can't write. A lot of work is on the stocks, but I waste day after day.

Sincerely yours,

H. L. MENCKEN

Dumbarton, November 8, 1920

Dear Holt:

Yesterday I sent you a signed contract for *Figures of Earth.* . . . You will notice I am retaining the copyright on this book, just as a general precaution against I know not what: have, by the way, the copyrights been taken out on the new *Cords* and *Domnei?* Also I amended the author's guarantee, for several reasons, one of the most obvious being that as it stands it is idiotic: you reserve the right to pass on the book, and still ask me to guarantee it contains nothing immoral! I note that in the Harper contract the corresponding clause is more sensible, in that it covers only "injurious and libelous matter." Besides, I can no longer endorse my own notions of morality, nor, for that matter, yours—— Have you no changes to suggest in the *Figures?* I had looked for at least a modest handful. At all events, I would like your notion on the dedication scheme.[3] My idea was that I wanted to acknowledge my debt to each of the six, and it is not possible to give them a book apiece. To the other side, it looks a little skimpy, it even looks conceited to esteem a fraction of one of my books as worth dedicating, as a quite appreciable something. What do you think? . . .

---

[3] *Figures of Earth* was dedicated to Sinclair Lewis, Wilson Follett, Louis Untermeyer, Henry L. Mencken, Hugh Walpole, and Joseph Hergesheimer.

I have had of late a vast deal of good reading matter, as in *Main Street* (previously recommended to you) and Mencken's new *Prejudices,* which is, I believe, a really great book in its first 150 pages. Perhaps my interest flagged after he had ceased mentioning me, but I am sure the first part of this book is as good stuff as you find anywhere. . . . My friend [John] Gunther writes me, from Chicago, that—I quote—"Mr. Robert Herrick in his annual course on contemporary literature at the University of Chicago, devoted more time to you than to any other American novelist. He even went so far as to have me read the *Bookman* article to his class" &c. All this to me is Greek, but you, who are familiar with Chicago, may comprehend. . . .

I sent you an advertisement of the Miller & Rhoads book fair, which really passed off splendidly. Miss Duzan, and incidentally Mrs. Cabell, is profoundly enraged with you for having none of my books in. Luckily I had some *Domneis,* a few *Cords,* and a stray volume or two of my other works, which I let Miss Duzan have for my afternoon. I must proudly record that I autographed and sold out every Cabell book in the house, so that dozens were turned away lamenting. I too was lamenting that I had not brought in all the *Domneis* I had at Dumbarton, and also that you had not got in a stock of my books, for we could easily, I think, have sold 50 more books if only we had had them. What happened? Anyhow, I relished letting Miller & Rhoads repurchase at $2 and as a favor, the volumes I had at odd times bought from them at .35 and .25.

Yours faithfully,
JAMES BRANCH CABELL

From Sinclair Lewis

Washington, November 15 [1920]

Dear James:

In beautifully tranquil evenings I have been reading, have now just finished, *Cords of Vanity,* & *Domnei,* for whose coming I have not yet thanked you. They are extraordinarily beautiful—& true—— Despite the beauty of Joe's decorations—despite his sharp, startling perception of shadows, deep browns, & clean kid gloves, I rather think that you alone in this country are giving us "perfected speech"—& doubtless we have not yet even begun, we dullards, to have the wit to recognize & revere it.

You have been so completely honest in expressing Townsend! I wonder only if it isn't because he has had so much of Charteris & coats-of-arms

& lovely ladies of Lichfield that he finds it so hard to be convinced about himself? I wish he could have a year—well, a month of Gopher Prairie. You know that I wish this not because, like all decent & reasonable persons, I regard the 100% Americanism & God's-countriness of G.P. as desirable, but for quite the opposite reason. I'd like Townsend to stop, for a moment, his absorption with golden ladies, & discover how many other things there are to damn. Jurgen damned them—& so did Perion—they put sword to all the world, not just to the Aunt Marias of Lichfield—the Lichfield that least of all the world could value Townsend.

But this is tangential babble & the real (not genuine) matter is the serenity I have found in these two books—& my debt to you for them.

As ever
SINCLAIR LEWIS

Dumbarton, November 15, 1920

Dear Rascoe:

The *Maupin* is a beautiful book with a delightful preface. . . . The preface, of course, does but substantiate my contention that many of your *Tribune* articles would figure advantageously in a book. . . . The Mencken pamphlet I delighted in, more deeply, I suspect, than you joyed in the Cabell pamphlet—— I wonder too if you saw the article about me by your protégé Gunther as it figures in the current *Bookman?* To me it is an ingenious and rather effective dovetailing of you and Mencken and Follett, with an at times disastrous soldering of Gunther, but upon the whole very, very good. There is to be an astonishingly competent chapter about me in the Moffat Yard *Short Story Writers,* by Blanche Colton Williams. I have read it in proof, and was candidly astounded, the more so in view of the author's paramount responsibility for the O. Henry Memorial collection of short stories, since that to me was an even more flagrant exhibition of perverted taste than the O'Brien volume.

You see no hope for this country in literary matters, but I am rapidly falling into the optimism of senility. Therefore I call to your attention Lewis's *Main Street,* which is as near what I had hoped it would be as could, in a world wherein my own books are never that, be endured. A fine, honest and satisfying piece of work, I take it to be, the more readily of course for that my name is on the dedication page. Even so, I think you will agree with me it is a nearly perfect example of that particular "method"—which "method" is peculiarly abhorrent to me for personal use, to be sure, but that does not prevent my admiring the bringing out of its best features by others—— Then Mencken's second

volume of *Prejudices* I would unhesitatingly call great, at all events in
the first 154 pages. One or two of the papers thereafter would be no
overwhelming loss if omitted, and tend to sketchiness. But the opening
consideration of "The National Letters" is, I think, absolutely the best
treatment of this topic by anybody anywhere—— Here again, I am probably beguiled into an unwontedly charitable frame of mind by being
called a scarlet dragonfly, but even so—! Yes, I protest the book is magnificent.

So there are at least two books to brighten your outlook. Hergesheimer's book about Cuba also looks promising, but I have not yet
read it, being now swamped in books. I have just finished Walpole's
Captives, which troubles me by being just a well elevated plateau, where
I would much rather find a mountain or two. By the way, do you know
his very earliest books, particularly *Mr. Perrin?* I sometimes wonder if
Walpole is not obstinately traveling away from the natural bent of his
talent—— Anyhow, he is English. Here, Holt has lighted on a really
promising young fellow, in a Robert Nathan. Also, I hear—not from the
natural source, I grieve to say—that a really notable novel is now being
written in Seminole, Oklahoma. Why, then, despair of the literary outlook. . . .

You speak in your last letter of a paper which sounds very interesting
indeed. But as to my knowing aught of the Greek writers of the ultimate
decadence, I can but recall to you, not for the first time, that I am a quite
uneducated person of entirely Jurgenic erudition. I can invent you an
excellent book about these writers if you like, and at a pinch quote
it, but that is all.

I almost regret you have been bothering with my writings in *McClure's
et als.* for these are but bits of the complete *Figures of Earth,* which will
be out in February, Holt promises upon oath, so that I dare say we may
really look for it some time next year. It is, I really think, a good book—
not at all cosmic, as I remember foretelling to you a long while back,
but vital, and with very lovely bits of gymnastic writing, which upon
Untermeyer's suggestion, I shall henceforward describe as contrapuntal
prose—— However, you can best judge the book when it appears. To
Holt it was a hideous and pathetic disappointment, because nothing I
could say to him in advance could prevent his looking to find in this book
an attempt to re-write *Jurgen,* and when he found no shadow of such
attempt he grieved, as will, I know, a many others—— Then in the
autumn we reissue the revised *Line of Love* and *Chivalry,* and I am
hoping you will do me a preface for the latter. Mentally I have assigned
the *Line* to Mencken, who has kindly proffered a preface to any book
I select, because I think that is the book he would handle best. But if

you prefer that, or would rather wait until next year (1922) for *Gallantry,* or would do no preface at all, pray state your preference. I do not offer you *The Eagle's Shadow,* which evidently I must reserve for my own prefacing, under the title probably of *Vingt Ans Après.* Any of my literary friends, even you, would handle the book too ferociously.

Let me hear about this. You got, I hope, the *Domnei,* and properly admired the beautiful send-off which Hergesheimer gave it. I hope too you will write Holt some feeling and fervent observations as to the unexampled vileness with which the new *Cords* was printed. I still think that a good book, but the "method" was well-nigh fatal. In revising I found there was absolutely no way in which really to convey anybody's character except Townsend's. You see, he misunderstands almost everyone all through, and I am bound to give only his impressions—which results continually in an impasse. Even so, by hook and crook I managed a little to realize the women, as best I could.

Yours faithfully,

JAMES BRANCH CABELL

From Burton Rascoe

Seminole, Okla.
November 20, 1920

Dear Cabell:

I shall, with delight, write a preface in my very best manner to any book you suggest. In fact, I have deemed it something of a right that I should be asked to do so, and I have been a little grieved that no such suggestion has been forthcoming. It has made me feel so painfully isolated, and I have been viewing the cotton fields with unwonted intimate concern, wondering wistfully whether therein were not fitter employment for my "very capable hands." You see, I read the Hergesheimer preface with its shimmering adjectival opulence and its beautiful attribution to Plato of ideas that Plato never remotely had, and I read Follett's delightful divagation around the theme of possessing an unique original version of a book now given to the public. And I have timidly inquired of myself whether I could sustain these heights——But I shall try my best.

I have not yet seen *Main Street,* but from all the tidings I have had of it, a very great pleasure is in store for me. Lewis has the stuff in him and he needed only to be deflected from his fancy that it were "better to please humble Minnesota farmers than a handful of literary posers." They tell me, too, that Floyd Dell's *Moon-Calf* is a good piece of work, despite the letter I have today from F. Scott Fitzgerald denouncing it a shade too fervently to be disinterest[ed]ly as "a wretched thing, without a hint of glamour, utterly undistinguished." (From what I have been able to gather the themes of *Moon-Calf* and of *This Side of Paradise* are parallel, Dell's being only, as Fitzgerald puts it, without glamour.)

Mencken is to send me his second *Prejudices*. I have not yet read it. "The National Letters" is a revision, is it not, of the article which appeared in the *Yale Review?* A very fine, meaty essay, which I hope he has pruned of its defacing vulgarities and extravagances—— While we are on the subject of Mencken, can you help me in resounding this only idea of his which has ever stumped me? Wherein does his oft-repeated *code of honor,* as he explains it, differ essentially from the fundamentals of Christian ethic? I have studied his enunciation of it very closely and I can find no amazing disparity between his code and the code he so vehemently decries. One should expect in it some definite iconoclasm, some radical precept, some diverting variation. But, no, it becomes, as he states it, merely a code whereby a man of honor will not make sentimental overtures to a friend's wife or sister in that friend's absence and whereby a man violates his sacred honor if he shows up ten minutes late at an appointment.

I am acquainted with Walpole's *Green Mirror,* but not with *Mr. Perrin,* and, of course, I have not seen his *Captives.* Holt has told me nothing about Robert Nathan and his new book; this is, I suppose, the same man who wrote the rather enthusiastically noticed book about Andover or Exeter and Harvard last year [*Peter Kindred*]. I dipped into it, found the style tedious, and turned it over to a reviewer. At the same time I was highly pleased with another book in kind, *This Side of Paradise,* which reminded me in some respects of the earlier *Cords of Vanity.* Fitzgerald is, I think, worth keeping an eye on; he is only 24 or 25 and his first book, as well as some of his stories in the *Smart Set* are very well done.

The printing of *Cords* is, as you say, abominable. The book looks like a Home Library reprint from very damaged plates; but Guy's troubles appear to be too depressing already for me to increase them by strictures on a situation which, doubtless, he would help if he could. You are wrong, though, about his being disappointed in *Figures of Earth.* He tells me he has read it four times and that it is "heart-breakingly beautiful." And my reading of the fragments confirms that judgment. Here is an ineffable beauty, and the magic of your touch transcends anything I know of in literature.

I do not get the *Bookman,* and, naturally, I missed Gunther's article. But I read it in manuscript some months ago and found it very well done, indeed. There were one or two glaring impertinences, as I remem-

ber it, but I am glad he got it published, and, above all, I am glad of his
courage in choosing that as his term paper to be submitted to J. W. Linn
and Percy Boynton. Do you know where he may be reached? I should like
to write him a note.

My essay on Decadence was suggested to me by re-reading after twelve
years Pater's *Marius the Epicurean,* a book which I once honored, I believe, above all others and concerning which I lately found myself wondering if it might not be translated into English by a competent proof-
reader and issued in the series I am editing. Here buried beneath a slough
of colons and semicolons, dashes and half-stops is much meat and many
intimations of beauty. And Pater perceived rather better than he stated
the spectacle of the rich flowering of the decadence, the importance to the
sensitive reader of such a writer as Apuleius, that Cabell of the period——
My paper, in its final form, will in reality be concerned with the phe-
nomena of contemporary civilization, and therein you will figure rather
extensively.

Meanwhile I toil in anguish over a book which writhes out a sentence
at a time under the constrictions of an ideal of perfection. The *"prélude
d'un oratorio achevé dans le silence"* at all events it may be—— And the
accouchement threatens to be stayed or aborted by the necessity of earn-
ing cheese and milk for Hazel and the children. Spring probably will see
me seeking a job in New York. Write me candidly whether you actually
think it worth while to make the *Tribune* articles into a book. I read
certain of them over every four months or so and seem to think they
would not be so bad, and to them I could add some stuff I have lately
concocted. But there is a superfluity of mediocre books and I am not sure
that this may not add to that superfluity—no more, I choose to think,
than much of Mencken's work, Squire's, Holliday's and I know not how
many others. But write me truly. The trouble is that since no one seems
to have perceived what I fondly imagine are the special excellences (with
the difficulties involved) of my various prefaces and articles which I especially liked, they may, after all, not exist.

Yours ever,
BURTON RASCOE

Dumbarton, November 20, 1920

Dear Joe:

This is but a note of my indebtedness to you for a very beautiful book.
Knopf here, in passing, has prodigally contributed his quota, of more
than Oriental splendor.

For yourself, I believe you have made a book which is unique. I certainly do not know of anything at all like it. You have rendered the love-affair between Havana and yourself very, as Mencken would say, caressingly, and have admirably depicted the two participants. . . .

I thank you, of course, for the kind mention of *Jurgen*. And I wonder how *Steel* fares, and *The Bright Shawl?* and where I am to look for "Scarlet Ibis?" when for "The Meeker Ritual?" when for the booklet about you? and what, in general, you are doing apart from moving picture superintendence?

I have no prospect as yet of being screened, but Clark, as I believe you know, has made a comedy of *The Rivet,* which is now scheduled, they tell me, for production next autumn, so that I too shall invade the stage. [The play was never produced.] *Figures of Earth* at last is in the printer's hands, and a part of it is dedicated to you. Some day I hope to proffer you an entire book. But, you see, in the *Jurgen* mess I have been so generously befriended by some five or six persons (*quorum magna pars fuisti*) that any dedication to any one of them would, to my mind, involve an implied slight to the others. So I have disposed of the trouble by dedicating the divisions of the book to individuals. It is perhaps a queer extension of my theories of Economy, carried too far to involve any great compliment to the dedicatees. But it is the fair solution, to my thinking, and at all events I have awarded you the most beautiful portion, for the sufficing reason that I think you will appreciate it.

In re those fractional dedications, I wonder if you comprehend just how good this *Main Street* really is? I have gone back to the volume after the first complete reading, to dip into it, taking chapters at random, and have been astounded by the rich satisfyingness of the texture throughout.

Yours faithfully,

JAMES BRANCH CABELL

From Joseph Hergesheimer

West Chester, November 23, 1920

Dear James,

The devil of it is that, not going to Richmond immediately on the inspiration, I have been again involved and caught. This annoys me excessively, since I am tired and very low, and could think of nothing more desirable than such a party as we would have. Thank you for dedicating anything in *Figures of Earth* to me; I am most impatient to get at it. About *Main Street*—it is a very courageous and fine undertaking;

and I understand it is selling much better than you and myself put together. For its success I am honestly and wholly glad. With messages to Mrs. Cabell and affection for yourself,

JOSEPH HERGESHEIMER

From Sinclair Lewis

Washington, December 2, 1920

Dear James:

I am vastly pleased—I am more flattered than I dare reveal to you—by my inclusion among the dedicatees of *Figures of Earth*. Only *should* you have my name first when Barrett Clark & Guy Holt have done such stout service to *Jurgen?* Please—I sha'n't at all mind if you retire me to the rear, since my service to *Jurgen* was very meager—consisted mostly in one letter to *Jurgen & the Censor*, which letter, as I now re-read it, is notably ill-written & overuses the word "high." But do as you will, & believe that I shall be more than content.

A charming & quite voluntary letter from Galsworthy about *Main Street* has come & of course much pleases me.

I am writing—trying to write—for the *Post*, but all the while planning another not-to-be-serialized novel at least as ambitious as *Main Street*. I shall be too poor to begin it until some time next year.

May one send Christmas Greetings early as well as shop early? What a joyous Xmas it will be in Belgium, Ireland, Haiti, Korea, Mesopotamia, & all the other brave-little-nations which have been liberated & self-determined by the forces of light & democracy!

Afmo.

SINCLAIR LEWIS

From Deems Taylor

159½ East 83rd Street
New York
December 24, 1920

Dear Mr. Cabell:

I spent a week in Richmond not long ago, and almost went out to see you; but I lost courage, and didn't. I wish now that I had. Not that I had anything in particular to say, except that I felt vaguely that I must somehow manage to thank you for having written *Jurgen*.

Even now, with plenty of time to say it in, I find it almost impossible to put into words what *Jurgen* means to me. It is a great and beautiful book; and the saddest book I ever read. Even now I can't read it without tears, though there are whole chapters that I know almost by heart.

The censorship I don't mind so much; but I do resent the book's defenders. You can't defend it, any more than you can defend *Les Contes Drolatiques*, and *Leaves of Grass* and *Tono Bungay* and *Through the Looking-Glass*.

What is there to say, except, "if you don't like it, God help you"? It's a far greater book than the Balzac, by the way, for the *Contes* lack beauty, and they lack wisdom.

I suppose it's the masculine verity of the book that makes it so poignant. We have each of us his Dorothy and his Chloris; and we do teach mathematics the night before we go to Hell—in our heads at any rate.

There isn't anything to say, after all, is there? I was afraid there wouldn't be. Well, let me say "thanks" again, and go back to your book. Forgive this letter, if it seems intrusive.

Sincerely,
DEEMS TAYLOR

Dumbarton, December 29, 1920

Dear Mr. Taylor:

It is a real pity you did not let me know when you were in Richmond, but, to the other side, you have written me such a delightful letter that I incline to forgive you.

Delightful though it be, however, it is such heady reading that I must temperately wave aside all the fine things you say about *Jurgen*, save only your statement that it seems foolish and futile to "defend" the book. There we are heartily at one. So many friendly persons have written this, that and the other laudation which troubled me more vitally than any onslaught. And there is no possible reply wherein I might combine civility with sincerity. But I, at least, do not "defend."

I do, though very cordially enjoy such—in my partial eyes—intelligent appreciation as yours, and give therefor due thanks. You have been most kind, and I am grateful.

Yours faithfully,
JAMES BRANCH CABELL

From Mrs. F. Scott Fitzgerald

38 West 59th St.
New York [date?]

This is me—so don't you think I rate this
one colossal favor?   [*a snapshot of Mrs. Fitzgerald enclosed*]

Dear Mr. Cabell—

For a very young and pretty girl, won't you *please* do an amazing favor? I simply have got to have a copy of *Jergen,* [*sic*] and don't you know where I can find one? Its absence is spoiling a perfectly good Cabelliana—and anyway, I want to give it to Mr. F. Scott Fitzgerald for a Christmas present.

I've grown weary and musty with ransacking book-stores—and I've also tried to steal Mr. George Nathan's copy: under pretense of intoxication—all I got was a Toledo blade fencing foil. Judging from the kick he's raised about it, I presume it's priceless so if you know anybody who doesn't think your pen is mightier than Nathan's foil please tell the goofer that I'd like to exchange—

This is very important, so please write me awfully quick—PLEASE

Presumptiously,
MRS. F. SCOTT FITZGERALD

Isn't *The Rivet in Grand-Father's Neck* the best of all? It makes me so sorry for myself—and you and all the rest—

I'm going to grow this thin   if you don't know where I can—

Dumbarton, December 20, 1920

Dear Mrs. Fitzgerald:

It is not possible to resist an appeal so picturesque, and a picture so appealing, so I am seeing that a *Jurgen* goes forward to you with my compliments. If it can in any way add to the Christmas of the author of *This Side of Paradise,* who is, between ourselves, the most interesting young man that I know of anywhere, I shall be deeply pleased.

No, I cannot truthfully say that I think *The Rivet* the best of my books, but in the same breath I must remind you that I am the worst possible judge.

Yours faithfully,

JAMES BRANCH CABELL

From F. Scott Fitzgerald

38 W. 59th St.
New York City
Christmas 1920

Dear Mr. Cabell:

It was the surprise of my life when Zelda handed me an autographed first edition of *Jurgen* this morning. You can imagine how I felt when I tell you I haven't even been able to borrow it. Whenever I go to George Nathan's I finger it covetously but I could never get farther than the door with it. People have a way of regarding it as infinitely precious. I want to see anyone try to borrow mine!

I once fingered a copy of it in a New Orleans bookstore one year ago and I've been cursing myself ever since for not buying it. I'd seen Menken's [*sic*] review but was very broke at the time. I read a wretched article on you in the *Bookman* by someone last month. Menken and water. It must amuse you to have whole book review sections devoted to you after years of comparative neglect. Do you remember Samuel Butler's

> *Oh critics, cultured critics*
> *Who will praise me after I am dead*
> *Who will see in me either more or less*
> > *than I intended*
> *How I should have hated you*

—only you have the ironic good fortune of being alive.

I have just finished an extraordinary novel called *The Beautiful Lady without Mercy* which shows touches of your influence, much of Menken

& not a little of Frank Norris. Up to now such diverse writers as you, Menken, Drieser [*sic*], and so forth have been held together more or less by the common enemy, philistia, but now that good books are, for the moment, selling almost as well as bad ones I wish Menken would take a crack at such bogus masterpieces as *Mooncalf,* a book without glamor, without ideas, with nothing except a timorously uninteresting report of a shoddy and uninteresting life. I'm all for *Salt, The Titan* and *Main Street.* At *Poor White* I grow weary—but at *Mooncalf*—My God!

The only two books I've ever known my wife to weep over were *Ethan Frome* and *The Rivet in Grandfather's Neck.* I appreciated your qualified tribute to Tarkington in *Beyond Life.* I agree with it perfectly.

I hope we'll meet in the near future & meanwhile I'm looking forward to *Jurgen* as I have never looked forward to a book before.

Most admiringly and gratefully

F. SCOTT FITZGERALD

Dumbarton, December 29, 1920

Dear Mr. Fitzgerald:

When I received your wife's delightful letter telling of her need of a copy of *Jurgen* against your Christmasing, I was doubly glad of my forethought in having laid in a small "private stock" between the time of the book's suppression and the time the news reached the Richmond dealers. It enabled me, you see, to express tangibly the interest and hopes awakened by *This Side of Paradise*—— Oh, yes, I admired a great deal and quite cordially, but I optimistically insist upon regarding the book as prophecy forerunning even finer books.

I hope—though probably that is asking too much of human nature at your time of life—that you will not be very much spoiled by the book's, quite merited, success. I can imagine no book which, in view of all the circumstances, could be more interesting reading than your second novel will be perforce. For you seem to have all the gifts——

But I have no desire to preach from my coign upon the gloomier side of forty. It is but that my interest is very lively.

No, I have read neither *Moon-Calf* nor *Poor White.* Floyd Dell, in particular, has been at such pains to express his abhorrence of all my ideas that his book hardly allures me with any prospect of congenial reading. But of my half of the dedication page in *Main Street* I am justly vain. That now is an excellent title, but I believe *The Beautiful Lady without Mercy* is better. . . . I shall look forward to it, as well as to at least a glimpse of you when I am next in New York.

Yours faithfully,

JAMES BRANCH CABELL

From F. Scott Fitzgerald

New York City, December 30, 1920

Dear Mr. Cabell:

Can't resist telling you that I have finished *Jurgen* & think on the whole that it's a finer novel than *The Revolt of the Angels*—tho at present I'm inclined to rank your work as a whole below both Conrad & Anatole France. However you're a much younger man.

My wife doesn't agree—you are by all odds her favorite novelist.

Please don't bother to answer this but if you'd let us know next time you're in N. Y. we'd both be very flattered.

Yours

F. SCOTT FITZGERALD

[Postscript]

" . . . Then Joe * read us . . . his poem at which both David * . . . and I laughed appreciatively

> " *I'm sending a cable to Cabell*
> *To cavil at callow callants*
> *Who callously carped at the rabble*
> *For caring for amours gallantes*
>
> *For each pious burg out in Bergen*
> *(a county in Jersey) has spoke*
> *For jerking the joy out of* Jurgen
> *And judging* The Genius *a joke!"*
> (From Margot Asquith's Diary, Vol 9. P. 273)

* King Joseph the III of Patagonia
* David Balfour, M.D., D.D.

Dumbarton, December 31, 1920

Dear Holt:

A letter . . . informs me that you have received the manuscript of *The Taboo in Literature,* upon which I await your opinion. The title of the volume, if published, by the way, should obviously be *Indecency*—— I hope you have had also the doll which Ballard sent Cicely in your care. Her picture came in perfect shape, and he treasures it, explaining to all that it is "Guy Holt's little girl." It is a most taking photograph, I think myself. . . .

I began this letter last year, and was interrupted by Miss Frances New-man coming a-calling. She has, I think, real gifts, and, certainly, a proper sense of literary values. She has begun a novel for which you might advantageously look out. . . .

> Yours faithfully,
> JAMES BRANCH CABELL

Dumbarton, January 26, 1921

Dear Holt:

Herewith a suggestion for the catalogue. It is tentatively rendered, to do with as you like. Of course there are at least two other available "lines": to play up the continuous reliance of mankind upon appearances, as the book's theme: or to assert that the main question raised is, What is success? Grandfather Death ultimately suggests that success consists of being yourself, but there is no reason to suppose that Death is the best possible judge of life—— It is distressing to be the author of books so multiplicative in significance that you cannot swear they mean anything in particular. . . .

Don't bother about *The Weekly Review,* as I managed to acquire a copy. It is rather a good paper, by the way, though Boynton seems ungraciously unwilling to concede what he does concede.

Taboo, do you know, with luck ought to irritate almost as many persons as, I think, the *Cords* will render peevish?

> Yours faithfully,
> JAMES BRANCH CABELL

From F. Scott Fitzgerald

New York City, Feb 23 [1921]

Dear Mr. Cabell:

I was delighted to get *Figures of Earth.* I had just ordered it at the book-store, which copy I shall present to some unworthy charity.

I am cancelling all engagements to read it today and tomorrow.

Having finished my second novel née *The beautiful lady without mercy* but now known as *The Beautiful and Damned* I am about to sell my soul . . . and go to the coast to write one moving picture. . . . "Well," as Codman says in his touching monograph on Anchovies "there is no movie in *Jurgen.* It just won't fillum."

—Incidentally given free reign wouldn't it be a treat to see it unexpurgated in the movies.

That was an idiotic review of *The Cords of Vanity* by Richard LeGallienne—which reminds me I must order France's new book *The Fall of the Angels*. It must be a sequel to *The Revolt of the Angels*.

Still hoping that we may meet soon.

Faithfully
F. SCOTT FITZGERALD

From Sinclair Lewis

Cincinnati, February 26, 1921

Dear James:

Gracie writes me from Washington that *Figures of Earth* has come. I am excited, eager to get it. . . . I am, mildly & tentatively lecturing—6 talks in Chicago in which I picked on 'em & told 'em to read Cabell, Hergesheimer, Sherwood Anderson, Wharton.

John Farrar, that charming boy now running *Bookman*, telegraphed asking me to review *Figures of Earth* but I refused because, as it is in part dedicated to me, it would savor of log-rolling &, really, do no good.— And this bullying lecturing does quite as much gospeling as any review.— I come back to civilization about April 1st. I hope to God we see you before we go off to Europe.— Good letters from Walpole & Galsworthy re *Main Street*. I don't know, but I don't *think Main Street* is as bad as the sale (over 100,000) would indicate. It is, I think, an accidental sale—& very comfortable to the plans for novelizing of an ex-hack named

SINCLAIR LEWIS

From Deems Taylor

New York, March 10, 1921

Dear Mr. Cabell:

Having finished *Figures of Earth* and *Beyond Life,* and being about to begin *Domnei,* I was seized with an ill-advised impulse to write you baldly and flatly what I managed not to say when I first wrote you about *Jurgen*—i.e. that I think you are a great man—saving perhaps Conrad, the greatest writer of English now living.

But then I realized that that wouldn't do at all. Such things aren't said. It would be unrestrained and gushy, and would annoy and embarrass you horribly; for there would be nothing to say in reply except "thanks," which wouldn't be modest, or "nonsense," which wouldn't be polite.

So I didn't, after all, and decided to content myself with pointing out merely that the way you cleave to my notions does you great credit, and that *Figures of Earth* will not be popular.

Also, privately, I wish to God that if you're going to use anagrams you'd label them. Having solved Vel-Tyno and Ageus and Sesphra, I am slowly going insane trying to turn all the names in both books into something else.

It's curious how your stuff seems to infuriate reviewers. If they'd sneer, now— But they roar so, and beat upon the table. Do you ever come up north?

Sincerely,

DEEMS TAYLOR

I think I'll do a *Jurgen* suite. [He did.]

Dumbarton, March 12, 1921

Dear Mr. Taylor:

Nothing could please me more than to have you do a *Jurgen* suite. And Heaven be my witness, but the three gods of the Philistines are my sole essays in anagram. So you need search no further.

And—well, just as you point out, there is really nothing I can gracefully reply to the things you say about my books in general: but that vocal disability does not interfere with the existence of considerable internal gratitude and contentment. Reptiles are not more silent and lively.

Which naturally suggests reviewers. It is a curious and to me inexplicable fact that of all my books reviewers react to *The Cords of Vanity* most vigorously and viciously: what any of the others evokes is in comparison a lullaby.

Yours faithfully,

JAMES BRANCH CABELL

Dumbarton, March 15, 1921

My dear Mr. [Carl] Van Doren:

This is a rather inadequate word of thanks for the review of *Figures of Earth*. In view of the uniformly pleasant things therein said of my work, I hesitate to think it a really thorough-going review. Even so, I recognize with delight that you have taken the book in the spirit in which I meant it to be taken; and that at least one reviewer has recognized in Manuel the deflected artist. It is also a rare boon to find a criticism of this book not entirely devoted to *Jurgen*.

For all which reasons, and for yet other reasons, I am properly grateful.

Yours faithfully,

JAMES BRANCH CABELL

From H. L. Mencken

The Smart Set

March 26, 1921

Dear Cabell:

The other day I sprained my wrist, and am now magnificently bandaged and quite unable to write by hand. These few lines are dictated,—a difficult matter for me. I used to dream of employing fifteen or twenty stenographers and writing two or three books a week, but I found by experiment that it was much easier to do one book a year by hand. . . .

These are hard days for magazine editors. The printers are getting all of the money. Whatever is left over goes to lawyers employed to defend literature against the postoffice. Last week we were actually hauled up on a charge of printing an obscene cover. I was quite unaware of the obscenity until the postoffice experts pointed it out.

Figures of Earth tickled me materially less than *Jurgen*, but what are the odds? Obviously every reader must like one or two of any given man's books more than he likes others. My firm belief that *The Genius* is not as good a book as *The Titan* is a subject on which Dreiser and I exchange hostilities at least once a month. The old boy regards my heresy as a proof of intrinsic depravity. I believe that some of the best writing you have ever done is in it. . . .

Sincerely yours,

H. L. MENCKEN

Dumbarton, March 18, 1921

My dear Miss Newman:

. . . When it comes to enjoyment . . . all else pales before the delight I got from your review of *Figures of Earth*—— Your guess as to the ten gods was 90% correct: for "Apollo?" read "Agni," and all is right, even to the tenth Mexican blend, in which having selected one god, I could not resist the feathers that grew upon the leg of the other. As to the animated image, you may be interested by the enclosed letter, printed along with portions of the present fourth book, when these portions figured as a short story in the last October number of *Romance.* Viewed in some of his aspects, I suspect that Sesphra is the book called *Jurgen,* but then allegories interpret themselves so variously once they are set agoing. As for my women— Well!, and, besides, there is Bettie Hamlyn in *The Cords* to confront you with, and, I believe, one or two others in the different short stories, and, anyhow, I have nowhere disputed the existence of clever women. Sixthly and lastly, I must protest that not an illusion was lost between *Jurgen* and the *Figures.*

And, really to conclude, I am unspeakably appreciative of that review. . . . I only hope I can retaliate before long by reviewing your novel.

Yours faithfully,
JAMES BRANCH CABELL

From Hugh Walpole

London, Regents Park, N.W.1
March 28, 1921

My dear James

I was just beginning to curse you for having forgotten me altogether when that charming reminder came in the shape of *Figures of Earth* with part of it all to myself. I can tell you I was a proud man and a pleased one.

And all your many sins of omission were forgiven you.

I have now read the work and am immensely pleased with parts of it. Some things are too hard for me and I propose very shortly to read it all again. It has to my mind the supreme advantage of improving all the time just as *Jurgen* did. It has great beauty and pathos but I do wish that sometimes you were a little clearer. I have many questions to ask you of it that I can't ask until we meet— When is that to be? When are you coming here and why not this year? There are many people who will like to meet you. Do come soon. I miss you surprisingly at all sorts of odd times.

I am very well and very happy. *The Captives* has sold here better than any of my others and for next Autumn I have a novel that is a great deal more romantic than it would have been if I had never met you. I never think of *America* with longing but of certain individuals with poignant wish for their company,—you, Joe, and one other above all the rest. I have a rather charming little anthology from my books coming out next month and Conrad has written a preface to it. Dear James why are we not seeing more of one another?

Life is short and is skipping past. We ought to be together. Now answer this, you lazy devil, and believe me always

Your loving friend
HUGH

Dumbarton, March 31, 1921

My dear Nathan:

Herewith, in accordance with Mencken's instructions, you have *The Jewel Merchants*.

I am heartily glad you can use it. The thing seemed to offer a chance of expressing my real gratitude to both of you, and I could not be sure that the polite speeches accompanying its return were not just polite speeches: so all ends well. In the autumn McBride is to make a booklet of this drama, for Little Theatre use, and with that end in mind, I have made the "final text" centre upon a duel with daggers, as more practicable for amateurs. Hence the sable erasures.

I have ordered, but have not yet seen, your new book, wherein, they tell me, you give [me] some free advertising, for which I may have to thank you later. But you are always more than generous to

Yours faithfully,
JAMES BRANCH CABELL

From Sinclair Lewis

Washington, D. C.
Cosmos Club
[date?]

Dear James:

I have at last been able (It sounds vilely ambiguous—able!) to read *Figures of Earth*—with delight in its grave & insinuating humor, with admiration for its swift summaries of the futilities of life—as the War to End War—with joy in its beauty always. I think you grow ever. It is so universal a comedy— Why the devil do you, once, use "to suspicion,"

that colloquial brother of "dark-complected?" Perhaps to give Stuart
Sherman a chance to bark? . . .

As ever,

SINCLAIR LEWIS

From Donald Ogden Stewart

Yale Club—New York
April 1, 1921

My dear Mr. Cabell—

For some reason, known only to Frank Crowninshield and God—respective (and respectable) editors of *Vanity Fair* and the earth—your delightful letter of March fifteenth has just reached me, and truly, messire,
I know not how to tell you of the pleasure and pride with which it was
received. Needless to say, it has been forwarded to the old homestead
where it will be deposited, with fitting honors, amid great grandmother's
wedding dress and grandfather's shoulder straps.

And if you will be so kind as to make the following note on your calendar—say about the middle of October—"write to Don Stewart"—for, you
see, I have but lately decided to leave the profitable profession of stocks
and bonds for the unprofitable indulgence in the task of writing more
or less perfectly of more or less beautiful happenings. And *"nescis quid
certe est"*—hence my request for another word from you in October, for
I imagine that my enthusiasm and money will last just about that long—
and *"Hylax in limine latrat"*—so that while a certain amount of flagging
courage can undoubtedly be revived at that time by a re-reading of *Beyond Life et al.,* yet nothing would be quite so thankfully received as
another gracious epistle from Dumbarton Grange.

Meanwhile, I meditate more mischief—in the pages of the *Bookman*—to
wit, a series of parodies based on the idea of an Outline of American
History,—addenda, you see, to H. G. Wells' work, describing American
history as it would be outlined by American novelists.

The introduction—"America's Glorious Heritage and History"—is to
be by William Lyon Phelps with appreciative and illuminating footnotes
by H. L. Mencken. Oh, droll will it perhaps be to see what I can have
Henry do to the brave enthusiasms of the Professor Doctor of Yale.

Then, with due reverence, I shall once more try my hand at your style
—in dealing with the Christopher Columbus legend. The possibilities are,
I believe, good—I hope the work fulfills them. The main motif, of course,

would be the disappointment of Columbus when he really discovered America—for as you have so often said, it is the dream of America and not the actuality, which is eternal. "Now," said Columbus, "Is it not somewhat droll that I who have dreamed a beautiful dream must henceforth live only as a discoverer of a rather stupid country?" Of course, there is also an opportunity for a few anti-Sumnerite subtleties regarding the curious manner in which Columbus demonstrated to Queen Isabel that the earth is not entirely flat.

The inspiring explanatory footnotes to your theme are to be written by Dr. Frank Crane.

Sinclair Lewis is to describe the "Landing of the Pilgrims" and Scott Fitzgerald the "Courtship of Miles Standish."

Other contributors will be Harold Bell Wright, Ring Lardner, Joseph Hergesheimer, Opal Whiteley,—Dreiser, and others. If the thing is well done, I hope it to be an American *Christmas Garland*—but at any rate I shall have much fun in the doing. The first of the series is to appear in the June *Bookman,* I believe.

Some day, or rather, some night—I hope to sit late with you over a flagon of Strong Drink where I may clear my mind of many thoughts— as for instance your opinion of this *Main Street* which seems to epitomize all you hold most abhorrent. I am as wonderful of your enthusiasm (which is, perhaps, as you say "gratitude") for Sinclair Lewis as I am of Anatole France's socialism, and furthermore I might at that time convey to you more of an idea of the pleasure which your letter gave me than is perhaps apparent in this, my well-meant acknowledgment.

Sincerely,

DONALD OGDEN STEWART

From Joseph Hergesheimer

West Chester, April 24, 1921

Dear James

There's just no dam' use trying—I can't begin to get back to Richmond now. My mother, who is very old, after being pretty much the same for ten years, is dying, and—aside from feeling—there are many small sub-legal difficulties, with relation to her income. The moving picture people are, at long last, moving, and seem to think that they own me, collar and necktie; proofs are here—but no secretary—for reading; I have novels to rewrite, articles to compose, correspondence—this I detest—to keep up, and God knows what else. In addition to the happiness of being with you, you did me good—but I suppose I wouldn't have any feeling for you if you didn't—and in return, and anyhow, we are anxious more than ever to have Mrs. Cabell and you at Dower House. Don't stick an eyebrow up and compose yourself into a mask of contrary determination. James, you ought to, you should, you must, do this. It is a part of your responsibility as, hereafter, we sit writing about each other. The place has never been lovelier, the birds more musical, the drinks better. We have the rooms, the servants, the strawberries, the asparagus, heaped cold with French dressing, and the spirit to welcome and entertain you both. You can stay in a chair on the porch, drive through the greenest hills on earth, talk or not—— In other words we're fond of you and should like to have you in our house. You'll find me, for about six weeks, doing nothing extended or new, nothing to interrupt, and I must shoot Mrs. Cabell around in my little Fiat. I have been decidedly low in my mind since my return—one of the premonitory fogs of old age has enveloped me. . . .

Affectionately

JOSEPH HERGESHEIMER

Dumbarton, April 27, 1921

My dear Miss Newman:

The bulletin arrived nearly a week ago, but I am still blushing—— And my little boy was so delighted at receiving his copy that he has since seized on all pamphlets that have come in the mail, on the ground that "Newman sent it to him." I must tell you that you made a marked impression on him the day of your visit, and that he talks of you constantly as, for reasons best known to him, "Newman."

It would have been tactless of you, though, to get the bulletin to me on my birthday—— It happened that Hergesheimer was then here, and your sister had lunch with us that day, and we talked much of you, rather than of depressing mathematics. I now wonder if Hergesheimer has written you. He had previously enjoyed your Library Notes, and said he meant to send you a line—but since leaving here, has been, I gather, neck-deep in moving picture enterprises—— It was a delight to have him hereabouts for some two weeks, and I plan to visit him in return toward the end of May——

And, no, don't send me the new Beerbohm. It is to be out in an American edition this spring, and then I shall procure a copy to read and keep. You see, I shall want the book, but if I read it beforehand I may be troubled to justify the extravagance of buying it. My conscience about book-buying is tender now that every new book acquired means the ousting of some older one to make room for it on the shelves.

Besides, I have just finished *They Went* [by Norman Douglas] (with vast enjoyment), and am confronted with the manifest duty of reading *Moon-Calf, The Age of Innocence, The Narrow House* [by Evelyn Scott], and three or four other "new" books, now that I have owned them for weeks and weeks——

Yours faithfully,

JAMES BRANCH CABELL

Dumbarton, April 29, 1921

Dear Hal:

Time and again I have intended to write you, but you know how it is yourself. Meanwhile I become a bit overawed by your prominence—who am I to molest you in your glory? But I derive a deal of satisfaction from having foretold what a good thing *Main Street* was going to be so long before it was published. And I really rejoice in your success with no more jealousy and envy than is human—— And you appear, too, to be winning almost equal laurels at the lecturing—wherein, by the by, you are proving the best advertising agent I ever had, and considerably increasing my bill at the press-clipping bureau.

The things you commend, though—well, I reserve judgment. For some weeks now I have been the owner of a *Moon-Calf* and a *Narrow House,* which I intend some day to read on your say-so, but the general look of the first does not allure, whereas the second's aspect rather actively repels. If time and an actual reading prove me wrong I will apologize. And some day too I shall read all these short stories that have of late pullulated in every other magazine on the bookstands, "by Sinclair Lewis."

What, I wonder, will you do next in the book line? To follow up *Main Street* with anything is an appalling undertaking. I must certainly try to see you, any how, before you leave this country. At present, we rather vaguely plan to go to New York by motor some time after the middle of May and, the plan being carried out, I shall hope to see you when we pass through Washington. But of that you shall hear more later.

Hergesheimer was recently in these parts, for some two weeks, and I enjoyed it, though he keeps me dizzy by working on three novels simultaneously. The notion flabbergasts me. But Joe at bottom is a dear—there are a great many upper strata, I grant you,—and if only he preserves the old don't-give-a-damnativeness may build permanently. That observation, to be sure, applies to most of us—— Anyhow, I have done a monograph on him which the *Bookfellows* are to bring out this spring, and therein my general notions about him will be made accessible to all.

About *Jurgen* I don't know. I do not—now—especially object to being suppressed, but am inclined, rather, to regard the fact as a buttressing of my general philosophy. That *Jurgen* was suppressed proves a great deal that *Jurgen* merely hints. As for your flings against the verb "to suspicion," a fig for them!

Yours faithfully,
JAMES BRANCH CABELL

In April, Maurice Hewlett (whom Cabell had idolized in his youth) attacked Cabell violently in the New York *Post*, under guise of a review of *Figures of Earth*. Many of Cabell's authorities and gods were from the first pure invention, and this he was the first to admit, faced with the accusation by a knowledgeable person. But unfortunately for Mr. Hewlett, he happened to light on various matters about which he was evidently ignorant, but which were well known in folklore and fable. Mr. Cabell replied in a letter to the *Literary Review* which listed the various deficiencies in Mr. Hewlett's knowledge, and added: "Plain honesty compels me thus publicly and modestly to admit that when Mr. Hewlett accredits to me the invention of (and blame for) all these, and other, matters he honors me beyond my due. And while these deficiencies in Mr. Hewlett's knowledge are interesting, why, after all, should his naive confession of them be printed as a review of a book written by somebody who does happen to know about these things?"

Dumbarton, May 4, 1921

Dear Holt:

. . . The Hewlett letter would probably not have appeared but for the fact that last Saturday was Walburga's Eve, when almost anything &c. And it was not prompted by lumbago but rather by the profound psychological truth that nobody is interested in a defense, whereas everyone delights in an attack. So that the best defense of my maligned *Figures* was, in the circumstances, to call attention to the fact that Hewlett is nowadays a jackass who writes balderdash. But I am still overcome by, and properly grateful for, his astounding slips. By the way, Untermeyer wrote (unknown to me) a hot reply, which Canby refused to print, on the ground that my letter was sufficient and "savage." So you see!

I was much pleased by Mrs. Becker's cream-puff, and guessed who supplied the filling. Mrs. Cabell bears out the preposterous statement that I never laugh,—to my amazement. I shall begin practising a half-hour every morning before the looking-glass. . . .

Yours faithfully,
JAMES BRANCH CABELL

From Sinclair Lewis

May 16, 1921

Dear James:

And after all—I *shall* miss you, damn it. We sail for England tomorrow, instead of June 15. A million good fortunes to you.

As ever,

SINCLAIR LEWIS

On the day Cabell received Lewis's note, he wrote to Hergesheimer that possibly they could stop by West Chester the end of May and ended with a wail: "I am cross this morning. There is in the field opposite a cow who does not have to play the Jack pudding with her brain, and I envy her. Besides, put to the test, she could write quite as well as I just now."

The visit with Hergesheimer took place amid much acclaim and many comings and goings. Pictures were made for rotogravure sections of the papers, and altogether Cabell was quite exhausted before he reached home again. In a letter to Holt he protested "I find the responsibilities of being, belonging to and owning so-and-so perfectly damnable: what I need is a desert island with a good mail service."

From H. L. Mencken

Baltimore, June 8, 1921

Dear Cabell:

. . . Schönemann was formerly an instructor at Harvard; he has now gone home and is professing at Kiel. Some time ago he printed an article about me in one of the German reviews. His wife is a well-known German poet. But Scheffauer is far more likely than any of them to handle your books effectively. He actually has a publisher on the hook, and a good one. Maybe I overestimate the effect of translations, but my feeling is that they do a lot of good. The native critical boobery is powerfully impressed by them. I believe that a success for *Jurgen* on the Continent would enable you to grab the Comstocks by the tail at home. I suggest that you write to Scheffauer, telling him of the forthcoming English edition, and then see that he gets an early copy of it. Don't break into your store of genuine firsts! I gave away four or five copies of *The American Language,* and now curse God, for it is selling for $25 or $30 a copy.

The Dunciad against Hewlett, Le Gallienne *et al.* was excellent stuff. Lay on! My head is on the block. But you'll never escape the clipping bureau. Every time some ass preaches your funeral sermon, the Cabellistas near and far will come to the bat again. The war is on forever.

I have begun a long treatise for the *Smart Set* on the present state of the fine arts in the South.

Sincerely yours,
H. L. MENCKEN

The man to do the French *Jurgen* is Leon Bazalgette. I believe that Walpole could reach him. He is now engaged on one of the Dreiser books —I forget which one.

Dumbarton, June 25, 1921

Dear Dr. Van Doren:

You have given me much pleasure, and roused a really lively gratitude, by your sixth article in the "Contemporary American Novelist" series. It seems to me all actually sympathetic, in the preciser meaning of that adjective, and you have missed hardly one pet notion of mine, with the sole exception of a whim which, since it has never yet been put into printed words, you could not well have "got"—— Be patient, and some day that prodigious secret will be revealed.

That "tawdry and baroque," though. Well, I knit brows over that, in the main, because I have just completed rather thorough revisions of *Chivalry* and *The Line of Love;* and while, heaven knows, I found enough to blush at the while I extirpated it, yours were not the exact epithets with which I justified my re-tailoring of these volumes—— Anyhow, it may be that we objected to the same deformities, whatever we called them: and anyhow, my faith is cordial that you may find the revised versions describably as improvements.

I hope this series is to be a book before too long? I have thus far felt so in touch with you that I plan to unearth and re-read the Wharton article, which, I begin to suspect, I must have read obtusely. To that alone was my response not instant and vivid—— The Hergesheimer paper, I must tell you, I liked almost as much as he did, and encyclopaedias could not say more. And even so, I vaingloriously think that you continue to improve.

Yours faithfully,
JAMES BRANCH CABELL

From H. L. Mencken

Baltimore, July 3, 1921

Dear Cabell:

I am glad you liked it. [His paper on the fine arts in the South.] It was cunningly designed to provoke both the *Reviewer* crowd [a literary review published in Richmond] and the *Double-Dealer* outfit [a literary review published in New Orleans] to atrocities against seemliness. Miss Clark [4] writes that Hergy advises her to avoid bellicosity and aim for charm. I fear that Joe is full of that automobile-polish gin. Back to Poe! His literary articles are models.

Van Doren's stuff seems to me to be very good. In the *Nation* for July 6th I have a review of his book on the earlier novelists. It is very well put together, and I'd have praised it more if it had not been for the danger of being accused of a brother act. He is a reformed professor, and headed straight for Hell.

By the direct help and intervention of the Blessed Saints, to whom be glory eternal, I have driven the last golden spike into *The American Language* [first revision]. All that remains is to correct the stenographer's singularly dirty copy, to read the galley and page proofs and to make two enormous indices—a trivial business after the book itself. No more philology, as God is my witness!

I shall stir up Holt in the matter of the proofs. When I last saw him, two weeks ago, he was intoxicated.

Sincerely yours,

H. L. MENCKEN

I didn't accuse you of lack of courage; I simply accused you of wasting your cannon on three damned foreigners. America forever! Think of Jack Dempsey! By the way, I saw him murder the Frog yesterday afternoon. It was a noble spectacle. All the hoors were present.

Dumbarton, July 5, 1921

Dear Joe:

You have, I see, been at it again—I allude to the pernicious practice of reading Henry James,—and so figure in *Vanity Fair* rather shamelessly reeking with the telltale aroma of what you have been up to. Otherwise, I liked the paper immensely, and if you really enjoy reading James I merely marvel without exhortation. But the "Feminine Nuisance" is quite a different couple of sandals. . . . I beflood it with an approval

4 Emily T. Clark was one of the editors of the *Reviewer*.

that seeps into every detail. It is a paper which I am frankly proud to be mentioned in, because it seems to me (in everything else, anyhow) so entirely right and just and adequate.

I hope I do not miss your *Saturday Evening Post* story, I have watched for it as best I might, but the *Post* is now sold here in such limited shipments that it is usually "all out." If the worst befalls, you will have to send me a copy.

We plan now to go to the Alum on the twenty-sixth of this month. It has only recently been settled that the place is to be "open." That means, there will be a half handful of impossible persons subsisting on farm fare and backbiting, in some perfectly finished mountains. It is not a collocation to which I could with a clear conscience invite you. But if your plans should permit you to come that way I would be delighted. In fine, I doubt if you would be able to stand the place, and I hope you will come to it. That is my honest stand.

Mencken has done a ghastlily truthful paper for the August *Smart Set,* in re the awakening of literary interest in the South, and therein deals at once tenderly and inflexibly with the *Reviewer.* It is an article which I hope to see do them good alike internally and with the public. It is really, I think—seduced, no doubt, by sundry personal compliments therein let drop,—a notable paper even for its author. And the maddening part is that the persons for and at whom it is designed will never see it. If only Mencken could acquire the *Southern Churchman,* and so reach the public that has the actual and dire need of him!

Anyhow, what are you doing toward any definite book? I am just sending off the book form of *The Jewel Merchants.* That will be a little book this autumn, along with the revised *Chivalry* and *Line of Love,* and my monograph upon Joseph Hergesheimer is due, I believe, in October: and then, next January *The Lineage of Lichfield* is to be yet another little book. So I have a variety of irons in the fire, and fret daily over the unconscionable slowness of the printers. There is so much, you see, to be out of the way before I can get down to a really new book.

As ever,

JAMES BRANCH CABELL

9

ACQUITTAL

Early in 1921, there had been launched in Richmond a small magazine called the *Reviewer*. Mencken in March, in reply to a suggestion by Cabell that he contribute something to the publication, wrote: "I'll be very glad to do something for the *Reviewer,* once I get the sand out of my eyes. It is the first Southern magazine ever to be *printed* decently. All the rest look as if they were done by country job-offices. But I am in the midst of such a mass of work that I begin to show mental symptoms. If you hear of me running amuck in the streets, don't be surprised. . . . I have asked the pastors of all the Baltimore churches to order prayers for me. If the Richmond clergy will join in the pious work, so much the better.— Some day I shall write a notice of the *Reviewer* for the *Sun.*"

After helping the young editors with both advice and articles, Cabell offered to edit three issues beginning with October; whereupon he wrote to various friends for contributions.

From Frances Newman

Atlanta, August 10, 1921

My dear Mr. Cabell

By a most distressing coincidence, your note was sent out from the library while I am languishing at home with a cold just in process of descending into a cough. And perhaps it is due to my enfeebled state that I can't seem to think of a subject on which I could be very acrimonious. . . .

But I am very anxious to write a paper on those writers who take life seriously and find it good—the Mesdames Porter, Charles Dickens, Robert Browning *et al.;* those who take it seriously and find it bad—Conrad and Hardy, of course, and some others; and those evolved beings who find that not quite all is right with the world. Of course, there are some others, but I should like to take yourself and Norman Douglas and Ana-

tole France as types of it and work out a little about the natural effect of
nationality on such a temperament. I should try not to let my support be
embarrassing to you, and I really think I might be fairly vicious about
the first two classes. Probably there is also a class who take it cheerfully
without finding it flawless—Jane Austen, for example—but who nevertheless think it good.

I gather that you have seen my strictures upon Mr. H[ergesheimer]'s
strictures, of which I am far from proud. But I still think that between
the ordinary man and the ordinary woman there is little choice, except
that the woman is always anxious to assume a culture though she have
it not and that this occasionally changes her from a Lord George Hell
into a Lord George Heaven. It is exactly between the exceptional man
and the exceptional woman that there is a gulf most mortifying to a
woman. If not an American woman could read, I think our novels would
be different, but probably no better, which I call the war camp libraries
to witness. . . .

I hope you saw the *Times* Supplement and the *New Statesman* on Mr.
Mencken—even I could have asked no more. And Mr. Murry in the *Athenaeum* on poor Mr. Walpole's novel was murderous—"Ouidesque."

Please let me know if this subject would distress you and if you want
an article for the October number. I hope your cold is routed.

Very sincerely yours

FRANCES NEWMAN

Dumbarton, September 27, 1921

Dear Holt:

First, let me relieve your auctorial suspense, and in my editorial capacity, assure you that I like "Coda" tremendously. It came too late for the
October issue of the *Reviewer,* so I am going to lead off with it in the
November number. . . . And for the excellent sonnet, too, my best thanks:
it shall adorn the December number, and gild my exit from editorship. . . .

[Robert] Nathan has kindly permitted me to use the verses as to man's
growing up in quietness, and a prose selection from the book [*Autumn*]
—— I am in despair about that book. It is crammed with beautiful things,
with page after page of music. But it does not hold together. It does not
draw you on connectedly, and you are annoyed by the sense that the man
is being satirical about you don't know what. In fine, it has interested me,
I have enjoyed and very cordially admired it, and I advise you to publish
something else by the same author. And I shall hold the MS. till I have
copied out the excerpts, and will then return it to you. He has genius,
you know—— And by the way, so has this Donn Byrne, about whose

Messer Marco Polo I cannot say more or less than that it is the only new book I have read in I don't know how long that I wish I had written just as it stands.

I hope your vacation has done you good. You seemed all in. Your spectacles seemed to be of ebony, so far as talk revealed your outlook, and I trust the vista now appears at worst only a dark gray. I tried and failed to write you at Woodstock, but the *Reviewer* has pre-empted all my time. I shall be heartily glad to get that December issue to press. But it is rather amusing, too——

Yours faithfully,
JAMES BRANCH CABELL

Dumbarton, September 28, 1921

My dear Carl Van Vechten:

For the while—you may or may not know—I am helping the *Reviewer* "make up" their numbers; and thus I have seen "An Old Daguerreotype," upon which you have, first of all, my warmest felicitations. It is very beautiful.

But the rub is, that it is just twice too long for the *Reviewer*. The obvious solution is to run it in two parts. The alternative, which I think preferable, is to run it as two articles, "The Tin Trunk" and "An Old Daguerreotype." Thus, the second article would begin at the bottom of page six, and is perfect as it stands. The first would then end with the pig coming squealing to the door to greet you—which, as it stands, is a little abrupt.

So can you not round it off with a sentence or two? It can be done easily and effectively, I suggest, by lifting the thought from page ten, "It gives one a curious sensation" through "made up of such stuff?" But that is only a suggestion.

I hope you can do this forthwith, in time for us to use the first paper in the November issue,—and am, in any event,

Yours faithfully,
JAMES BRANCH CABELL

From Carl Van Vechten

New York City, September 29, 1921

Mon chèr maître,

My principal sensation this morning is that I have received a letter from James Branch Cabell in which he refers to a paper of mine as "very beautiful." For the present I ask nothing more.

When Miss Clark wrote me that you were considering serializing this paper made up of memories and mists, I was, I admit, a bit terrified, but your suggestion of dichotomy has relieved me. It seems, indeed, to divide very neatly. By all means, end "The Tin Trunk" with the phrases from Page 10. . . . And, of course, omit these phrases from the subsequent paper—as it seems to read all right without them.

When, I wonder, am I to meet you? Joe has promised me this pleasure for years, and his easy, delightful talk of you has become an aggravation, since the promise has not been kept. Do you ever come to New York? And when you do, could you find time for a lunch or a dinner—or a goblet of sacramental wine?

sincerely,

CARL VAN VECHTEN

Dumbarton, October 5, 1921

Dear Miss Newman:

I saw Mr. Holt only the other day, and then for the first time heard of their decision as to your book, as well as of the misaddressed letter. He is really, let me say, quite honest in his admiration for the manuscript's— I quote—"damnable cleverness." But they all judged, very much as he wrote you, that the cleverness would worry the persons who would like the story, and the story not appeal to those who would appreciate the cleverness. So the book did not appear—just viewed cold-bloodedly—a promising business venture—— That is the McBride decision. But, not for a moment, ought you to regard them as infallible. I would, in your place, now send the book to Knopf, and thereafter—in the event of the worst befalling—to Harcourt. And remember that rejections mean less than nothing. I cite from personal history: *The Cream of the Jest* was rejected by fifteen publishers: *The Rivet* was returned without comment in a contest in which the prize was awarded to Miss Dalrymple's *Diane of the Green Van:* and I might extend the harrowing history even further.

So! it is good to know you will soon be in Richmond. My wife has talked of taking me on to New York about the seventeenth, in which event I will not be here when you are: but I do not think she will succeed, and even in that event we must manage to arrange for a chat in New York.

The *Reviewer* has probably reached you, and I trust you have pardoned the unavoidable cuts. We have had to set seven pages as the absolute limit, and, I believe, I amputated only the least essential parts. Please, though, send the paper for the November issue the moment this reaches you: we are to make up the contents on the tenth—that is, to ratify them in a full meeting, and then to allow me two days wherein to "edit" before we go to press—and I have reserved the space for you, with everything else actually in hand. So mail it now! . . . As to *Autumn*—it is in many places quite beautifully written. The man has real gifts, and I have persuaded him, too, to help out the *Reviewer*. I shall wait, anyhow, a month or two before reading *Erik Dorn* [by Ben Hecht].

Yours faithfully,

JAMES BRANCH CABELL

Some time before Cabell began the editing of the *Reviewer,* Ben Ray Redman had sent to the little magazine a paper called "Bülg the Forgotten." This purported to trace the origin of the story of *Jurgen* to a volume about medieval legend by Gottfried Johannes Bülg. It was of course a piece of fabrication throughout, but Cabell wished it published and put it in the November issue that he was editing along with the second installment of his own *Lineage of Lichfield*. In the December issue he states in a note to what he had always intended to be the last installment of his *Lineage* in the *Reviewer:* "In view of Mr. Redman's article entitled 'Bülg the Forgotten,' as published in the November issue of the *Reviewer,* it has appeared advisable to discontinue these genealogical papers. The reader will readily comprehend that, were there nothing else, the unique policy pursued by the editors of the *Reviewer,* of using one portion of the magazine to disparage the contents of the remainder, creates an impossible situation." He went on, however, to answer with the quoting of more numerous and more formidable authorities than Redman had used to buttress his argument. Cabell did not deny the existence of Bülg nor his debt to him; he merely said that he was fully as aware as Mr. Redman of his debt to this ancient authority. Many people were taken in by the controversy, including gentlemen of the legal profession, and it was obviously Redman's paper that Judge Nott had seen and was to refer to in his decision from the bench in the *Jurgen* case.

From Joseph Hergesheimer

West Chester, October 18, 1921

Dear James,

Again I've been away, and when I got back both the tall and the short copies of your paper were waiting for me. Someone, I can't remember who, told me that it was your impression I didn't like this when it appeared in the *Bookman:* but this was such nonsense I didn't even try to correct it. You well enough know how I feel about your continued appreciation. About *The Happy End* your view, of course, may very well be far clearer and more correct than mine. Any exact weighing of my short stories is, at present, impossible, except to this extent—they are honest. An aesthetic lack in them, to whatever extent it may exist, is a faithful reflection of the same thing in myself. I have never vulgarized my work, and my philosophy in the field of magazines is simply the recognition that out of a whole possible circle of life and experience but a small segment can there be treated. However, within this limitation still something remains adequate and important. I could go into this more fully with you were it not for the always present danger of a hinted excuse. So far as The American Institute goes, as I wrote Mencken, I have no objection, as a simple and immoral novelist, to such an innocent advertisement. I have never, I think, met any of its members except Tarkington; I never go to meetings, literary or other; and if they still care to subscribe to such an attitude toward the whole works they're welcome. There is a great deal of talk about my having arrived, standing in the giddy and dangerous forefront of public approbation; but unfortunately this is nonsensical. In 1920, for example, I wrote three short stories, and spent the rest of the time trying to perfect certain phases of my books. What fortunately floated me was the chance sale of a story to a moving picture corporation. During 1921 I have written five short stories, any one of which stood a better chance of being refused than accepted and spent three months completely re-writing *Cytherea;* for which, on the material side, I may get a small return in a year or so. In this time at least two-thirds of the public scribblers hardly lost an opportunity to have a knife in me, including an attack by practically the whole American press following the Bergen lecture at Yale. So far as I'm concerned I should gladly tell anyone what my books paid me, but that is not exclusively my concern. But the smallness of the sum, in comparison to the loudness of the suppositions gathered about it, would surprise and appall you. You mustn't feel that I am complaining about this, that I feel in any way injured. Indeed I am rather on the side of the public: why should they support a writer who distrusts practically everything connected with them; and more particularly for the reason that I have never missed an opportunity to say this. After I had spoken at the Boston Book Convention, where I was by no means drunk in the manner reported, those gentlemen cut what sale my books had eighty per cent for something like eight months. Well, here is a letter of various clues; I write to you without premeditation, and you must make out of it what you will. On the whole I'm quite happy about my position, happiest perhaps in my friends; in them I have actually arrived, in them and by them, and the rest can go where it likes. But every now and then when one of them refers to me as swaying on the verge of a golden pit, in view of my bank book, it does a little disturb me. My dear James, if you choose to regard me as an investment of your affection or integrity of opinion you need have no fear; I can promise you better things rather than worse.

Faithfully,
JOSEPH HERGESHEIMER

Dumbarton, October 24, 1921

Dear Holt:

. . . I can but conclude that I am to have nothing from Rascoe for the *Reviewer:* I am sorry for this, and in fact I had rather counted on you to see that he helped out with something—— Hergesheimer is much upset and aggrieved by the article about him: I think, unreasonably, and anyhow——! Well, I recognize that I am just as morbidly self-conceited as he, but I swear I hide it better. Van Doren writes me that he is going to review the paper in the *Nation.* . . . *The American Novel,* by the way, is marvelously good. Van Doren has the best sense of form, I mean in what he himself writes, of anybody now criticizing. His papers on the current novelists have been in this respect to me a joy and wonder. . . .

Yours faithfully,
JAMES BRANCH CABELL

From Joseph Hergesheimer

West Chester, October 28, 1921

Dear James,

All things are worse than mutable, but it is our present plan—Mencken's and mine—to come to Richmond about November twenty-fifth. We have been madly corresponding about this for a number of weeks, and the result seems at last to have emerged. I see nothing about me here but endless galley proofs: white from Alfred and yellow from the *Post*. The weather is beautiful—no better subject exists than the weather—golden like an orange and sweet like an orange from the Indian River. If you find this sentence too much like the Belgo-India school I'll change it to the simple phrase that every day it's possible to play golf.

Faithfully,

JOSEPH HERGESHEIMER

Dumbarton, November 2, 1921

Dear Joe:

It will be fine should you both come. I shall be turning out a debutante step-daughter at just that period, and you might help me to stand it.

The first of your "Tintypes" is excellent, and my sole complaint against it lies in the fact that you sent it in too late for the December issue, which is my last number. Expedition would hardly have helped, though, as Miss Clark had previously warned me that anything "he" sent in she meant to hold over for her own number. . . .

Yours faithfully,

JAMES BRANCH CABELL

Dumbarton, November 4, 1921

Dear Joe:

Your telegram has just been telephoned out to me. But of course do you and Mencken come just as you had planned. We are giving on the evening of the twenty fifth a dance, for the younger set, at the Woman's Club, and this I shall have, I suppose, to attend. But it would be to me a joy, and a very real comfort in tribulation, if both of you would come too. Invitations are duly going forward to both, and to all the Reviewers, and I shall reserve the library for the literary guests, so that we can withdraw utterly from the dancers when we so elect. It would be an addition to the party, I candidly confess, should you bring something on the hip, as by force of circumstances the affair will be Saharan.

So come. I really want you to. And all the remainder of that week-end is quite free.

Yours faithfully,

JAMES BRANCH CABELL

From Joseph Hergesheimer

West Chester, November 7, 1921

Dear James,

There was no question of my staying away because of a debutante dinner, but since Mencken had written contra dress clothes I wasn't sure that he would go on with the dance. However, a letter from Harry this morning still commits him to our plan. We shall therefore appear toward dinner Friday, the twenty-fifth. Anything that we should know we'll discover by a note from you waiting for us at the Jefferson. I am looking forward to this party with the greatest possible anticipation— you may rely upon us in the direction of that metaphorical hip.

Faithfully,

JOSEPH HERGESHEIMER

From Guy Holt

New York, November 4, 1921

Dear Cabell:

. . . I read and marveled at your review of *Marco Polo* in the *Nation*. Do you know that your sentences daily become more and more involved? I am becoming afraid that in your search for the perfect cadence you will begin to write your verb at the beginning of the sentence.

I haven't had a chance to read the Hergesheimer monograph yet. I have been out almost every night these last three weeks and so have read nothing which was not prescribed. . . .

"Coda," upon the whole, came out astonishingly well. I am not nearly so ashamed of it as I thought I should be and so far as the original of one of the characters is concerned not nearly so embarrassed. From the other two I have not yet heard. Well, it encourages me to believe that I can write dialogue at any rate. . . . I shall try to do some prose things for them, the Reviewers. I can write much better when I know there is no possibility of my getting any money for what I do.

Lane's New York office is vague as to the publication date of the English *Jurgen*. It is expected "at any time." There is some reason for the fear that the package containing our copies will never get through the customs but seizure is improbable.

Finally, I am delighted with Miss Newman. She is an amusing person and an amazing one who has thus far outtalked everyone in New York.

We have had three encounters at the first of which she confessed her love for you. Yesterday I saw her for a few moments and she informed me that she had met Mencken and had capitulated. You are forgotten. No less you are to be in her new novel which, I think, will be first rate. . . .

. . . More imposters are coming along with autographed Cabell books and so far as I can see your only protection is to refuse to inscribe books, except for people whom you know. One method of avoiding annoyance of this sort is to adopt the Hardy-Kipling custom of demanding that persons who wish your autograph should donate five or ten dollars to some charity which you select. . . .

Faithfully yours,
GUY HOLT

Toward the end of the fall Cabell asked in a business letter to Holt: "What, by the way, is the status of the *Jurgen* case? and what imports the nomination of this Garrard Glenn for the defence?" It was explained that Mr. Glenn was with Goodbody, Danforth & Glenn, the firm of lawyers who had been engaged to take over the defense deserted by Quinn.

From Joseph Hergesheimer

West Chester,
Monday, November 14, 1921

Dear James

Everything, as you now know, has been arranged. Mencken and I are reaching Richmond late Friday afternoon, going to Emily Clark for dinner, and then——on with the dance. I have great hopes of this party, it ought to be chaste, refined and elevating, noble in thought and deed. Burton Rascoe and his Hazel were here from Friday till Monday; she is quite nice and I like him as well as ever. What do you think of a paper called "Beauty in Women" for *McCall's?* Well, already I am passed the middle of it; I can't tell about it yet, except that it's hell to do.

Faithfully,
JOSEPH HERGESHEIMER

The gathering came off with great success, causing more pleasure to the *Reviewer* crowd probably than to the debutantes dancing in the ballroom. For the group in the library promised increased help to the little magazine, whose reward to contributors was "in fame not specie," as printed on its inside cover.

Dumbarton, December 3, 1921

Dear Dr. Van Doren:

Your paper in the current *Nation* came as the pleasantest of surprises, in every way. I had not looked to have the two revisions reviewed at all, and now feel mildly guilty for having sent them to you, in which action my motive was, really, a desire to let you see my efforts toward elimination of the baroque and tawdry. I omit, you see, the quotation marks.

Now, as to several grounds for gratitude. What you say about *The Jewel Merchants* is, of course, true, and, I believe, I concede as much in the Prologue. But I can assure you that the dialogue was very imposing indeed, before we gradually brought it to the plane of being speakable. And I have already made clear my reason for being enormously thankful for what you say about the Hergesheimer pamphlet, apart from the handsome things you say concerning my "writing" therein.

But the main point is—barring the fiendishness of your illustrative selections—your utter comprehension of what I was trying to do with the two revised books. Nothing could please me more, nothing could more reassure me as to the pains squandered on these resurrections, than the complete understanding, and, I think, sympathy, with which you and Mencken have already appraised the result. It makes one feel that all this profitless labor may not have been quite wasted, and that one's unthriftiness has palliations. But I do wish you would get rid of your earlier versions, and make no more of those uncomfortable textual comparisons. They set me to wriggling.

Even so, I am tremendously pleased and grateful, and as such subscribe myself

Yours faithfully,
JAMES BRANCH CABELL

From Joseph Hergesheimer

West Chester, December 16, 1921

Dear James

So much had piled up while I was away that it is only now I am reaching my personal affairs: in the first place I am thanking Mrs. Cabell and you for your hospitality; and in the second——but there are numbers of small things. The next, however, isn't small—too many of your books that I own aren't autographed. If I send them to you, properly prepared for return, will you do this? The *Domnei* you gave me was stolen with four other valuable books, so I am forced to include a fresh one; and I am so happy at owning two *Jurgens* that they are both going to you. . . . I have just completed four papers on women for Rascoe and *McCall's*. These, I believe, begin in February; and they were, in manner, conditioned by their audience; but for all that they are not contemptible. The paper on John Partins was read at the Academy of Music for the benefit of the Charlotte Cushman Club; and there were two thousand or more people present. It was taken absolutely seriously, superficially seriously, and the book stores and local literary editors have been a lot bothered by inquiries about Partins. The usual number of people were annoyed at me. Mencken has absorbed my liking for Richmond, and we promise ourselves another trip in the Spring. Why you are so firm in not coming to Dower House I can't gather. Indeed, you'd be happy here—old house, books, quiet, rum, admiration. Well, that's that! *Cytherea* will make her remote bow January third, and it is my hope that my friends will like her. I assure you that I paid—in coal and chops— for whatever excellence you may discover in her. Soon, now, I hope, I can retire into the uninterrupted composition of novels. I have less and less inclination to spread what water I have over broad and shallow places. . . .

Sincerely

JOSEPH HERGESHEIMER

"The Life and Works of John Partins," a paper on a nonexistent writer, also appeared in the *Reviewer* for January 1922. Perhaps it seemed a little derivative from *The Cream of the Jest,* in which the unwritten novels of so many fictional writers were listed. But it was delightful, and Mencken said some years afterward to one of the editors of that departed publication that they had published the only thing of Hergy's he had ever really wanted to print.

From Louis Untermeyer

[date?]

Dear Cabell—

It is amazing to observe what your few additions, amendments and substitutions have done to *The Line of Love.* All the Pylishness has gone and Manuel's progeny actually resemble their quondam creator. I reserve my first reading of *Chivalry* until this Christmas mail is answered & the last of the Yule log-rolling disposed of.

Heavens, the series of critical parodies of which I wrote you, is on Harcourt's list for late Spring. (About one third of it will appear in

Kreymborg's beautiful Roman *Broom*.) Your particular Nirvana contains a full-fashioned ballade—refrain & all—a proper triolet and three fourths of a kyrielle—all more or less disguised as conversational prose. I hope to bring proof of it to Richmond when I leave these parts in about a month. . . .

By the way, I hope to dedicate *Heavens* in this way:

> "Putting up his blunted lance and deserting,
> for all time, the ensanguined lists of
> Parody, the author dedicates these
> skirmishes in that field to
> JAMES BRANCH CABELL
> HENRY LOUIS MENCKEN
> CARL SANDBURG
> AMY LOWELL
> ET AL.
> with the comforting observance
> that to the victims belong
> the spoils."

May I?

Cordially,
LOUIS UNTERMEYER

Dumbarton, January 3, 1922

My dear Joe:

You need have no doubts about *Cytherea*. She strikes—oh, at least, thirteen or fourteen without any faltering. It ought, too—for really this is a merit of quite different order—to be your greatest commercial success, for it is pre-eminently what the jargon calls a readable book. I mean, it raises a question, and then goes forward without dalliance or byplay toward a solution. I am almost tempted to state that the story grips the reader.

It is, though, when you ascend to unblushing allegory in Savina's death at Cobra, that I lie upon the floor and stretch my legs and purr. I do not know of anything anywhere that impresses me as being more disgustingly beautiful. But in everything Savina and Fanny are conveyed as being all there—— It is a book, in short, wherein I find hundreds of things to applaud, and upon my conscience, no one thing with which I am yet prepared to pick fault. . . . You have done a wholly admirable thing in this book. I am very proud to know you. . . .

Yours faithfully,
JAMES BRANCH CABELL

From Joseph Hergesheimer

West Chester, January 5, 1922

Dear James,

Your letter, I will admit, was looked for with anxiety. Indeed, the night it arrived I had driven in to the post office to see if it might be there. My dear James, you know how happy I am about all this. Turning so flatly from magazines, from the easy magnificence of their returns, I must have three things at least: the support of a small handful of friends, something not entirely foreign to a degree of satisfaction in myself, and then a number of books sold. As I have told you I am not rich but extravagant. However, I think I am more or less safe now, certainly I shall continue to write as well and as completely independently as I am able, and there will be something for Dorothy at that lamentable finality which undoubtedly I shall meet first. Thank you. Now here is a widely different affair—on the seventeenth I am leaving on a journey which shall include literally everything in the United States, north and east and south and west. I have wanted to do this for a long while, to see the forests and mines and plains, the isolated villages in the northwest woods, the old adobe towns strung along the Pacific, the interior, and that long French trail strung from Quebec to New Orleans. Privately, Lorimer is sending me, and I am to write in a pattern entirely to my own liking and of my own choice. What I plan is a very strongly aristocratic attitude, without any sentimentality, and—like the dash of Angostura bitters in an old-fashioned whiskey cocktail—with such bitterness as I am pleased to shake into the whole. This, which I find irresistibly promising, is quite aside from any consideration of the magazines as such. Dorothy is going with me, we hope to be returning at the end of April, when we shall come up from New Orleans through Georgia to Richmond.

Faithfully,

JOSEPH HERGESHEIMER

From Louis Untermeyer

New York, January 10, 1922

Dear Cabell:

It is good hearing that you are to be in these mad parts sometime this month. Surely, this time there should be no bars to our long-deferred meeting. The evenings of the 24th and the 23rd (the fifteenth anniversary of my wife's marriage!) are taboo. But practically any other morning, afternoon or evening that you may name is free for intellectual, alcoholic or scandal-mongering stimulation.

Meanwhile, I am enclosing a fragment of the forthcoming *Heavens*. It is not, I realize, nearly as humorous, *per se,* as Stewart's but I have tried to do the thing from a somewhat different angle; endeavoring to capture, beneath the superficial verbal nuances of a tricky style, the inherent and pervasive Cabellian poetry. How far I have failed I leave to your charitable eye. But will you cry out at any particularly gross injustice? By that I mean will you not return this proof, correcting any phrase that may seem to you a false or malicious libel on your art. I promise to make the necessary changes before the volume gets to the page-proof stage. . . .

The English edition of *Jurgen* has finally come from The Bodley Head. It is, in many ways, a beautifully made volume. But it is an unevenly illustrated one. Some of Papé's drawings display a neat pen yoked to a nimble imagination; others show his pencil breaking down beneath the burden of your nimbler fantasy. He seems to me to be unhappy in the deeper moments, even his "straight" serious illustrations smack of the poster—the picture of Anaïtis might have been made for Mr. Anargyros's cigarettes. But, in spite of a few cheap inserts and tail-pieces, it is so far superior to what we have been offered as "gift-books" that I am grateful for it. . . .

Who *is* Frances Newman anyway?

Cordially,
LOUIS UNTERMEYER

In a letter from Paris about the English edition of *Jurgen,* Galantière says that he personally has great hope for the future of American writing. It is interesting to compare Galantière's letter with what Wilson Follett wrote Cabell about this time: "One encouraging thing seems to strike me: a change in the signs of the times. For some reason or other, a determined onslaught on Realism draws ten times as much response, from all over the lot, as it did a few years ago (I wonder if you and others are not finding it so, too). And I rather think there is, in our published fiction, a slow shifting of the center of gravity— a shifting in the right direction. I am not young enough to be sanguine about anything; what I think I see is probably only a minor eddy, not indicative of the main current; but at any rate a certain kind of good book—e.g. *Messer Marco Polo*—has a better chance to-day than it did at this time last decade, and when you challenge the reporter novelists to-day you find that a good many persons unexpectedly want to elect you their champion. Even in Alabama, so Thomas Beer writes me, there is a woman who objects to 'the transcribing of yesterday's washing and the carrying of coals to the Wellsian Newcastle.' This same Tom Beer, by the way, seems a likely recruit, among the youngsters—*The Memoirs of a Midget,* though, if it catches on at all, will do more for sound fiction in a year than the sum of criticism will in ten."

Dumbarton, February 11, 1922

My dear Mr. Beer:

You have made me your debtor in divers ways. First, and most important, by writing a peculiarly vivid and interesting book, which I read last night, at a sitting, with vast enjoyment. Next, for your kindness in sending me *The Fair Rewards* so handsomely inscribed, for the free ad of *Jurgen* in the text—for all these am I quite properly grateful, and this is a paragraph to say as much.

I must say too that I have been interested in your work for some while, certainly since I read "The House of Atreus," and that I have been looking forward to this novel. I feel now that my anticipations were justified. . . .

Yours faithfully,
JAMES BRANCH CABELL

From Louis Untermeyer

310 West 100th Street
New York City
February 11, 1922

Dear Cabell:

You needn't have been so skeptical about it. I *have* the Italian Chocolate *Beyond Life* and, what's more, it looks as if I will procure a copy of *The Eagle's Shadow* which my secret agents have been searching for. With the exception of the Genealogical Opera, I will soon have a complete Cabelliana!

Meanwhile, I need a bit of information for my projected essay on "The Psychogenesis and Submersion of a Poet." (The article, I can promise, will have another title and will enlarge on the theme of my paper on "Cabell, the Masquerader," published in the *Post* about a year ago.) I began to speak of the matter across your steak à la Brizola but the conversation twisted it away from me. Tracking down your disguised rhymes, I fell, with particular suddenness, over those in the seventeenth chapter of *Figures of Earth.* The rhymes in this incantation of the Image Makers are obvious, not to say dexterous, even though you try to throw your reader off the scent by switching your rhythms. And I believe I recognize the first chant as a Browningesque version of "Four and Twenty Blackbirds" whereas the third voice is obviously Swinburne's declaiming "Mary Had A Little Lamb." But who, if any particular poet, is the second wizard whose neat couplets describe the commercial king and the bread-and-honey eating queen? And can it be Meredith or Morris who pictures the maid about to be assailed by a blackbird? I throw myself upon your patience even though I may be asking too much and seeing too little.

That was a fine day, Wednesday, and a memorable cocktail at Dumbarton. When you arrive here, if ever, I will make reparation. In the linen-closet—— But you shall see. And, I hope, soon.

My salutations to All Concerned.

Yours more than ever,
LOUIS UNTERMEYER

From Sinclair Lewis

London, February 14, 1922

Dear James:

A thousand times I have thought of writing to you, but between working rather steadily on the new novel (it will presumably be finished about June first, be out in September) and gravely viewing London, Cornwall, Kent, Paris, Lago Maggiore, Rome, now London again, I have been rather engaged.

The new book is the portrait of a good business man who is forward-looking, one hundred per cent, and all sorts of things which you lamentably aren't, in a Typical American City—there really are "typical" cities, in America; cities like, say, Cincinnati, Omaha, Kansas City, Minneapolis, Rochester.

I don't know that I have very definitely "got anything out of" almost a year in Europe—out of trattorie in Roma, a half-timbered cottage in Kent, crush teas at Lady Colefax's in London—except the important thing of having enjoyed myself. I remain, I suppose (perhaps to my advantage) incurably a brash and provincial American. It's not at all that I prefer Americanism, or advocate it; I simply am it. I could be happy in Europe the rest of my life; in a year I could be speaking at least a comprehensible Italian, and altogether happy in a villa at—oh, perhaps Rapallo, or on Lago Garda. But throughout I remain cheerfully conscious of Middle-western wood-boxes and wheat-shocks, of New York elevateds, of the traveling salesmen with whom I feel so natural.

But why—in—hell you, who are of essence European, whom I can so beautifully see in a vettura (and in an eye-glass) on the Pincio, or on the Place Vendome, or on Piccadilly—why you should remain in America is beyond me. Hugh and I quite arranged it, the other evening. We have a Tudor cottage for you—a neat little place with twenty bedrooms—and a rose garden and a library collected for ten generations, and the whole damned thing costs about what a two-rooms-and-bath does in America, and the neighboring baroness (beer by origin but books by quite real instinct)—comes round and *begs* you to come to tea, and you have much more fun out of not going than you have out of not going places in Richmond!

I have seen the English *Jurgen,* and I hear of it everywhere. May God in his everlasting mercy totally damn and blister Jack Squire and Shanks for their treatment of it in the *London Mercury*—— You, who have a Freudian martyr complex, doubtless enjoyed (if you saw it) Shanks' reference to Wardour St. in his review, after your years of having brite young American reviewers make the same sage allusion. But me, being quite without complexes (in Minnesota we have neither complexes, ancestors, nor proper corn bread)—I was sore as the devil. And Hugh was equally so, and through the hedge of his milk-white teeth he spake exceeding winged words.

Last summer I thought of the Alum. Even in Kent, with shadows forever crossing the North Downs just above the Pilgrims' Road, I longed for that little porch, and the cornfield, and the hills. Oh well, perhaps I shall see it again. I expect to be back in America in, say, May, and be there for a year or so; then—God knows——

My obsequious respects to your wife, and to you only an undiminished and furious query as to why you aren't here in England, where you belong, where people would love and understand you—— It's a good land, this. I love it deeply—damn it!—but me, I am of the busy Western streets—damn it!

Servant,

SINCLAIR LEWIS

Dumbarton, February 24, 1922

My dear Scott Fitzgerald:

Having thoughtlessly failed to keep the wrapper of your book, with the Minneapolis address, I am sending my thanks perforce in care of your publishers. I have of course been following *The Beautiful and Damned* in the *Metropolitan*—with pleasure and admiration. I have found it gratifyingly solid—moving, human, brilliant at times, and always nicely ironic.

Your ending could hardly be happier. Now I find that in the serial publication there seem to have been considerable cuts, so I am going through the novel again with, I foresee, augmented delight. Meanwhile I forward my thanks both for the sending and the writing of this book.

Yours faithfully,

JAMES BRANCH CABELL

From F. Scott Fitzgerald

626 Goodrich Ave.
St. Paul, Minn.
March 4, 1922

Dear Mr. Cabell—

Thank you for your letter. I am tremendously sorry you followed *The Beautiful & Damned* in the serial because it was cut to pieces. But I appreciate the compliment of your doing so. And the final book version was considerably revised. However it isn't worth going through again, for you, I mean.

Hergesheimer, that charming egotist, came through this swollen Main Street awhile back. He didn't like it.

When do we meet?

I have just finished a comedy for the commercial stage.[1]

When do you publish another book? Please do soon as I am bored with all current fiction including my own.

(This is yours. I believe I'll
use it for awhile)

Yours faithfully

F. SCOTT FITZGERALD

I appreciate your kindness in saying those things about the book. I cut part of the ending in the final revision, as you notice. I hope it wasn't the part you liked. I liked the other ending but it seemed to spoil the general *hardness* of the book.

[1] Probably *The Vegetable or From President to Postman* which Scribner published in 1923.

From F. Scott Fitzgerald

St. Paul, Minn.

[date?]

Dear Mr. Cabell:

I feel that by asking your permission to quote a private letter I have not acted in the best of taste. There have been, of course, innumerable precedents of late, but that does not excuse it. I appreciate your exceeding kindness and courtesy.

It seems that [Maxwell] Perkins of Scribners had heard from some editor in Richmond that you liked the book. He had tried to get in touch with that editor to see if it was quotable—realizing how invaluable a word from you might be. For some reason he evidently failed, and he wired me Monday night—or Sunday—asking me if I had a letter from you which was quotable. I wired you immediately.

I've had the pleasure of a three day amour with an Exquisite Case of Spanish Influenza, and like all such illicit affairs it has left me weak and chastened. I hope you are *not* the same.

Faithfully,

F. SCOTT FITZGERALD

Dumbarton, March 18, 1922

My dear Scott Fitzgerald:

... It was a pleasure to be quoted as an admirer of your new book; of course if I had written something expressly for that purpose, I would gladly have been more loud in phrase. I believe that, upon the whole, my feeling as to the book is pretty accurately—with one exception—summed by Mencken in the April *Smart Set*. The exception is the incredible dictum about "the thing is botched at the end"—I having particularly joyed in the end,—but all the last part of Mencken's review is the most accurate possible statement of my reasons for liking *The Beautiful and Damned.*

Perhaps by good luck, I had not seen the last installment in the *Metropolitan* when the book came, so that the only ending known to me is the book version; I shall not look into the other, as this one I find amply satisfying.

You ask about my new book—I shall, D.V., begin on it two weeks from to-day, but as yet even its subject matter remains unknown. All that the at all near future promises is the new *Gallantry* and the little *Lineage of Lichfield,* which I think more important than anybody else appears to, and which therefore will be limited to 365 copies—I mean, on account of my publisher's failure to appreciate the book's "universal appeal."

Yours faithfully,
JAMES BRANCH CABELL

From Carl Van Doren

The Nation
New York
March 20, 1922

Dear Mr. Cabell:

I have just come back from a dimly hortatory week in what some might call the academic shades of my alma mater, the University of Illinois, and I find I must write to tell you what a hero you are there. For all the brightest boys and girls your books are the current bible: the Book of Beauty, the Well of Wit, The Handbook of Courtship, the Serious Call to the Devout and Holy Life of Art. Perhaps rather too many, after the fashion of too many older amateurs, identify you with *Jurgen*. But I was pleased to note that such fellows sat below the salt, above which were the souls who had seen some of the allegory in *Figures of Earth*.

In my own days there—I mean at the University, not either above or below the salt—we had no such fine tastes. Those undergraduates who had ever read a book had ordinarily gone little deeper than Stevenson or Kipling. So you see you have done some "good"—as has also Mencken, whose fame reverberates over the prairies.

Very sincerely yours,
CARL VAN DOREN

From H. L. Mencken

Baltimore, March 21 [1922]

Dear Cabell:

I find by my records, greatly to the distress of my conscience, that I did *not* send you *The American Language*. Well, blame Knopf: he got the whole matter of the advance copies horribly balled up. But God will not forgive me. At the least he will send me the great pox. I enclose a slip to glue into the book. Also a copy of the confidential Credo.

Fitzgerald blew into New York last week. He has written a play, and Nathan says that it has very good chances. But it seems to me that his wife talks too much about money. His danger lies in trying to get it too rapidly. A very amiable pair, innocent and charming.

I have had no news from Hergesheimer, save a telegram. Gouverneur Morris, who is at Monterey, has laid in 100 jugs against his coming. I have a suspicion that he will try them all.

I am tackling *Prejudices III* and it is very hard going.

Sincerely yours,

H. L. MENCKEN

Dumbarton, March 25, 1922

Dear Dr. Van Doren:

There were at least two excellent reasons for rejoicing over your letter —first, the kindliness which prompted you to write it, and second, the news it contained. There is not of course anything preferable to being viewed without disfavor by the young; the plastic mind takes an impression,—I know by the light of memory,—which endures as a matter of habit rather than of reason; and I would not care to confess all the authors of whom I still think tenderly because I read them before I had more or less jelled—— So for very obvious causes your news from the prairies is pleasure-giving.

To the other side, it is disappointing to have no news whatever of the treatise upon the living novelists. It was scheduled, as I recall, for March, and here March is practically done with. And it is a book to which I look forward with the liveliest sort of curiosity as to how you will shape the whole.

Some day I too hope to bring out a new book. In the meanwhile I have revised *Gallantry,* and have made of it a thoroughly immoral performance.

Yours faithfully,

JAMES BRANCH CABELL

From F. Scott Fitzgerald

The Plaza, New York
March 27, 1922

Dear Mr. Cabell:

Am dictating this and it is the most profound agony I have ever gone through. The Stenographer embarrasses me because I feel that I have got to think quickly and in consequence everything comes in broken clauses. But I simply cannot let your very kind letter go unanswered any longer. You were very nice to allow me to place such an endorsement in the advertisements of my book. It has gone up beyond 30,000, in fact it will touch 40,000 within the week, but I doubt very much if as many people will like it who liked *This Side of Paradise*. I saw Mencken and Nathan for a minute the other morning. Mencken seemed nervous and tired, but Nathan is his usual self, albeit developing a paunch and losing a bit of his remarkable youthfulness. Why do not you publish a geography of the lands of your own creating on the inside, front and back covers of your next book, much as Conrad has in the last edition of *Victory*. I think it would be very amusing both for you and for your public, or would it, in the case of an imaginative country appear too obvious?

Am in New York, having rather a poor time and will return to St. Paul Sunday.

As ever,

F. SCOTT FITZGERALD

From H. L. Mencken

Baltimore, April 20, 1922

Dear Cabell:

Certainly I'll be glad to review *The Lineage of Lichfield*. Where is the book? It has not yet reached me. I am delighted to hear what you say about Untermeyer. His parodies seem to me to be genuinely first-rate. He is miles beyond J. C. Squire.

I am sweating through *Prejudices III*, a fearful job. Theoretically, the book is simply a series of reprints, but actually I am rewriting most of it. The opening chapter will be a treatise on Americanism, with a philosophical glance at the chivalrous attitudes visible during the war. I am in no mood for work. I hope to go to Europe in August, and the great mass of routine that I must get through before then paralyzes me.

No news from Hergesheimer save a telegram and a letter. But from various agents I gather the following: In Seattle he was robbed of his diamond-mounted toothpick. In Portland he came down with wood alcohol. In San Francisco he won $17 shooting dice, and then blew it upon a hand-painted shirt. In Los Angeles he drank 40 cocktails in 40 hours. He seems to be having a roaring time of it.

Isn't your annual pilgrimage to Babylon almost due?

Sincerely yours,

H. L. MENCKEN

Dumbarton, April 26, 1922

My dear Van Doren:

You have most triumphantly evaded the one danger I foresaw. As the papers appeared one by one, there was a queer effect of your ranking all your authors on one plateau,—as if all were about equally important, and Herrick, for example, "wrote" as adroitly as Hergesheimer. But now you have arranged your matter with clearness, coherency, and a certain low cunningness, upon which I make you my most hearty congratulations. You have made a perfectly symmetrical book [*Contemporary American Novelists*]; and your division between Argument and Art of your chosen ten is a master stroke exceeded only by your artfulness in dodging responsibility for choosing this especial ten. . . .

Some of your dicta, I confess, rather bother me. Floyd Dell, for example—I read what you say of him, and feel that I ought in duty to have another go at *Moon-Calf*, which I found absolutely impervious. For you have not an over-kind heart; your mockery in Old Style is too delicately devilish to permit the suspicion.

I shall not ever take your advice, though, I suspect, as to that modern comedy of Virginia. (In passing, I have never laid the scene of a book in Virginia.) I distrust the contemporaneous, for the reason that one's conclusions about it—exactly—"wither in the light and fire of time." I distrust it because of—exactly—the feeling which prompted you to write pages 34-7 in the book. In fine, you give me advice and therewith irrefutable reasons for not taking it. And you give me too some pride and a great deal of pleasure.

Yours faithfully,

JAMES BRANCH CABELL

From Thomas Beer

227 Palisade Avenue
Yonkers, N. Y.
May 2, 1922

Dear Mr. Cabell—

In Sicily there is a demon named Celerri, whose feet are luminous on the soles. This makes his nightly forays doubly interesting as he is obscure when standing flat footed. He also smells of bitter almond. These facts have been made known to me by Clefante Visella, my gardener. The matter, in view of the May *Century,* appears not too remote from the field of your present speculations. So I forward the annotation for your files.

Yours obligedly
THOMAS BEER

Dumbarton, May 6, 1922

My dear Mr. Beer:

But that is indeed a delightful demon! I must certainly make use of him, and I am heartily obliged to you for the introduction.

I am doubly glad for that it gives me an opportunity to say that "The Bridge"* seemed to me a peculiarly vivid and convincing writing. It is really nice of me to like the tale after Burton Rascoe has announced that the May *Century* contains a new story by me and a fine story by you, for the statement has implications—— You had, I hope, my letter as to *The Fair Rewards,* of whose success I hear with joy.

Yours faithfully,
JAMES BRANCH CABELL

* Error in the title for which, upon the whole, I need not apologize. [The story's title was "Enemy."]

From Thomas Beer

Yonkers, May 8, 1922

Dear Mr. Cabell,

If I didn't answer your letter about *The Fair Rewards,* I am a dog and the descendant of innumerous, inferior, inequitable dogs with a strong prevalence of Mississippi hound in the breed—I probably didn't. I was, about that time, a mere container for some fifty agitated gallstones. As for your kindness to "The Enemy" it had been more truly merited if the hareem in the *Century* office hadn't removed some references to the girl's outline—a warrant for the fool's preoccupation. Burton has gone to Princeton to spread LIGHT and TRUTH among the ephiboi. At least, I think he has gone there. My life is in considerable danger and I don't dare go to town—— Let me warn you that the least safe task you can take upon yourself is to review a novel by Waldo Frank. I did so and the results are terrifying. Virgins of Canaanitish aspect whose noses are as towers looking toward Jerusalem and fragile youths in need of shaving pursue and execrate me. All the pleasures of persecution are mine. *Vanity Fair* for June will, I think, print some observations by myself on your library and household decoration.

Yours,
THOMAS BEER

Dumbarton, May 11, 1922

My dear Van Doren:

The vexatious press of private matters has prevented the earlier expression of my delight in your review of the *Lineage*. I am the more grateful for that I still insist, in the teeth of my publishers' scepticism, that the opus is an illuminating, if not indeed an actually requisite, approach to the shape and sum of my writing. It is, in fine, like all cantraps, really potent when properly used.

Upon the whole, too, it makes a volume of satisfactory appearance, though I now regret that I did not provide for more initial letters in red, if but to palliate the book's unconscionable selling price.

Yours faithfully,
JAMES BRANCH CABELL

From Carl Van Doren

New York
May 17, 1922

My dear Cabell:

I am remarkably glad that you like my little note on *The Lineage of Lichfield*. The temptation was to write a great deal more about it than the pounds and ounces of its bulk might seem to warrant. To my thinking it is an indispensable Gradus ad Cabellem.

Don't you suppose you could write me a review of Arthur Machen's new book which Knopf has published? This particular collocation of Machen and you seems to me irresistible by the readers of fine literature.

Sincerely yours,

CARL VAN DOREN

Lord, how I like what you said about my new book!

Dumbarton, May 19, 1922

My dear Van Doren:

No, you must not tempt me to write now about Machen. I am already tied up with family affairs and disordered vision—I shall have to shut the left eye when it comes to signing this, but typewriter keys are luckily easy reading—and these arranged, there is still a story to be done before I can get down to the writing of that long-overdue book. So I cannot undertake anything else, much as I would like to see the *House of Souls* attain the success it has so long deserved. I in particular hanker to point out that the stories should be read in precisely inverse order to that in which they are printed; and throw out the suggestion that the book's failure to find many readers is largely caused by the fact that this arrangement has never been made typographically.

So I can but thank you, and attempt the signature of

Yours faithfully,

JAMES BRANCH CABELL

Dumbarton, June 17, 1922

Dear Holt:

At home awaited me an enormous pile of not very important letters, one of which I send you [from Aleister Crowley]. Read and return with your opinion as to the advisability of investing (what?) books in him. Then I can answer him. But what is the *English Review? . . .*

Your note came yesterday. I shall be glad to see the case settled. Then we can talk of divers matters. But in the meanwhile, I count on you to keep me informed—and prefer, upon the whole, to have the case thrown out. . . .

Yours faithfully,

JAMES BRANCH CABELL

Dumbarton, June 17, 1922

Dear Hal:

On the afternoon of the thirteenth, that proverbially unlucky day, you were seeing someone off on the train at Forest Hills, so that I, already on the train, passed helplessly within a foot or two of you, on my way to New York and home. The maddening part is that I was for a week at Nassau Boulevard, while you were, to appearances, at Forest Hills and were supposed by me to be in New Hampshire. It is what I have heard described as "romantic irony" for accident to have brought us thus close together at the exact end of my stay on Long Island.

At all events, I know you are now in thrall to *Babbitt,* and this is just to wish luck to the book, and, however belatedly, to bid you welcome to these States.

Yours faithfully,

JAMES BRANCH CABELL

From Guy Holt

New York, June 20, 1922

Dear Cabell:

The *English Review* is, or was, a sort of superior *Dial* which Ford, Madox, Hueffer started about twenty years ago. At that time it published some of the best work of the now no longer younger Englishmen. I see a copy occasionally and it still publishes excellent stuff, although it has grown staid with the years and is superior to the *Mercury* only in that it is not in the hands of a clique.

Crowley is, as you know, an ingenious charlatan whose praise will do you no particular good but probably no harm. It would probably be all right to send him the *Rivet, Domnei, Gallantry* and *The Cords of Vanity* say.

No news has come from downtown. The 26th is now set as the official date but we are mentioning that to no one as there is a strong possibility that matters will be quietly dropped. We may not learn of this latter development until the day before the trial.

Faithfully yours,

GUY HOLT

From H. L. Mencken

Baltimore, June 26 [1922]

Dear Cabell:

. . . In my memory sticks a picture on your wall: a view of my person, horribly like. What I propose is that if you will (a) give it to the nearest colored church and (b) send me an elegantly autographed landscape of yourself, I'll send you by return mail movie gals. Monroe made a very pretty fellow of me. I promise to hang your picture between Ibsen and Kay Laurell.

I hope to sail on August 8th, and am trying to get enough work done ahead to let me leave with a clear conscience.

Sincerely yours,

H. L. MENCKEN

From Joseph Hergesheimer

West Chester, July 1, 1922

Dear James:

For the past seven or eight weeks, ever since I got home from the West, I have been absolutely lost in the preparation and beginning of the book I went out for to get. In plan it did not seem too complicated, but the actuality turned out to be beyond any words. In putting together and writing the first third, now practically completed, I simply lost every other connection and responsibility with earth. This in explanation of what you must have thought of as my very uncivil silence. *The Lineage of Lichfield* came safely and I think it is a very romantic and charming affair: it is the essence of romance. What you clapped on at the end was in a very nice ironical vein, but I'll be goddamned if I would have hung Hewlett's name at the end of those other lovely titles. You were, I heard, in New York; your silence with me on that point was more than justified by my apparent silence about your book. I should like to have seen you. I cannot now get away and there I am. I shall go nowhere this summer, work on *The Magnetic West,* and live as sparingly as possible through the heat.

Faithfully,
JOSEPH HERGESHEIMER

From H. L. Mencken

Baltimore, July 7, 1922

Dear Cabell:

Thanks for the view of you. A noble likeness! The morons of the Postoffice piled crates of eggs on it, and it is cracked like an old master, but only in the lower part. The face is undamaged. I have handed it over to the secular arm to be framed, and shall hang it between Mary MacLane and Ibsen.

I met Lewis in New York the other day. He was magnificently soused. He promised to send me the proofs of his new book within a week or two. I am very eager to see it. He reported some curious encounters with Squire *et al.* in London. I shall take a close look at them in August. They are ripe for a rough round in the ring.

Sincerely yours,
H. L. MENCKEN

From Sinclair Lewis

July 20 [1922]

Dear James:

It is infuriating that we should have been within shouting distance on Long Island, yet have missed each other. I wish it were possible now to be with you on a porch at the Alum. I am writing from Charles Flandrau's house in St. Paul. I have been viewing my aboriginal Main Street again & driving about with my father. Day after tomorrow Gracie joins me in Chicago & we go motoring round—God knows where. The proofs of *Babbitt* are all in, & I am rather vacuous after the let-down following a year & a half of work which, even while I was in Europe, was rather steady & demanding. Writing seems to me just now an occupation improbable & inconceivable—pretty girls & whiskeys & soda the only sure excellences—& for them I have no talent whatever. Yet I know that before long I shall again be (with my quite characteristic 100% Pep & Vigor) wildly hammering out messages of cheer for morons, all in that photographic & journalistic manner the good critics so justly attribute to me.

My greetings to you & your family, James, & my high esteem.

Ever—
SINCLAIR LEWIS

Mountain Lake, Virginia
August 10, 1922

Dear Holt:

It is needless to say I was delighted to have your recent long letter, with all its news, in that I was glad to get the full account of the *Jurgen* case which you wrote me when on your Western trip. In any event! I want you to send to M. Edouard Bernaert, 34 rue Lohmond, Paris (5), France, a copy of: *The Line of Love, Gallantry, The Certain Hour, The Cords of Vanity, The Rivet,* and *The Cream of the Jest.* He, I may tell you, is to make a complete translation of my works which Lafitte is to bring out, on the same terms as the German *Jurgen.* The affair seems virtually concluded, the only hitch being that, it appears, an American book after remaining untranslated for ten years becomes in France public property, so that these may have to be *"des arrangements spèciaux"* to prevent a rival firm bringing out my earlier books in their unrevised form. This point cleared up, they want to begin at once with *Beyond Life* and bring out the set in its proper order. I will later let you hear when the promised contract arrives, which should be about a month from now. The German *Jurgen* is to come out in May 1923—— It has been a great drawback to me, this having no real publishers, in the struggling with all this French and German correspondence, and I have often thought of how convenient Alfred, say, would be to manage these matters—— We will, of course, divide the profits, in the event of there being any.

But we will straighten out all these matters when you come to Richmond in September. I have made a fair start on *The Place That Ought Not to Be; A Comedy of Wickedness* (?), and would have done much more but for unfavorable conditions here which have interfered with work. The book should be done, now, by Christmas. I do not know what it will be like when completed, but the worst, the frame-work, is over, and I have the skeleton ready for decoration and festoons.

I wonder if you saw my story, "The Bright Bees of Toupan?" The Marriage Symposium has resulted in the most appalling drivel from the (ahem!) other contributors. I have now five stories (one untyped) toward *The Silver Stallion*, to appear in book form in, with good luck, 1924, and begin to master my new "form." We shall remain at this place until the twenty-first, and then return to Dumbarton.

That seems all.

Yours faithfully,

JAMES BRANCH CABELL

From Guy Holt

New York, August 14, 1922

Dear Cabell:

It was good to have your letter and—yes, as you imply, I owe you many apologies. When I got out of town I found that I had no more news of *Jurgen* than I had already communicated to you. The trial, as I wrote you, was postponed until fall because of the crowded condition of the courts. Any other settlement was made impossible by the religious convictions of certain of the prosecuting staff. For a day there was some serious speculation about a possible third arrangement. "There may be another way out," said our counsel, looking mysterious and mentioning a moot point of law; but this came to nothing and I was never told the details of the scheme. It was this I had in mind when I promised to write you more fully. For the rest, I was hot, distracted, at war with the world as I ever am when I'm obliged to sell things, and put off writing until I should have had some word from you which would give me occasion.

The books have gone to M. Bernaert. It is good news that Lafitte will do a complete set of you; also that the German *Jurgen* is to go through at last. Do you know that you are somewhat unjust about this affair? You have given me practically no information about the German negotiations, merely informing me that they were "under way" and of the present French arrangement I have had no hint until now. We should have been glad to act for you. I assumed that you preferred to conduct the negotiations yourself. . . .

Faithfully yours,

GUY HOLT

Dumbarton, September 21, 1922

My dear Hal:

It was a grievous error to delay my acknowledgment of *Babbitt* until I had read the book with the leisure it merits and so prodigally repays, for now I can but feel each bit of personal praise to be indistinguishable in this week's freshet of paeans. I strive for originality, however, by not voicing the obvious truth that *Babbitt* is better than—the book whose name I leave unmentioned, and so gain uniqueness.

Babbitt seems to me sound and very, very excellent. Beyond that I do not venture into detail, not even into the plain duty of thanking you for the ad of *Figures of Earth*. But I think that you ought to be proud, and I know that your friends are.

Yours faithfully,

JAMES BRANCH CABELL

From Guy Holt

New York, October 3, 1922

Dear Cabell:

I returned home to leave town again immediately or I should have written you before this. Many, many thanks for *Curious Popular Delusions*. It's a grand cantrap book and Redman is planning to assassinate me in some mysterious fashion in the hope that he will inherit it.

. . . Apropos, Saturday morning Mr. Goodbody phoned to say that Mr. McBride (whose steamer docked Saturday) and I must be in town on Monday; that our motion to examine the minutes has been refused; and that in a very few days we shall know just when and in what fashion our trial is to be conducted.

I am terribly sorry about your eye. I hope you are not blaming me for your troubles as you once did when your ear drum broke. As for me, the affliction which was beginning when I was in Richmond has progressed unreasonably and I am now, in my small way, a veritable Job.

Oh, yes, I am now ensconced in a handsome studio in Macdougal Alley —and it was, as it always is, more than pleasant to see you.

Faithfully yours,

GUY HOLT

Dumbarton, October 8, 1922

Dear Holt:

What in the name of all the fiends is going on at your office? You spend the working day within some fifteen feet of Mr. McBride, with whom you presumably stay on speaking terms. You have all written out in your Law's Serious Call &c., absolutely all the information which he and Mr. Glenn are at this late date demanding. The whole thing seems absolutely the last word and straw in the way of incompetence.

It would perhaps not so utterly madden me but for our present family circumstances. My wife's eldest daughter—whom you never saw, for she has long been an invalid—died here on Thursday, and it is with the corpse in the house that I begin to receive these requests for my presence in New York to tell you again who was Harpocrates and what were muntrus, and so on, when you have it already written out. It causes me furiously to think, I can assure you, of the talk I had with Knopf last week—— But that can wait. What I want to say is that, if you insane people consider it absolutely necessary, I can manage to be in New York Wednesday from morning until midnight, with every inclination to get you all in jail. You will readily understand the upset condition of everything here, and of my wife in particular, which causes me perhaps to write with some jerkiness or even harshness. But apart from that, and the lack of any previous intimation that you wanted me to come on to New York, you are all insanity-provoking people to have dealings with.

Yours faithfully,

JAMES BRANCH CABELL

From Carl Van Doren

The Century Company
New York
October 14, 1922

My dear Cabell:

In telling you how pleased I am at your grief over my leaving the *Nation*, I think I shall undertake to give you what pleasure there is in my latest critical decision: that "In The Second April" is the best short story I have read in two years.

I am glad to have your best wishes at my new address. I shall be glad also to have some of your best stories.

Very sincerely yours,

CARL VAN DOREN

Dumbarton, October 16, 1922

Dear Holt:

Your note, received this afternoon, gives me just time to catch the late mail.

I do not know that at the present time there is much to be said. Mr. Glenn's brief appeared to me excellent, for the adopted line of defence; and I can but hope the judge may agree with me.

As for my coming on—but to what end? You have but to wire me . . . and I will come. But I doubt if I would ever enjoy it, and, as I have said, I decline to defend *Jurgen* in any way or to protest the goodness of my intentions. But you are familiar with the preface to *Jurgen and the Censor.*

Things here have bettered considerably, and Mrs. Cabell, now that the first shock is over, has wonderfully recovered her poise. So my presence here is no longer indispensable. But—! Well, you, I imagine, can comprehend my attitude without any explanations.

Yours faithfully,
JAMES BRANCH CABELL

Three days later Holt wired Cabell that the indictment was dismissed and *Jurgen* acquitted of all charges.

Dumbarton, October 19, 1922

My dear Holt:

Your telegram when received this morning was—need I observe?—good reading matter, the best that your firm has put out for a long while. I must, while I think of it, ask for a copy of that thaumaturgic brief, which, in its final form, I never saw.

Well, what is to be done next? I mean, for one thing, is it possible to put the book again upon the market at once? and will the firm bring suit against the society? . . . I await your plans, and tender in turn my warmest congratulations. . . .

Now I must get down to addressing cards acknowledging sympathy with our recent bereavement, and bring, I am afraid, incongruous cheerfulness to the task.

Yours faithfully,
JAMES BRANCH CABELL

McBride immediately issued the following:

FOR IMMEDIATE RELEASE

New York
October 19, 1922.

The proceeding for the suppression of James Branch Cabell's book "Jurgen", instigated by the New York Society for the Suppression of Vice, and Mr. John S. Sumner, its secretary, was brought to trial before Judge [Charles C.] Nott and a jury on Monday, October 16th, in the Court of General Sessions. The defendants, Robert M. McBride & Co., Robert M. McBride, President, and Guy Holt, Secretary, were represented by their attorneys, Goodbody, Danforth & Glenn, 27 Cedar Street, New York City, with whom was associated as counsel, Mr. Garrard Glenn of 42 Broadway. The defendants did not dispute the fact of publication but, at the close of the People's case, moved for the direction of an acquittal. Judge Nott took the motion under advisement and this morning handed down a decision granting the motion as follows:

JUDGE NOTT'S OPINION

PEOPLE

VS.

HOLT, MCBRIDE & CO. ET AL.

"The defendants herein, at the close of the People's case, have moved for a direction of acquittal and the dismissal of the indictment on the ground that the book "Jurgen" on the possession of which the indictment is based, is not an "obscene, lewd, lascivious, filthy, indecent or disgusting book" within the meaning and intent of section 1141 of the Penal Law, for the alleged violation of which the indictment has been found.

"I have read and examined the book carefully. It is by Mr. James Branch Cabell, an author of repute and distinction. From the literary point of view its style may fairly be called brilliant. It is based on the mediaeval legends of Jurgen and is a highly imaginative and fantastic tale, depicting the adventures of one who has been restored to his first youth but who, being attended by a shadow in the guise of the shadow of his old self, retains the experience and cynicism of age which frustrates a perfect fulfillment of his desire for renewed youth.

"The adventures consist in wanderings through mediaeval and mythological countries and a sojourn in Hell and Heaven. He encounters beings of mediaeval folk-lore and from classical Mythology. The most that can be said against the book is that certain passages therein may be considered suggestive in a veiled and subtle way of immorality, but such suggestions are delicately conveyed and the whole atmosphere of the story is of such an unreal and supernatural nature that even these suggestions are free from the evils accompanying suggestiveness in more realistic works. In fact, it is doubtful if the book could be read or understood at all by more than a very limited number of readers.

"In my opinion the book is one of unusual literary merit and contains nothing "obscene, lewd, lascivious, filthy, indecent or disgusting" within the meaning of the statute and the decisions of the courts of this state in similar cases. (See Halsey v. New York Society, 234 N. Y. 1; People v. Brainard, 192 App. Div. 116; St. Hubert Guild, v. Quinn, 64 Misc. 336.)

"The motion, therefore, is granted and the jury is advised to acquit the defendants."

ROBERT M. McBRIDE & CO.'S STATEMENT

The Publishers made the following statement:

"Judge Nott's decision, acquitting *Jurgen* of the charge of being an 'obscene, lewd, offensive, lascivious and indecent' book, is gratifying but not unexpected. Throughout the two years in which we have been awaiting trial, we have held to our original opinion that *Jurgen* is a work of great literary merit, which we were and are proud to have published, and that its suppression would be not alone a personal loss, but a severe blow to American literature. It was unthinkable that any court could sustain the charge brought by the overzealous Mr. Sumner."

ROBERT M. MCBRIDE & COMPANY

From Louis Untermeyer

New York, October 19, 1922

Dear Cabell:

I was almost expelled this morning for rising to my feet when his honor charged the jury (you should have seen those twelve hundred percenters!) to bring in a verdict for Holt, McBride *et al.* I was about to congratulate the justice upon his excellent decision as well as his discovery that *Jurgen* (which he pronounced Yourgen) was founded on a well-known mediaeval legend.

As it was, both Redman and I felt cheated. Had the case gone to the jury, Redman, as you know, was going to read—God and the Smith Brothers willing—the entire work to the twelve (technically) good men and (legally speaking) true. The recitation would have taken six and one-half hours. At the very conclusion, just as Redman was tottering from the stand and the jury was being waked by the clerk of the court, I was to tower to my five feet seven and cry *"Encore! Encore!"*

As I say, I feel that Justice Nott has cheated me of a brilliant and dramatic jesture. In spite of which I congratulate you, as I have already congratulated Holt, not only on the delayed evidence that Truth, Beauty and Allied Generalities will prevail but on the adroit and altogether admirable brief prepared by Garrard Glenn. My renewed felicitations.

Cordially,
LOUIS UNTERMEYER

From Guy Holt

New York, October 20, 1922

Dear Cabell:

I am sending you, at once, a copy of Mr. Glenn's brief. I think it a very remarkable production and we have decided to issue it as an additional volume in the series of Cabell scholia. Our notion is to call it *Jurgen and the Law,* to preface it with a brief foreword recounting the history of the *Jurgen* suppression and explaining the importance of Glenn's brief, in that it presents in the most cogent form possible the arguments for the differentiation between literature and pornography and also pointing out its intrinsic interest as a piece of polemic literature. We should also include in the book Judge Nott's decision.

And of course we are going to reprint immediately. We have not yet received the court order releasing the books but we expect to have them by Monday and we have already disposed of the major portion of them in the city. . . .

Finally, although we are not announcing this publicly, our counsel are now investigating the various charges upon which we can bring suit against Sumner and we are attempting to estimate the damages we have suffered through the loss of the book. We want, however, to say nothing at all about this at the present time as it seems wise to avoid publicity until we are actually ready to bring suit. . . .

This is all for the moment. I am glad it wasn't necessary for you to come up and I need not tell you how heartily delighted we have felt over our victory. We have had congratulatory messages from all manner of people in town, who have asked us to pass them on to you also. Heywood Broun stopped me today and, after offering congratulations, heaved a sigh and said, "You do not know what a load this has taken off my conscience. I have felt uneasy the last three years ever since I printed that fool letter of Kingsley's."

Faithfully yours,

GUY HOLT

Heywood Broun in his column in the New York *World* of October 21, quoted Judge Nott at some length, and added: "The decision of Judge Nott atones for the most conspicuous blunder in literary censorship of which America has been guilty in recent years. . . . The acquittal of *Jurgen* removes from our own shoulders a heavy burden. When Mr. Sumner brought action against the book he stated that his attention had first been called to it by an article on the *Tribune* book page, which we were editing at that time. This article was a letter from Walter Kingsley, who stated that *Jurgen* was by far the most popular book among the chorus girls of New York. According to the letter, competition was raging up and down Broadway as to which girl could dig out of the book the greatest number of hidden meanings. This seemed to us innocent enough. It was easy to imagine ever so many ways in which chorus girls might be employed to worse advantage."

A day or so later Broun had the grace to admit: "A gross injustice was done to *Jurgen,* and it can't quite be made up now. That, of course, is the unfair part of many of the proceedings undertaken by Sumner. Even when he loses his case eventually in court, irreparable damage has been done to the book which he attacked."

Young Thomas Caldecott Chubb wrote Cabell: "I can only wish you, then, that since *Jurgen* will no longer have some of its appeal to that sort of a public to whom Mr. Sumner, perhaps unintentionally, serves as a procurer, it will speedily find another one which does not need his indirect recommendation, which considers and is pleased by other things. That I am sure it will." But McBride commented that so many people had borrowed and read *Jurgen* during the three years of its suppression that he doubted if they would find a wide market for the reprinted volume. However, he went ahead vigorously and did all that could be done.

From Robert M. McBride

New York, October 25, 1922

Dear Mr. Cabell:

In the rush of events here I have neglected something I intended to do —to offer my felicitations on the outcome of the *Jurgen* case.

It was a sweeping vindication. I do not believe that any jury, and especially the one that was impaneled for this suit, would have rendered a decision for conviction. Nevertheless, it was a great relief and an even greater victory to have the indictment dismissed by the Judge. Moreover, the decision that we secured puts us in a much better technical position to bring suit against Sumner, which we are strongly tempted to do and which I think we shall do. We probably could not collect very heavy damages from the Vice Society even if the outcome of the suit was favorable to us, but we might collect something and the publicity would be of no little help in keeping up the interest in *Jurgen* and in your other books. . . .

Faithfully yours,

ROBERT M. MCBRIDE

Dumbarton, October 25, 1922

Dear Holt:

—But, no, I do not want to write to you. I desire merely to reread and yet again reread Mr. Glenn's brief and Judge Nott's decision as to those mediaeval legends of *Jurgen*.

My sense of duty, though, compels me typewriterward. I had the brief this morning, and have just read it, for the first time in its glorious entirety—— It should certainly be published, as you suggest. . . .

Yours faithfully,

JAMES BRANCH CABELL

Cabell was much moved by Garrard Glenn's brilliant brief for the defense, from which the following quote is particularly significant: "Under our common law there has not been, since the abolition of the Courts of Star Chamber and of High Commission, nor will there ever be again, such a spirit in our law as may result, thru statute or decision, in the institution of a censorship of the mind in its modes of expression."

In reply to a letter of gratitude and appreciation, Mr. Glenn wrote from New York:

From Garrard Glenn

New York, October 27, 1922

Dear Mr. Cabell:

I cannot tell you how much I appreciate your letter. It went so far beyond my deserts that I am almost ashamed to look it in the face; but nevertheless I am going to preserve it for my children. I feel that the whole occasion was an immense privilege for me; an opportunity to touch spaces and concepts that hitherto had rolled along far beyond the reach of my circumstances. I appreciate the memory, but I shall hold fast to the connection. The professional delicacies do not interfere in this regard, because the case is finished, and our ancient Norman-French phrase *autrefois acquit* and the common law doctrine which it expresses, will protect *Jurgen* from any further attempts of Mr. Sumner in the courts of New York. Our common law,—not our statutes, for the modern ones are of Philistia,—has its own grand aspects, but the difficulty is that so few can be made to realize them. Now *Jurgen* is free, and I am therefore privileged to commune with its author; and I shall probably in the future abuse that privilege excessively.

You may be interested to know that I received a letter from the Dean of Columbia Law School [Harlan Fiske Stone], who, in addition to his cultivated learning in the law, is also one of the best judges of etchings in this country, in which he says of the *Jurgen* case:—

"I am glad you are in this case. I think the whole country is in danger of being ruined by a smug Puritanism and that intelligent people with liberal ideas, especially lawyers, ought to fight this tendency."

Sincerely yours,

GARRARD GLENN

❧ 10 ❧

AND SO TO CONCLUDE

Jurgen was once more put on sale and, thanks to Mr. Sumner, became a phenomenal success. With the irritation of the case behind him, Cabell could wholeheartedly continue his writing. During the next ten years letters passed back and forth between members of the group, but each became more and more involved with his own work and, depending perhaps on hasty trips, corresponded less and less often. All of them stood almost at flood tide, with great productions ahead. Hergesheimer was to do *Quiet Cities, Swords and Roses,* and *The Limestone Tree;* Sinclair Lewis was to write *Arrowsmith* and *Dodsworth* and was to become the first American to be awarded the Nobel Prize in Literature; Dreiser had *The American Tragedy* in front of him; Carl Van Vechten, *The Blind Bow-Boy, Nigger Heaven, Spider Boy;* Rascoe, *Titans of Literature* and *Prometheans;* Mencken was to write *Treatise on the Gods,* enlarge *The American Language,* and add continuously to the great series of *Prejudices;* while Cabell with *The Silver Stallion* and *Straws and Prayer-Books* brought to a conclusion his saga of Poictesme, and launched into the second period of his work with several books of essays and the first volume of the Dream Trilogy. All of the group wrote furiously and obviously enjoyed living, even in a world of which they could not wholly approve. But the technique of their craft enthralled them, for certainly they felt that truth, in order to endure, must be beautiful.

Men changed jobs, created new magazines, and dropped the old. Rascoe left the Chicago *Tribune,* and via a stop with *McCall's,* turned up as literary editor of the New York *Tribune.* Mencken wrote from Baltimore in 1923: ". . . The Day of Judgment is upon the Republic, i.e., I am to launch into a new monthly review toward the end of the year. The name: *The American Mercury.* The publisher: Knopf. Format: the most chaste and dignified possible. Contents: a general survey of the national scene, realistic but never indignant. The field is wide open. To one side the Liberals chase butterflies; to the other side the Otto Kahns

277

and Henry Morgenthaus and other such great patriots sob and moan for endangered capital. Certainly, there must be room in the middle for an educated Toryism—the true Disraelian brand. It exists everywhere, but in the United States it has no voice. I want to liberate the young serious writer as the young poet has been liberated. The former is still greatly hobbled. Where would he sell his stuff, imagining him to have it on paper?"

Cabell was interested and contributed occasionally to the new publication. His main concern, however, was to get the stories of the life of Manuel and his descendants in a uniform edition and he turned to Holt with suggestions for an introduction to a reprint of *The Eagle's Shadow,* saying: "The point is, of course, that twenty years ago some persons were shocked by *The Eagle's Shadow,* just as to-day their children were shocked by *Jurgen:* and the moral, that the grandchildren will blankly wonder what, in either case, the pother was about.— Also, the sceptical will think I am faking the whole thing." And again to Holt: "Yes, I have now definitely decided to go ahead with *Straws and Prayer-Books—* which, to be sure, for symmetry's sake ought to be called *Before Death,* a title which I put aside in chief because of its probable depressing results upon prospective purchasers. . . . I have all the framework done excepting only two considerable gaps. It is still, of course, the most halfwitted sort of reading: and I am in the usual state of uncertainty as to whether my intelligence is really gone this time or may yet be retrieved."

Retrieved it was, however, and when the book appeared, Carl Van Vechten wrote to Cabell: "I had just finished—so far as seemed humanly possible—writing a novel called *Firecrackers,* which seemed to me very imperfect, so far short did it fall of my intentions regarding it, when *Straws and Prayer-Books* arrived. In this ironic mood I read your perfect book. Perhaps a novel by Floyd or Ethel Dell—priceless junction!—would have served better as an antidote to my complaint. However that may be, I must say to you that this book is you at your very highest water mark and that is very high, indeed. And it is some small solace to realize that I know a man who writes perfect books and is kind enough to send them to me—even if I cannot write perfect books myself."

The Silver Stallion was in the making, and Cabell remarked to Holt that he wished, if possible, to sell some of it to magazines before publishing the book, and added: "It seems mere honesty to state that, after allowing you a reasonable number of years wherein to write it, I myself have written your story of the lover who won the princess by not doing anything, and have disposed of it to the *Century.* . . . My best thanks for the Wharton book [a short appraisal of Edith Wharton by Holt]. It seems to me pretty good, but in a way that emphasizes the need of having

your skeleton clearly thought out before you begin such a book. And I
hope you will not, either, give way to outbursts of unmanly petulance.
It is in his miraculous sense of form that Van Doren excels when he
comes to shape any of his criticisms: the symmetry of each is as perfect
as that of a sonnet. Take profit!"

Through the years, Dreiser and Cabell had both experienced an attack of the censor,[1] and now Mencken was to have his share. On April 3,
1926, he wrote to Cabell: ". . . As you have doubtless heard, the Comstocks in Boston have raided *The American Mercury* April number.
They allege, not that it is obscene, but that one article by H.[erbert]
Asbury is 'immoral!' I am going to Boston on Sunday to accept responsibility, submit to arrest and go on trial. If I'm convicted, you will have
the pleasure of sending me a Bible in jail. If I'm acquitted, half the
Methodists of Boston will face suits for damage in the Federal Courts."
A week later Mencken wrote: "The victory in Boston was sweet and overwhelming. I am now entertaining the Comstocks with a damage suit for
$50,000. It is to be argued in the Federal Court on Monday." Again
Mencken won: ". . . I suppose you have heard of our new victory over
the wowsers in the Federal Court in New York last Tuesday. Judge Mack
gave us an injunction against the Postmaster General. In addition the
learned Judge delivered an eulogy of *The American Mercury* from the
bench and said that he was a charter subscriber and proud of it."

Before many months, Guy Holt decided to leave McBride. This posed
a real problem for Cabell. His deep affection for Holt, both as a friend
and as a publisher, conflicted with his ruling desire that the books of
the Biography, as he called the many-volumed story of Manuel of
Poictesme, be issued in a uniform edition. So many of his books had already come out under the McBride imprint that after much consideration he felt it would be best to remain with the publisher who had issued
the major portion of the work. But the decision was not easy, as Holt
knew, and as Cabell made plain. How could he tell with whom he would
be dealing, or that the people in the office might not take his fault-finding seriously? "I merely repeat that, after eleven years, I feel so utterly
at sea as to be almost seasick."

The Silver Stallion was dedicated to Carl Van Doren, and when he received his copy, Van Doren wrote to Cabell: "For half a dozen years I
have envied Burton Rascoe the dedication to *Jurgen* as I have never envied any other man any comparable laurel. Now, however, the acrostic
porch to *The Silver Stallion* completely removes from my character the

[1] Dreiser's *The Genius* had been suppressed in 1916.

last trace of that particular Deadly Sin. It has never been possible for me quite to decide which of your books I like best, but I have no dimmest doubt that *The Silver Stallion* is the one I take most pride and delight in being associated with.

"This is not merely because I have a taste if not a gift for delicate blasphemy or because I suspect all Redeemers. It is primarily, I think, because the *Stallion* seems to me, at least after two scrupulous readings, the most interwoven of all the chapters in the Biography. Much is said; all is hinted. I was constantly struck, as I read, by the glint of meanings, of the widest application, which appeared not in the sentences themselves but in the very constitution of the work. I was not, I felt, reading a book. I was sitting at the side of immeasurable Koshchei and with my own wits, you generously allowed me to imagine, studying the odd ways of his strange creatures. You allowed me to perceive these larger bearings of the story, and yet yourself gave the appearance of being interested solely in the play over the surface of the lightning of fine fancies, the phantasmagoria—if one may still use that word—of shining, biting colors. I have seldom come so near to being one of the gods, and I must thank you, as I abundantly do, for the opportunity."

In September, 1928, the *Bookman* published brief notes from various writers under the title "Statements of Belief." Theodore Dreiser ended his statement with the words: "As I see him the utterly infinitesimal individual weaves among the mysteries a floss-like and wholly meaningless course—if course it be. In short I catch no meaning from all I have seen, and pass quite as I came, confused and dismayed."

Cabell's statement immediately followed: "I have already summed up such comment as seemed necessary upon my own works in *Straws and Prayer-Books*. I doubt if I could put the matter more succinctly.

"I am sure, in any case, I could add nothing to the paragraph which Mr. Dreiser has written for you. Sincere and strong as has always been my admiration for his colossal sincerity and strength—and, above all, for his tenacious faithfulness to his art—it has not always been possible for me to agree with all the ideas of Mr. Dreiser. Hastily be it added, that any such uniform agreement would have been bad for both of us. But here I find him phrasing my own half-apprehended notions quite perfectly. I elect therefore to say, with extreme admiration and equivalent meekness, just 'Ditto.'"

When presently Dreiser acknowledged the statement, Cabell replied: "It was excellent to have your letter. In that *Bookman* note I did but avail myself of an opportunity hitherto denied me. For some while I have been annoyed by the prevalent notion that you and I are necessarily in exact and complete opposition,—and that, as Thackeray said about himself and Dickens, if the one set of books are true, the other must be false. I do not see it. To the contrary, I have always felt that you and I regarded, as it were, the universe from very much the same point of view, and have been honored with, through many years, the same opponents. What to do about it? is of course a question which we have tackled differently. But I think the real comradeship, and our sense of it, must exist in any case. . . . By all means, let us take it that we are already friends, as go affairs of the mind, and trust to the future as concerns our bodies."

Guy Holt had never settled into what either he or Cabell felt was his natural medium, and when in 1929 a small volume, Cabell's farewell to Poictesme, reached him, Holt sent a word of recognition: "I have sat down during these past two months many times to write you about *The Way of Ecben,* and I cannot—— For *The Way of Ecben* touched me too closely to permit me to look upon it as anything but the tragic end of a chapter—mine in a sense, though it is entirely your own. I know well enough that you cannot stop writing. . . . There [will] be a plenty of matters to record that you'll encounter. But you've closed a door on yourself. You've abandoned Poictesme, and that is a good thing as I see it; but you've said farewell to it—and that to me has been sadder than I can say. And I, who was the first to see so much of it created and settled and made fertile, can't help feeling a vital loss in its abandonment."

Not everyone was as discerning as Holt, and when Cabell continued to write and in 1930 published *Some of Us,* Van Vechten was moved to say: "On this particular occasion it was an added pleasure to learn that a former farewell was rather to a series than to the art of literature, and in the volume at hand the references to the author of *Peter Whiffle* were pleasant enough so that my only actual disappointment perhaps arose out of their infrequency. The book is charming and incisive. I cannot but think that you much overpraise Frances Newman, both as to acumen and as to performance. I think perhaps you underpraise Elinor Wylie in the same departments.— But who knows? The Hergesheimer paper is admirable."

And almost at once Sinclair Lewis added his comments: "We are enchanted to have *Some of Us.* . . . I have read again with joy all that I had read before and all that I had not; as for Dorothy, she has disturbed me in my writing room by devouring it with incessant low chuckles, and by reading aloud such impertinences as '—if any aspersions printed that far on in a book by Mr. More can be regarded as actually published.'

"I wonder if the appraisal of Elinor Wylie had hitherto been published. It seems to me singularly beautiful, and singularly just. As there are vast sections of the subjects of Hoover who have never regarded

Elinor, so are there cliques of Wylieites to whom every word she wrote was perfect, while, of course, you are so right about her terrible *Orphan Angel*. It wasn't merely an orphan; it was a bastard; and if it was an angel at all, it was of the sort that would be content for twenty-four hours a day, through eternity, to sit on a 22 carat golden cloud harping and discussing theology with Bishop Cannon."

And then in the early summer of 1932, telegrams from Ernest Boyd and George Jean Nathan proposed to Cabell a project of rather vague outlines. Finally a letter from Boyd arrived, saying: "The project about which I have been telegraphing is as follows: We propose to issue, monthly at first, a four page paper called *The Literary Newspaper*, printed in the manner of the better class dailies. It will deal only with the arts—politics and economics absolutely excluded. The publishers, who are ready to sign a contract, are the firm of Ray Long & Richard Smith. . . . Nathan and I will do the actual office work. The five editors will have shares in the enterprise *in lieu of salary*, & if we make any money editors & publishers will share proportionately. . . . Are you disposed to join us? O'Neill, Cabell, Dreiser, Nathan, Boyd makes an interesting group of editors and is regarded by the publishers as an attraction to the public. . . . If you are willing to be named as co-editor, I'd greatly appreciate a telegram from you."

Cabell was agreeable, and plans went forward. Presently Boyd and Nathan sent a joint report: "You will be glad to hear that the scheme which we discussed has now been settled. The paper is to be called *The American Spectator*, with the subtitle 'A Literary Newspaper.' We plan to bring out the first number dated November first, and hope that you will be able to let us have something for the first issue."

Cabell sent along some contributions, and toward the end of September wrote: "It is difficult to wait in patience for the first issue of *The American Spectator*, especially as people keep asking me what sort of a something it is, and appear to think I should know."

The editors kept in touch by a constant exchange of letters and one from Nathan ended: "It is grand news that you will be in New York the latter part of October. Dreiser has urged Boyd and myself to try to persuade you to spend an evening with us. He is most interested to meet you. Let us know in advance of your coming and we will arrange a quiet editorial party with appropriate tipples.

"We will have an advance proof of *The American Spectator* in your hands next week. It will not appear on the news-stands until October 20th."

When *The American Spectator* made its appearance, it was a single folded sheet of newspaper, bound with a band of bright-blue gloss listing the contributors to the first issue: Theodore Dreiser, Eugene O'Neill, James Branch Cabell, George Jean Nathan, Ernest Boyd, Clarence Darrow, Frank Swinnerton, Joseph Wood Krutch, Van Wyck Brooks, Havelock Ellis, Liam O'Flaherty, Ring Lardner, Lincoln Steffens, Louis Untermeyer, Calvin B. Bridges. The editorial began: "*The American Spectator* has no policy in the common sense of that word. It advocates no panaceas; it has no axes to grind; it has no private list of taboos. It offers an opportunity for the untrammelled expression of individual opinion, ignoring what is accepted and may be taken for granted in favor of the unaccepted and misunderstood. Sincerity, authenticity, and passion are its editorial criterion. . . . The essential editorial problem of the better and more ambitious type of monthly magazine is that it is much too large. . . . *The American Spectator* is limited to the size in which it here appears. That size will be increased only when and if the merit of sound copy on hand warrants it.

"Another defect of the average magazine is that its editor often permits himself to remain in harness long after his imaginative oats have given out. . . . The moment the editors feel that *The American Spectator* is becoming a routine job, is getting dull and is similarly continuing as a matter of habit, they will call it a day and will retire in a body to their estates."

On October 24, in a jubilant although restrained note from Nathan, Cabell was informed: "It will please you to know that *The American Spectator* has turned out to be an immense success. One hour after it appeared on the news-stands it was completely sold out and we had to keep the printers working all night long to supply the extra demand. That print order of 5000 copies also sold out immediately and on Friday night Smith had to put the paper on the presses again for a run of 15,000. Dreiser, Boyd and I got drunk."

The publication was to run about two and a half years, and during that time there were several editorial changes. Cabell insisted on being put below the line as associate, Sherwood Anderson was added, and in the final year Dreiser resigned to embark upon another scheme, which seems never to have matured. That spring Cabell wrote him: "Your letter as to your receipt of *Smirt*—a book which, in all honesty, is not designed to content anybody except its, as it were, relieved author—gives me the desired chance to tell you of my real and deep grief that you have left *The American Spectator*. It was a severance of which I had heard nothing until, very belatedly, I received the April issue. You comprehend, though, how tenuous is my conection with the paper.

"I feel that your going is a tremendous loss—and I grieve, too, that I can no longer play, without any sound warrant, at being your colleague."

Within the week, Dreiser replied: "Honors and satisfactions are *then* mutual and equal but do not cancel each other by any means. I shall always register, I hope, happy recollections of the year I spent helping make the next issue of that laughing monthly."

Cabell continued to correspond regularly, but he now addressed his *Esteemed Colleagues,* instead of Dear B D & N [Boyd, Dreiser, and Nathan], as formerly: "Returning home yesterday, after a week's absence, I found awaiting me, delectably, Boyd's handsome letter about *Smirt,* your joint letter as to the three papers, and the Year Book. Each one of these items has been to me a source of supreme satisfaction. Looking over the Year Book last night, I was surprised to see what an amount of sound and intensely good stuff we have published."

Having launched a remarkable venture in the middle of one of the greatest economic depressions in history, the editors of *The American Spectator* went blithely on, perhaps at bottom unaware of the real significance of the financial condition of the country. The end was not far distant, however, and when the final issue came out, it carried a supreme editorial, which read in part: "When we started *The American Spectator* . . . we told you that our purpose was simply to entertain ourselves and, we hoped, our readers. . . . And we told you at the same time . . . that when and if we got tired of the job, which involved no plans for any financial profits whatsoever . . . we would, as we expressed it, 'retire to our estates.' Well, we are tired of the job, although it has been a lot of fun, which we feel from your generous response you may have shared. So we are merrily concluding our performance.

"And here comes the strange part of it. At this moment *The American Spectator* enjoys the largest circulation of any literary and critical periodical in the United States. In the single month of December (the last for which complete returns are in) we jumped more than 6,000 in circulation over the previous month, which had shown an increase over the month preceding of 1,500 copies. . . . This isn't guff; it's the truth!

"We wish to thank you for liking our efforts so much and we hope that maybe you will miss our paper a little. Au revoir, THE EDITORS."

It is true that the original set-up of the *Spectator* showed that the editors had really nothing to do with the business management of the review, but to attempt to publish a newspaper for ten cents, without taking advertising (even in the last issues there was practically none), seems in itself to border on the realm of fantasy.

Cabell had been ill at this time with flu and pneumonia, and when Nathan wrote that he too had been a victim of the same troubles, Cabell answered: "Your good note of the eighteenth came . . . this morning, proclaiming you a fellow sufferer from this accursed malady which as yet keeps me derelict alike in all deeds and desires. While I would not wish this fact to be known generally, I rather fancy we are not so young as we once were—and that the sole cure seems mortuary." After reading Nathan's accounting of the debacle, he remarked: "Of the enclosed, I confess, I can make very little, except of course plain bankruptcy. I could have wished for a more glorious ending, but I agree with you that, taking matters by and large, *The American Spectator* has well served its purpose. . . . Nothing could well have been an improvement upon the concluding editorial, in any case." And later: "But, yes, in the *Herald-Tribune,* I had duly admired the superb publicity given to the demise of *The American Spectator*—and I found too some new grounds on which to wonder over the inexplicable way in which Ananias yet keeps his reputation."

When, as he usually did, Cabell sent to Baltimore a copy of his latest book in 1934, it drew a letter from Mencken that is significant in the light of their common experience with censorship: "When I came to page 9 of *Ladies and Gentlemen* it took me ten or twelve seconds to figure out what you were referring to. How much water has gone under the bridges since those insane days! The Comstocks are now down and out. In 1925 *The American Mercury* was barred from the mails for printing an article that might go today into the *Christian Herald.* I have always cherished the theory that our battle with the brethren in Boston helped to work that change. We beat them so badly that they were demoralized, and to this day they have never recovered their old bounce. If *Jurgen* was coming out today not a Methodist in the Republic would think of challenging it.

"I have been reading *Ladies and Gentlemen* with great pleasure. The old boy keeps his cunning.

"Joe Hergesheimer was here during the week, and we had much pleasant talk of you. I still live in hopes that you'll be induced to drop off in Baltimore some time and let me show you what remains of a great medieval city."

Turning to the page in *Ladies and Gentlemen* that Mencken mentions, we find Cabell stating:

"I at least have been writing now for the third part of a century. Throughout this while I have been permitted to write exactly what I wanted to write, and to publish as much of it as I desired. . . . Just once, I can recall also, I have found pressed against one of my books . . . a quite frankly trumped up charge of lewdness. Even at the time, the illogic of this seemed amusing. The upshot, at all events, was a collapse of the pious fraud, in due course, with no more harmful results than to advertise this particular book at the expense of its fellows, and handsomely to increase its sales. . . . It follows that (despite some large native talents for exaggerating any personal mishap) I am not able to feel martyrized by my American birth or by my dependency on an American audience. So far as goes my personal experience, the American writer, during the last thirty-three years, has been permitted, and to a certain extent encouraged, to do the very best of which he was capable. And if— just now and then—that best happened, after all, not to be in every one of its features an earth-staggering masterpiece, this outcome may well have been (I suggest diffidently) not so much the fault of America's cultural crassness as of its writer's failure to start life as a genius of the first order. Occasionally babies forget to do that."

POSTLUDE

by Padraic Colum

> *Joe and Jim and none beside*
> *Mark an age that quickly died.*

In the sort of doggerel that is often prophecy-bearing, Joseph Hergesheimer, drawing James Branch Cabell into it, announced a distinctive epoch.
It was to be a short one indeed.

> *Jim and Joe and none between*
> *Keep an age's memory green.*

> *Joe and Jim and only they*
> *Knew the spirit from the clay,*

> *Jim and Joe forever are*
> *With Linda Condon and Ettarre.*

The first couplet, we know as we read the correspondence it is included
in, has justification: it was an age that quickly came to an end—it would
be more proper to speak of it as a decade rather than an age. Its climax
was enacted in a court and was a vindication of a book and its author.

We can say, and give reasons for saying, that the period came out of
another trial, one held in London in 1878, when a painter, James Mc-
Neill Whistler, took action for libel against an art critic, John Ruskin,
and was awarded one farthing (the nine-hundred-and-sixty-thousandth
part of his claim for damages). This trial—it was so conducted by the
plaintiff that the verdict didn't matter—broke up the long armistice
that had existed between the arts and commerce and initiated a guerrilla
warfare on the part of the artists who had enough spirit to join up.
True, under the name of "Bohemianism" a war had been in operation
mainly on the French front. But from now on it was against an enemy
that was not so well supported. It was, too—and this was important—well
heralded; the dispatches from the front were brilliant and memorable.
In *The Gentle Art of Making Enemies* its conduct was announced by
Whistler. A preamble stated: "The serious ones of the earth, carefully

exasperated, have been prettily spurred on to unseemliness and indiscretion, while overcome by an undue sense of right."

So much of challenge, so much of dramatic gesture, had been put into the war initiated by that American of the South, James McNeill Whistler, that there were startled, defeating movements in the ranks of the enemy. The challenge, the dramatic gesture was repeated by that genealogist and resident of Richmond, James Branch Cabell. In England the enemy was "the serious ones of the earth." In this country they were the proponents of "Comstockery"; they were "the booboisie." It was fun to bear down on their ranks. What marks this decade is a personal and group enjoyment of the production of books. The writers feel they have a cause and an adversary; when they produce a book it forwards a cause and takes toll of an adversary. The combat was confident and joyous, and the era can be marked with an epithet: it was the Decade of High Spirits. The men and women who wrote to James Branch Cabell and were addressed by him were a happy lot. They were in a struggle and knew that in that struggle they were bound to win. With the verdict in favor of *Jurgen* they won a very honorable victory.

James Branch Cabell had already published seven books when he received a letter from a young editor in a publishing house, Sinclair Lewis—he, too, had published a few novels—declining a certain romance and giving very intelligent reasons for his decision. So the decade begins. It ends with James Branch Cabell's gaining celebrity, not only for a book but for a cause, and Sinclair Lewis's creation of new types in American literature and his going from the huge success of *Main Street* to the huge success of *Babbitt*.

A generation that is not altogether stodgy looks for an avatar, and with the publication of *Beyond Life* the sign is given that the avatar has appeared. From a bookshop, an editorial office, a critic's chair, young men emerge to turn to where the avatar is evident. That the three are domiciled in Chicago is interesting to notice. Chicago is a literary center and is aware of literary values: Edgar Lee Masters, Carl Sandburg, Sherwood Anderson are there; Theodore Dreiser has been an inhabitant. Also, in Chicago Harriet Monroe's *Poetry* and Margaret Anderson's and Jane Heap's *Little Review* are published. It could have literary expectations. Anyway, three of its young men, Lewis Galantière, Vincent Starrett, Burton Rascoe address themselves from it to the Richmond of James Branch Cabell.

There is something else to notice about the times: it was a decade in which there was an entente between literate publishers and authors of distinction—the names of Alfred Knopf, Horace Liveright, Ben Huebsch will come into the minds of those who belonged to that literary world.

And so it is not at all surprising that a publisher's representative, Guy Holt, should become not only a helper, but a disciple of James Branch Cabell. Guy Holt was a dynamic person still in his twenties; we can see that he had power with his pen.

A group formed, as Carl Van Vechten notes, but it is different from previous groups in America and different from groups in Europe. "Six men living in the same city who cordially dislike each other." This was George Moore's definition of the usual literary group. In this case proximity is out of the question. They have been magnetized by an individual. Burton Rascoe, the young literary editor of the Chicago *Tribune* spreads the word. He is the one most certain of the avatar. He devotes all his eloquence, learning, and youthful bellicosity to magnifying him. Rascoe's associations are with Henry Mencken and George Jean Nathan of *The Smart Set* and with the groups that frequent Mouquin's and the Algonquin. When we read his epistles we realize that for him there has been a shock of recognition and that it comes from the knowledge that here in America there is a writer who knows all the ways to spur to unseemliness and indiscretion the serious ones of the earth. It is interesting now to list the names of those who were so considered, the men who were often "overcome by an undue sense of right"—they are Paul Elmer More, Irving Babbitt, William Crary Brownell, Stuart Sherman, Paul Shorey.

The shock of recognition affects others, amongst them one who comes on the scene with the gusto of a man carrying a bottle of Bourbon during the prohibition era. He is Henry Mencken, whom Cabell recognizes as having "solidity under the pranks of the village cut-up." Then there is Sinclair Lewis whose "wholly charming, if wholly disapproving letter" Cabell cherished. When he reappears it is as an author, but not yet the author of a best seller.

And then there enters the ranks a forceful man of letters, Joseph Hergesheimer. Cabell is aware that there is something short of excellence in the work of this assured professional. But the man has a feeling for good surfaces—not meaning superficialities—for he has had a career as a painter. As he stands with James Branch Cabell, Sinclair Lewis, Henry Mencken, Burton Rascoe, there is something about "Joe" Hergesheimer that is quite commanding. And it is to the Pennsylvanian that Cabell confides his belief—"Writing I take to be a strategic retreat before unconquerable oblivion."

Eager to identify himself with some intellectual cause that will distinguish him from the successful delineator of a new generation, Scott Fitzgerald makes his way into the group that by this time contains Carl Van Vechten. Van Vechten is a moving spirit, not only in the literary but in

the whole artistic life of Manhattan, and has recorded its sophistica-
tion in *The Tattooed Countess* and *Peter Whiffle*. There comes in, too,
Thomas Beer, a writer who has left a mark on American letters because
of his personal style, and Louis Untermeyer with his flair for discovery.
And there remain Vincent Starrett, bibliophile and seeker after the rarer
things in literature, and Lewis Galantière, who, though an American, has
a stake in the new movement amongst French writers. And always there
is Burton Rascoe, attractive because of his excessiveness.

A cause had brought them together. It was made concrete when James
Branch Cabell became informative about the work which he wanted to
name *The Pawnbroker's Shirt* but which came into the world as *Jurgen*.
Its publication was hailed by those who rejoiced in the fact that in this
book erudition and uncommon writing were made entertaining. The attempt to suppress *Jurgen* as lewd and lascivious was so unfair that the
Comstocks and their ilk had a verdict brought against them in court,
and James Branch Cabell and his supporters were exalted. Very properly
this collection of letters that he wrote and that were addressed to him ends
with this triumph. Though those who wrote and those who received these
letters did not know it, an era comes to an end with this burst of glory.

A literary group? Maybe. But, anyway, they faced the serious ones of
the earth, and the Comstocks and "booboisie" with real authority. They
were magnetized and held together by the writer of *Beyond Life* and
Jurgen. Reading this exchange of letters, we are aware of a lack of som-
berness on the part of the writers. They are not concerned with the psy-
chotic and the maladjusted and a world on its way to Tophet because of
atom explosions or population explosions. They believe that order and
beauty can be promoted by good writing. They have, as writers of the
present era have not, a belief in style. They are confident that good
writing is possible, that a personal style can be achieved—in short, that
there is salvation for literate mankind. It seems a long way back to that
era. When we peruse this correspondence—it could be a discourse in the
form of correspondence—we have a feeling that we are looking back to a
happy time.

Not in any predictable time will we have another group of writers who
can confidently challenge the serious ones of the earth. They are not close
enough, these serious ones, to be affected by our discourse, however witty.
And those who indulge in such discourse, the men and women who believe that beauty and order can be promoted by good writing, are being
overawed by men doing top-secret work on space missiles and the like. Be
that as it may, we can read these letters for sense of a period that was
before cold wars and atom explosions and for character and opinion that
come directly over to us.

BOOKS BY

JAMES BRANCH CABELL

The Eagle's Shadow (1904) Doubleday, Page & Co.
The Line of Love (1905) Harper & Brothers
Gallantry (1907) Harper & Brothers
The Cords of Vanity (1909) Doubleday, Page & Co.
Chivalry (1909) Harper & Brothers
The Soul of Melicent (reissued as *Domnei*) (1913) Frederick A. Stokes & Co.
The Rivet in Grandfather's Neck (1915) Robert M. McBride & Co.
The Certain Hour (1916) Robert M. McBride & Co.
From the Hidden Way (1916) Robert M. McBride & Co.
The Cream of the Jest (1917) Robert M. McBride & Co.
Beyond Life (1919) Robert M. McBride & Co.
Jurgen (1919) Robert M. McBride & Co.
The Judging of Jurgen (1920) The Bookfellows
Figures of Earth (1921) Robert M. McBride & Co.
The Jewel Merchants (1921) Robert M. McBride & Co.
Joseph Hergesheimer (1921) The Bookfellows
The Lineage of Lichfield (1922) Robert M. McBride & Co.
The High Place (1923) Robert M. McBride & Co.
Straws and Prayer-Books (1924) Robert M. McBride & Co.
The Silver Stallion (1926) Robert M. McBride & Co.
The Music from Behind the Moon (1926) The John Day Co.
Something about Eve (1927) Robert M. McBride & Co.
Ballades from the Hidden Way (1928) Crosby Gaige
The White Robe (1928) Robert M. McBride & Co.
The Way of Ecben (1929) Robert M. McBride & Co.
Sonnets from Antan (1929) The Fountain Press
Townsend of Lichfield (1930) Robert M. McBride & Co.
Some of Us (1930) Robert M. McBride & Co.
Between Dawn and Sunrise (with John Macy) (1930) Robert M. McBride & Co.
These Restless Heads (1932) Robert M. McBride & Co.
Special Delivery (1933) Robert M. McBride & Co.
Smirt (1934) Robert M. McBride & Co.

Ladies and Gentlemen (1934) Robert M. McBride & Co.
Smith (1935) Robert M. McBride & Co.
Preface to the Past (1936) Robert M. McBride & Co.
Smire (1937) Doubleday, Doran & Co.
The Nightmare Has Triplets (1937) Doubleday, Doran & Co.
Of Ellen Glasgow, An Inscribed Portrait (with Ellen Glasgow) (1938) Maverick
    Press
The King Was in His Counting House (1938) Farrar & Rinehart
Hamlet Had an Uncle (1940) Farrar & Rinehart
The First Gentleman of America (1942) Farrar & Rinehart
The St. Johns (with A. J. Hanna) (1943) Farrar & Rinehart
There Were Two Pirates (1946) Farrar, Straus and Co.
Let Me Lie (1947) Farrar, Straus and Co.
The Witch-Woman (1948) Farrar, Straus and Co.
The Devil's Own Dear Son (1949) Farrar, Straus and Co.
Quiet Please (1952) University of Florida Press
As I Remember It (1955) The McBride Co.

Branchiana (1907) Privately Printed
Branch of Abingdon (1911) Privately Printed
The Majors and Their Marriages (1915) Privately Printed

INDEX